Advanced SAP ABAP
Comprehensive Techniques for Expert Development

© 2024 by Wang Press. All rights reserved.

No part of this publication may be reproduced, distributed, or transmitted in any form or by any means, including photocopying, recording, or other electronic or mechanical methods, without the prior written permission of the publisher, except in the case of brief quotations embodied in critical reviews and certain other noncommercial uses permitted by copyright law.

Published by Wang Press

For permissions and other inquiries, write to:
P.O. Box 3132, Framingham, MA 01701, USA

Contents

1 Introduction to ABAP and SAP Environment   **7**
- 1.1 Overview of SAP R/3 Architecture 7
- 1.2 Role of ABAP in SAP Ecosystem 11
- 1.3 ABAP Workbench Tools 14
- 1.4 Basic Navigation in SAP GUI 18
- 1.5 Understanding SAP Landscape and Transport System . 22

2 ABAP Syntax and Programming Fundamentals   **27**
- 2.1 ABAP Program Structure 28
- 2.2 Data Types and Declarations 31
- 2.3 ABAP Statements and Expressions 35
- 2.4 Working with Strings and Numbers 38
- 2.5 Control Flow in ABAP 41
- 2.6 Error Handling and Debugging Techniques 45

3 Working with Data: Internal Tables and Data Dictionary   **51**
- 3.1 Understanding the Data Dictionary 52
- 3.2 Creating and Managing Transparent Tables 56
- 3.3 Internal Tables: Definition and Usage 60

3.4	Operations on Internal Tables	64
3.5	Advanced Internal Table Techniques	69
3.6	Using Secondary Indexes and Keys	73
3.7	Data Dictionary Tools in SAP	78

4 Advanced Data Handling and Processing Techniques — 83

4.1	Working with ALV Grid Display	84
4.2	Handling Large Data Sets Efficiently	88
4.3	Dynamic Programming Techniques	92
4.4	Field Symbols and Data References	96
4.5	Data Selection and Access Optimization	100
4.6	Handling Exceptions and Errors	105
4.7	Parallel Processing in ABAP	109

5 Modularization Techniques: Includes, Function Modules, and Methods — 115

5.1	Understanding Modularization in ABAP	116
5.2	Includes and Subroutines	119
5.3	Creating and Using Function Modules	122
5.4	Parameter Passing Techniques	125
5.5	Methods and Classes in ABAP	129
5.6	Handling Exceptions in Modular Components	133
5.7	Packages and Naming Conventions	138

6 Dialog Programming and SAP GUI — 143

6.1	SAP GUI and Screens Basics	143
6.2	Screen Painter and Dynpro Programming	148
6.3	Working with Screen Elements	153
6.4	Module Pool Programming	158

6.5 Managing User Input and Validation 163
6.6 Implementing Navigation and Flow Logic 168
6.7 Enhancing User Experience with Custom Controls . . . 172

7 File Handling and Data Transfer 177
7.1 File Handling Basics in ABAP 177
7.2 Working with Sequential and Binary Files 181
7.3 Data Transfer Methods: Upload and Download 185
7.4 Using Application Server for File Management 189
7.5 Managing File Access and Security 192
7.6 Data Conversion and Formatting 196
7.7 Integrating with Legacy Systems 199

8 Object-Oriented Programming in ABAP 205
8.1 Fundamentals of Object-Oriented Concepts 206
8.2 Defining and Implementing Classes 209
8.3 Inheritance and Interfaces 212
8.4 Working with Objects and Instances 216
8.5 Encapsulation and Data Hiding 220
8.6 Polymorphism and Dynamic Method Calls 224
8.7 Exception Handling in Object-Oriented Approach . . . 228

9 SAP Enhancement Options and User Exits 235
9.1 Overview of Enhancement Framework 236
9.2 User Exits and Customer Exits 239
9.3 BADIs (Business Add-Ins) 243
9.4 Enhancement Points and Sections 247
9.5 Implicit and Explicit Enhancements 251
9.6 Switch Framework and Enhancement Implementation 256

9.7 Best Practices for Implementing Enhancements 260

10 Best Practices and Performance Optimization   267
     10.1 Coding Standards and Naming Conventions 268
     10.2 Efficient Database Access Techniques 271
     10.3 Memory Management and Internal Table Handling . . 274
     10.4 Using Performance Analysis Tools 277
     10.5 Optimizing Program Flow and Logic 281
     10.6 Implementing Parallel Processing 284
     10.7 Code Review and Quality Assurance Procedures 287

Introduction

In the realm of enterprise resource planning (ERP), SAP systems have long stood as a critical pillar for businesses seeking integrated solutions to streamline their operations. At the core of SAP's robust architecture is ABAP (Advanced Business Application Programming), a sophisticated programming language engineered for developing applications within SAP environments. This book, "Advanced SAP ABAP: Comprehensive Techniques for Expert Development," is meticulously crafted to deliver an expansive and methodical exploration of ABAP, catering to both novice programmers embarking on their SAP journey and seasoned professionals aspiring to refine their expertise in advanced SAP development.

ABAP is endowed with a powerful suite of features that empower developers to design bespoke reports, scalable modules, and specialized tools, ensuring that SAP systems are tailored to the unique needs of the organization. Mastery of ABAP's intricacies is essential for developers, functional consultants, and technical architects dedicated to customizing and optimizing SAP solutions to meet strategic business objectives.

The book unfolds through systematically designed chapters that delve into the essential facets of ABAP and its application within SAP systems. Beginning with foundational concepts such as ABAP syntax and data structures, it progresses to encompass more sophisticated topics including object-oriented programming, advanced modularization strategies, and techniques for performance optimization. The continuum of knowledge presented ensures a coherent and comprehensive learning experience.

As readers progress, they will garner profound insights into the SAP ecosystem, blending technical prowess with pragmatic methodologies for implementing enhancements and developing efficient applications. The exploration of advanced topics such as dynamic programming, effective data processing, integration techniques, and user exits forms the cornerstone of this book, equipping readers to tackle complex, real-world challenges inherent in SAP development.

Furthermore, an emphasis on best practices and performance optimization strategies will empower readers not just to produce superior code, but also to contribute significantly to the enduring efficiency and adaptability of SAP implementations within their enterprises. Embracing these practices ensures that SAP systems remain agile, responsive, and poised to meet the ever-evolving demands of the business landscape.

In essence, "Advanced SAP ABAP: Comprehensive Techniques for Expert Development" emerges as an invaluable resource for individuals engaged in the SAP ecosystem. It furnishes readers with the essential knowledge and skills to fully leverage the capabilities of ABAP, ultimately fostering the creation of scalable, high-performance, and innovative SAP solutions.

Chapter 1

Introduction to ABAP and SAP Environment

ABAP, or Advanced Business Application Programming, forms the backbone of SAP's robust application capabilities, offering a versatile language for tailoring SAP solutions to specific business needs. This chapter provides an essential overview of the SAP R/3 architecture and emphasizes the strategic role ABAP plays within the broader SAP ecosystem. It introduces the ABAP Workbench tools, key for developing, testing, and refining ABAP applications, and guides readers through navigating the SAP GUI. Additionally, it explores the SAP landscape and transport system, crucial for managing and migrating changes across various SAP environments. This foundational knowledge sets the stage for more advanced ABAP programming topics.

1.1 Overview of SAP R/3 Architecture

The SAP R/3 architecture represents a milestone in enterprise resource planning (ERP) software, characterized by its tiered structure and its ability to integrate comprehensive business processes efficiently. To fully appreciate the architecture of SAP R/3, it is essential to delve into the intricate balance and interaction between its various layers: the presentation, application, and database layers.

The architecture is often depicted as a three-tier client-server model. Each layer plays a distinct role in fostering a modular and scalable system environment. The model essentially separates each business functionality into distinct logical platforms, facilitating the management and execution of complex applications.

The **Presentation Layer** is the user interface of the SAP R/3 system. It serves as the intermediary between the users and the rest of the system. Typically, this layer is encapsulated by a graphical user interface (GUI), notably the SAP GUI, which runs on users' computers. This setup provides a user-friendly environment for performing tasks such as data entry and report generation. Users connect to the SAP system through this layer, making it the entry point for all transactions.

The communication protocol used in this layer is primarily Remote Function Call (RFC), a feature that assists in efficient client-server communication. RFC is SAP's proprietary version of a standard remote procedure call, which is designed to allow a program to execute a procedure in a remote system. This, in turn, makes it essential for seamless interaction between layers.

The **Application Layer** acts as the operational heart of the SAP R/3 system. It is where the business logic resides and is executed. This layer is responsible for processing all business transactions and computations. The application servers handle these tasks and their distribution depending on the workload. ABAP (Advanced Business Application Programming) programs, customized by users to meet specific requirements, are executed here.

The application layer makes extensive use of load distribution mechanisms to manage the execution of tasks efficiently. This is particularly essential in environments where numerous users perform simultaneous transactions. The design of the application servers allows for enhanced reliability and performance through methods such as load balancing. A dispatcher distributes tasks among the work processes within an application server, optimizing resource use and ensuring equitable task assignment.

1.1. OVERVIEW OF SAP R/3 ARCHITECTURE

A critical feature in this layer is the SAP Message Server, which facilitates communication between the application servers and provides load balancing. Moreover, the enqueue server ensures data consistency by locking the data that is being processed, thereby preventing any concurrent modifications that could lead to data anomalies.

The **Database Layer** functions as the data repository for the SAP system. It is designed to store all the data required by the SAP applications and handle all database requests submitted by the application layer. SAP R/3 supports multiple database platforms like Oracle, SQL Server, DB2, etc., allowing organizations to choose based on their existing infrastructure and preferences.

Data integrity and security in the database layer are paramount, necessitating robust transaction management. This includes operations such as commit and rollback, which ensure that transactions are completed successfully or reverted to maintain integrity. The underlying database management systems (DBMS) support Structured Query Language (SQL) to manage data efficiently.

Support for customization and extensibility in SAP R/3 is facilitated via **Business Add-Ins (BAdIs)** and **User Exits**. These elements provide hooks into the system's processing logic, allowing customization without altering the core software's code. This flexibility is crucial for tailoring SAP to individual business processes.

```
* Creation of a simple Data Element in ABAP
DATA: BEGIN OF it_mara OCCURS 0,
        matnr TYPE matnr,
      END OF it_mara.

PARAMETERS p_matnr TYPE matnr.

START-OF-SELECTION.
  SELECT * FROM mara WHERE matnr = p_matnr.
    WRITE: / it_mara-matnr.
  ENDSELECT.
```

The SAP R/3 architecture also incorporates advanced features such as **Batch Processing** and **Background Jobs**, allowing certain time-consuming processes to execute during periods of low system load. This enhances the system's overall efficiency and minimizes potential disruptions during peak usage times.

Security within SAP R/3 is of massive importance, and measures are ingrained throughout the architecture. This includes user authentication mechanisms, sophisticated role-based access controls, and audit logging to monitor system use and mitigate unauthorized data access. Security protocols such as encryption and secure network communication are implemented to protect sensitive business data.

Support for **Internationalization and Localization** is integral to SAP R/3, enabling adaptation to numerous languages and conventions across various regions. This is crucial for multinational corporations executing a globally unified business strategy. Localization includes adapting to regional legal requirements, which SAP achieves by pragmatically segmenting and isolating such variances.

```
REPORT zsimple_report.

DATA: country TYPE string VALUE 'USA'.

SELECT-OPTIONS: s_mara FOR mara-matnr.

START-OF-SELECTION.
  FORMAT COLOR COL_GROUP.
  WRITE: / 'Material Numbers:', country.

  SELECT matnr FROM mara INTO TABLE @DATA(itab)
    WHERE matnr IN @s_mara.

  LOOP AT itab INTO DATA(wa).
    WRITE: / wa-matnr.
  ENDLOOP.
```

The robustness of SAP R/3 Architecture allows it to support various modules such as FI (Financial Accounting), CO (Controlling), MM (Materials Management), SD (Sales and Distribution), and several others, each integral to enterprise operations. These modules are seamlessly integrated into the SAP R/3 system architecture, facilitating the comprehensive management of enterprise resources.

Finally, **Scalability**, one of the hallmark attributes of the R/3 architecture, permits incremental enhancement of system capabilities. This scalability is vital for businesses projecting growth, ensuring that information technology infrastructure constraints do not limit business expansion.

The SAP R/3 architecture's design demonstrates a clever orchestration of technical ingenuity and practical business functionalities. It combines a robust, secure, and scalable infrastructure with a flexible, customizable application environment. This synthesis not only supports present-day business processes efficiently but also adapts to the evolving technological landscape and business requirements. Understanding this architecture is paramount for leveraging SAP to its fullest capabilities, optimizing resources, and maximizing enterprise efficiency. Understanding technical nuances within each layer elevates one's ability to program and maintain a dynamic SAP R/3 environment. This understanding is crucial as foundational knowledge as one delves deeper into the customization and optimization of SAP solutions.

1.2 Role of ABAP in SAP Ecosystem

In the SAP ecosystem, ABAP (Advanced Business Application Programming) holds a pivotal role, serving as the cornerstone for developing business applications tailored to an organization's needs. ABAP is a high-level programming language created by SAP, designed specifically for the development of SAP applications. Its comprehensive integration with the SAP system allows businesses to extend, customize, and enhance their SAP environments effectively, thus aligning their IT capabilities with strategic business objectives.

ABAP was introduced in the 1980s, evolving alongside SAP's ever-expanding suite of enterprise solutions. It supports both procedural and object-oriented paradigms, offering flexibility and versatility to developers. This dual-paradigm approach is particularly beneficial, as it allows developers to choose the best programming style for their particular use case, enhancing the expressiveness and efficiency of code.

One of ABAP's primary functions within an SAP system is to facilitate the crafting of custom reports and applications. These are typically required when the standard out-of-the-box functionality provided by SAP does not fully meet a business's specific requirements. By writing ABAP code, developers can manipulate data from the database layer and present it through the application layer to the presentation layer in a manner that fulfills user specifications.

```
DATA: lt_mara TYPE TABLE OF mara,
      ls_mara TYPE mara.

* Select data from material table
SELECT * FROM mara INTO TABLE lt_mara WHERE matnr = '1234'.
```

```
* Loop through result set and display materials
LOOP AT lt_mara INTO ls_mara.
  WRITE: / ls_mara-matnr, ls_mara-maktx.
ENDLOOP.
```

ABAP's integration into the SAP ecosystem extends beyond merely fetching data. With its ability to handle database operations, ABAP facilitates powerful data manipulations—such as data selection, updating, and deletion—essential within any enterprise's lifeline processes. The efficiency with which ABAP executes these operations directly influences SAP system performance, highlighting the need for skillful coding practices.

The ABAP programming language is deeply embedded in various SAP modules, including but not limited to FI (Financial Accounting), CO (Controlling), SD (Sales and Distribution), MM (Material Management), and more. Each of these modules utilizes ABAP for crucial backend functionality. For example, Financial Accounting relies extensively on ABAP for generating detailed financial reports and enabling automated postings.

Moreover, ABAP is instrumental in crafting Form Layouts using Smart Forms or SAPscript, and creating sophisticated interfaces with the help of IDocs (Intermediate Documents) or BAPIs (Business Application Programming Interfaces). Both tools allow for integration and data exchange between SAP and non-SAP systems, providing versatile connectivity solutions and supporting heterogeneous IT landscapes.

SAP's NetWeaver platform, which serves as a technical foundation for many SAP applications, supports ABAP as a primary tool for extending SAP capabilities. The role of ABAP in this context is to enable seamless application integration across diverse application environments, encompassing HTML, XML, Java, and Business Process Management (BPM). This capability is crucial in present-day business scenarios where integration and interoperability determine the efficiency and success of IT investments.

```
DATA: lv_bapi_return TYPE bapiret2,
      lv_sales_doc TYPE vbeln_vf,
      lv_sales_doc_in TYPE bapisalesdocumentin.

lv_sales_doc_in-doc_type = 'OR'. " Order Type
CALL FUNCTION 'BAPI_SALESORDER_CREATEFROMDAT2'
  EXPORTING
```

1.2. ROLE OF ABAP IN SAP ECOSYSTEM

```
    sales_header_in = lv_sales_doc_in
IMPORTING
    salesdocument = lv_sales_doc
    return = lv_bapi_return.

IF lv_bapi_return-type = 'S'.
    WRITE: / 'Sales order successfully created with document number:', lv_sales_doc.
ELSE.
    WRITE: / 'Failed to create sales order:', lv_bapi_return-message.
ENDIF.
```

ABAP also plays a significant role in enhancing the SAP UX (User Experience) via the development of custom SAP Fiori apps. These applications, characterized by modern user interfaces and improved usability, are often built in conjunction with ABAP's capabilities to access and display backend SAP data seamlessly. The synergy between ABAP's powerful back-end processing and SAP Fiori's fresh front-end presentation forms a comprehensive development ecosystem facilitating user-friendly application deployment.

Object-oriented ABAP (OOABAP) has garnered increasing relevance in today's SAP developments for designing complex applications, promoting modular code, and enhancing maintainability. OOABAP facilitates encapsulation and data abstraction, integral to developing sophisticated software applications that are both robust and scalable.

ABAP Workbench, the integrated development environment (IDE) provided by SAP, offers all necessary tools to develop robust ABAP applications. It includes tools for creating dictionaries, source code, and various repository objects, alongside debug functionalities indispensable to developers. The Workbench's comprehensive nature highlights ABAP's role in supporting the lifecycle of SAP application development, from conception through deployment.

SAP has recognized the importance of cloud computing and adapting to new technology paradigms, thereby emphasizing the evolution of ABAP within the SAP Business Technology Platform (BTP). ABAP's cloud enhancements ensure that legacy systems integrate smoothly with contemporary digital transformations, contributing to future-proof enterprise strategies.

Performance optimization in ABAP applications is a critical consideration for developers working within the SAP ecosystem. Efficient data retrieval strategies, proper transaction management, and minimizing resource-intensive operations are essential practices for optimizing SAP application performance.

Security and compliance are inherently supported by ABAP through robust authorization checks and seamless integration with SAP's role-based security model. Developers must ensure that authorization objects and checks align with organizational policies, safeguarding sensitive business information and maintaining regulatory compliance.

ABAP's role in the SAP ecosystem transcends basic programmatic tasks to address broader functional and strategic objectives within an organization. By providing tools to tailor SAP systems, from backend to frontend operations, ABAP ensures an efficient realization of business processes. As SAP continues to innovate and adapt to technological shifts, ABAP remains a linchpin, guiding organizations through the dual demands of maintenance and innovation. Its ongoing evolution assures that it remains pertinent to the SAP enterprise landscape, empowering businesses to achieve their objectives efficiently while adapting to ever-changing technology demands.

1.3 ABAP Workbench Tools

The ABAP Workbench, a comprehensive suite of tools, serves as the integrated development environment (IDE) for SAP's proprietary programming language, ABAP. It is where developers create, maintain, and administer ABAP code. The suite is a cornerstone of SAP development, facilitating not only coding but also handling a wide array of activities essential for SAP applications, including designing data models, creating user interfaces, and managing objects within the SAP database.

The ABAP Workbench consists of several components, each tailored to different facets of SAP application development. Its expansive functionality promises seamless integration between various development processes, offering a robust infrastructure crucial for any SAP-based enterprise application development.

The **ABAP Editor** is at the heart of the Workbench, where ABAP code is written and maintained. It supports syntax highlighting, code autocomplete, and integrated debugging features, enabling developers to write efficient and error-free programs. The ABAP Editor adheres to SAP's standardized development practices, ensuring that all code aligns with SAP's best practices and protocols.

A quintessential part of the ABAP Workbench is the **Data Dictionary (DDIC)**, which facilitates the definition of data structures and database objects, such as tables, views, types, and domains. The Data Dictionary enables developers to manage metadata centrally, thus maintaining data consistency across the system. When an object is created or altered in the Data Dictionary, the alterations automatically propagate throughout relevant system components, reflecting instantly without requiring direct database interaction.

```
TABLES: mara.

SELECT-OPTIONS: s_matnr FOR mara-matnr.

START-OF-SELECTION.
  SELECT * FROM mara
    WHERE matnr IN s_matnr.
  ENDSELECT.
```

The **Function Builder** is another integral aspect of the Workbench, used for creating and managing function modules. Function modules enhance code modularity and reusability, enabling developers to implement processing logic in isolated units, which can be systematically called upon when needed. The Function Builder supports both synchronous and asynchronous remote function calls, crucial for creating distributed applications involving different SAP and non-SAP systems.

Debugging is a fundamental step in ensuring that software applications are functional and robust. The **ABAP Debugger** is a powerful tool that empowers developers to test and troubleshoot code by allowing them to execute their programs line-by-line. It provides various debugging techniques, such as setting breakpoints, watchpoints, and stepping through lines of ABAP code. Through a detailed examination of variable contents and the logical flow, developers can identify and resolve defects effectively.

Versioning and application lifecycle management are supported through the **Transport Organizer (SE09/SE10)** within the Workbench. This tool manages the change and transport systems (CTS) within the SAP landscape. The Transport Organizer ensures that all development objects are moved from one SAP system to another in a controlled and systematic manner, maintaining consistency across different environments. It is integral for successful development deployments from the development environment through quality assurance, finally to the production environment.

- Transport request types:
- Workbench: used for cross-system changes to ABAP objects.
- Customizing: used for modifying system behavior without direct coding interventions.

The **Screen Painter** is employed in designing custom user interfaces. It allows developers to create screens using drag-and-drop configurations, thereby streamlining the process of developing intuitive and user-friendly interfaces. It integrates with the SAP GUI, defining various screen elements like input fields, labels, and buttons.

```
MODULE status_0100 OUTPUT.
  SET PF-STATUS 'STANDARD'.
ENDMODULE.

* PAI module processed
MODULE user_command_0100 INPUT.
  CASE ok_code.
    WHEN 'EXIT'.
      LEAVE PROGRAM.
  ENDCASE.
ENDMODULE.
```

The **Menu Painter** complements the Screen Painter by allowing the creation of menu bars, function keys, and other navigation elements. It equips developers with the ability to construct logical user navigation paths, which are essential for enhancing the overall user experience within the SAP system.

An often understated yet powerful tool is the **Repository Browser**, offering a structured way to navigate the repository of all SAP objects. The tool aids developers in managing object dependencies and versions, thereby facilitating comprehensive object management and exploration.

Web Dynpro ABAP reinforces the Workbench's capabilities in building web-based applications. It is a framework for building structured web applications, offering a comprehensive suite of development and

1.3. ABAP WORKBENCH TOOLS

runtime capabilities. Web Dynpro ABAP strengthens SAP's UX strategy by delivering sleek, intelligent web applications that integrate tightly with SAP backend processes.

The ABAP Workbench also supports customizing reports and forms through **SAPscript and Smart Forms**, which are essential for creating and managing print layouts. These tools allow developers to define complex layouts for documents such as invoices and delivery notes, embedding graphical elements and dynamic content.

Furthermore, the Workbench incorporates **Code Inspector** and **Extended Check Tools**, integral for conducting static code analysis. These tools ensure code quality by enforcing adherence to standards, detecting potential performance bottlenecks, unnecessary complexity, and identifying security vulnerabilities.

ABAP Objects, the object-oriented extension to ABAP introduced with Release 4.6, is fully supported by the Workbench. ABAP Objects promotes cleaner, reusable code architecture via encapsulation and polymorphism, aligning with modern software development methodologies.

```
CLASS lcl_example DEFINITION.
  PUBLIC SECTION.
    METHODS: constructor,
             set_value IMPORTING iv_value TYPE i,
             get_value RETURNING VALUE(rv_value) TYPE i.
  PRIVATE SECTION.
    DATA: mv_value TYPE i.
ENDCLASS.

CLASS lcl_example IMPLEMENTATION.
  METHOD constructor.
    mv_value = 0.
  ENDMETHOD.

  METHOD set_value.
    mv_value = iv_value.
  ENDMETHOD.

  METHOD get_value.
    rv_value = mv_value.
  ENDMETHOD.
ENDCLASS.
```

Lastly, the Workbench encompasses **ABAP CDS (Core Data Services)**, enhancing data modeling capabilities and abstracting data layer complexities. This innovation offers developers a powerful query language for defining data models directly on the database layer, fostering effective use of data in applications.

The ABAP Workbench is indispensable for SAP developers, offering a coherent, integrated environment catering to all stages of the software development lifecycle. Its capabilities extend significantly beyond mere coding, encompassing database management, user interface design, testing, and deployment. As the SAP landscape evolves, the Workbench evolves concurrently, adapting to new technological paradigms and continually extending its functionality, thereby cementing its role as an integral component of SAP development pipelines. With SAP's move towards the cloud and new user experience models, the Workbench adapts, integrating modern development methodologies and paradigms, ensuring it remains relevant and impactful.

1.4 Basic Navigation in SAP GUI

The SAP Graphical User Interface (SAP GUI) serves as the primary access point for an end-user interacting with the SAP applications. As such, understanding how to navigate within the SAP GUI is fundamental for users, from entry-level clerks to experienced SAP consultants. SAP GUI is designed with user-friendliness in mind, balancing functionality with ease of use to help users perform their tasks efficiently across various modules and transactions.

First, it is vital to understand the structure of the SAP GUI, which consists of multiple elements: the title bar, menu bar, toolbars, navigation area, and the application area. Each of these components provides users with the tools to access system operations and commands conveniently.

The **Title Bar** displays the name of the application or transaction currently in use. This overview is crucial for users to know what part of the system they are interacting with at any given time. Alongside the title, system information like the client, user, session data, and server instance are displayed. This information is beneficial when troubleshooting or validating that the user is operating within the correct system client.

The **Menu Bar** presents a cascading array of options, echoing stan-

1.4. BASIC NAVIGATION IN SAP GUI

dard application behavior found in user interfaces worldwide. It typically includes system, edit, goto, extras, and help functionalities which aid in navigating, editing data, and accessing additional options within transactions. Selecting an option like 'System' or 'Help' opens further submenus, offering additional functionalities like logging off or accessing documentation and support.

The **Standard Toolbar**, located below the menu bar, provides quick access to frequently used functions such as save, back, exit, and command. Users can customize the toolbar to include shortcuts tailored to their specific needs, thus enhancing workflow efficiency. Each icon on the toolbar provides hover text, making it intuitive for users to discover the function it performs.

The **Navigation Area** typically appears as a side panel, enabling users to browse through transaction codes and a tree structure of available applications. This area is a central hub for accessing different areas of functionality within SAP and can be customized to show favorite transactions or user-specific application folders.

The **Application Area**, occupying the majority of the screen, is where users perform their primary work tasks. It is in this area that forms are filled, data is entered, and business transactions are processed. Depending on the module and transaction, this area can feature a wide range of input fields, buttons, and tabs, facilitating intricate interactions with the enterprise data.

A fundamental aspect of SAP GUI navigation is the understanding and use of **Transaction Codes (T-codes)**. Transaction codes are shortcut commands that allow users to access specific SAP transactions directly, bypassing multiple navigation layers. They are indispensable for SAP power users, facilitating rapid access to functionalities. For instance, the transaction code MM03 directly accesses the display material transaction in the Material Master module.

```
Commonly used transaction codes:
- SE80: Object Navigator
- SE38: ABAP Editor
- VA01: Create Sales Order
- ME21N: Create Purchase Order
```

The **Command Field** is located in the standard toolbar and enables users to enter transaction codes or system commands directly. Upon executing a command or T-code, the SAP system navigates immediately to the specified transaction. Users can toggle the display of the command field to maximize screen real estate or minimize distractions.

An additional feature enabled within the SAP GUI is the ability to open multiple **Sessions**. Running several sessions concurrently is extremely beneficial for users working across various transactions or modules simultaneously. SAP allows a maximum of six sessions to be open concurrently, with users able to navigate between them using the Windows taskbar or the Session Manager interface within SAP.

Field Help and **Dropdown Menus** further enhance user navigation, particularly for users unfamiliar with SAP system intricacies. Most input fields feature a dropdown button or a search help (F4) indicator alongside them. Clicking this button reveals a list or search criteria, assisting users in correctly entering data without having memorized specific inputs, which contributes significantly to reducing entry errors.

SAP GUI also supports **Personalization and Customization**, enabling users to adapt the interface to meet their needs. Users can tailor the color schemes, adjust visibility of fields, and create personalized favorites and shortcuts. Such personalization fosters an environment where users can work comfortably, knowing they can configure an interface that best enhances their productivity and reduces cognitive overload.

In day-to-day operations, using keyboard shortcuts in SAP GUI significantly expedites task execution and navigation efficiency. Shortcuts like Ctrl+S for saving, Ctrl+F for finding entries, and Ctrl+Shift+F3 for navigating between open sessions help enhance productivity by minimizing reliance on the mouse or navigation menus.

Examples of commonly used shortcuts:
- F1: Help
- F3: Back
- Shift+F1: Create new session
- Ctrl+P: Print

Understanding the **Status Bar** is equally important in SAP GUI navigation. The status bar is located at the bottom of the interface, communicating important contextual messages to users. These messages could range from success confirmations (e.g., "Document saved") to error messages requiring user intervention. The status bar thus serves as a crucial feedback channel between the system and the user, ensuring that they stay informed about the current operation's status and any potential issues.

The SAP GUI's security features should not be overlooked. The interface supports **Single Sign-On (SSO)**, streamlining the user authentication process while enhancing security. Single Sign-On ensures that users authenticate once, gaining access to all necessary applications without repetitive logins, thereby improving both security and user experience.

A thorough understanding of the **System Menu** reinforces SAP GUI basic navigation proficiency. Accessed from the title bar, the system menu grants users access to essential functions like creating a new session, obtaining system and user information, monitoring the SAP workplace, and accessing the clipboard.

For organizations deploying SAP across multiple languages and regions, SAP GUI offers broad-scale **Localization and Internationalization** features, allowing navigation elements, field labels, and system messages to be translated and customized according to the user's preferred language and regional settings. This inclusivity ensures broader user acceptance and mitigates misunderstandings stemming from language barriers, vitally important in multinational corporations.

Understanding basic SAP GUI navigation empowers users to make the best use of SAP systems' comprehensive capabilities, optimizing operational efficiency across business operations. By reducing the learning curve associated with SAP interfaces, users become proficient more quickly, allowing organizations to achieve a greater return on their SAP investments. As SAP GUI continues to evolve, tutorials and systematic guides remain pivotal, ensuring users remain adept at navigating this fundamental interface, maximizing their productivity, and aligning with ever-advancing SAP functional advancements.

1.5 Understanding SAP Landscape and Transport System

The SAP landscape is an intricate architecture designed to support complex enterprise processes, distinguished by its multi-tiered environments that facilitate development, quality assurance, and production deployment. Understanding this landscape is key to managing the lifecycle of SAP applications effectively, from initial development phases to production and maintenance.

At its core, an SAP landscape typically consists of separate instances or systems for development (DEV), quality assurance (QA), and production (PROD). Each of these serves a specific purpose within the development and operational cycle, providing a robust structure that ensures changes are systematically developed, tested, and deployed.

The **Development System** (DEV) is where initial customization, coding, and configuration take place. It is an environment tailored to creativity and testing, allowing developers to experiment freely with new features or modifications. Within this system, customizable settings, table configurations, ABAP programs, and interfaces are crafted. The integration of project-specific developments and enhancements takes place in this environment.

The **Quality Assurance System** (QA), or Test System, is a critical stage in the SAP landscape meant for robust testing of modifications and configurations transferred from the DEV system. Here, adjustments undergo stringent testing and evaluation before reaching production. The QA system replicates the production environment as closely as possible, providing a realistic testing ground to ensure the integrity and performance of changes.

The **Production System** (PROD) represents the live environment where the enterprise's business processes are executed. This system is the most critical, as end-users interact directly with it. Stability, security, and performance are paramount, thus any changes introduced must be verified and tested rigorously before application.

The nuanced architecture of the SAP landscape necessitates a structured, coherent system to manage changes, hence the introduction of the **SAP Transport System (CTS)**. The CTS is a fundamental frame-

1.5. UNDERSTANDING SAP LANDSCAPE AND TRANSPORT SYSTEM

work designed to handle the movement of development objects and system configurations across the SAP landscape. It ensures consistency and integrity by facilitating seamless transports from the DEV to QA and eventually to the PROD environment.

Transport Requests are at the heart of the CTS process. These are records of changes made within the SAP database, encompassing ABAP workbench objects, customizing settings, entries within T-codes, and more. Transport requests are created in the DEV system and are used to encapsulate alterations that need to be implemented across the landscape.

Transport requests break down into two main categories: **Workbench Requests** and **Customizing Requests**. Workbench requests manage repository objects and cross-client data, essential for technical modifications and new developments. On the other hand, customizing requests handle client-specific configurations, pivotal for altering settings that pertain to business needs without altering the core application code.

Once a transport request is documented, developers proceed to release it, guiding the package through the established transport route—from Development to Quality and then Production. This ensures a controlled and traceable pathway for changes, supporting compliance and governance within the software lifecycle process.

Transport Layers further introduce a degree of flexibility and control within the CTS. They define how the development objects are assigned and transported across the systems, essentially operating as predefined paths that transport requests follow. They ensure that developments are transported logically according to the company's requirements and project strategies.

The concept of **Layers** is complemented by the **Transport Control Program (tp)**. This program acts as an intermediary, facilitating the execution of transport requests by detailing the compilation, loading, and application of system changes. It acts in conjunction with the **Quality Gate Management (QGM)**, ensuring compliance with governance standards by setting quality checks within the transport flow.

Additionally, the **Transport Management System (TMS)** acts as a client-independent SAP system management tool, allowing administrators to configure and manage transport routes, layers, and strategies effectively. TMS provides an intuitive interface through which all CTS configurations can be managed, offering comprehensive insights into transport requests, transport logs, and troubleshooting mechanisms.

Below is a simplified example illustrating how one can view a transport request within TMS using SAP's ABAP interface:

```
DATA: lt_e070 TYPE STANDARD TABLE OF e070,
      ls_e070 TYPE e070.

SELECT * FROM e070 INTO TABLE lt_e070
WHERE trkorr = 'DEVK900123'.

LOOP AT lt_e070 INTO ls_e070.
  WRITE: / ls_e070-trkorr, ls_e070-as4user, ls_e070-as4date.
ENDLOOP.
```

Any successful transport strategy mandates a harmonious balance between automation and control, and toolsets like **SAP Solution Manager** enhance CTS by integrating monitoring, notification, and reporting functionalities. Solution Manager aids in harmonizing IT processes across the SAP landscape, making it invaluable for maintaining continuity and operational integrity.

Transport management in SAP is also fortified by a series of **Best Practices**. These include maintaining clear documentation of all transports, evaluating dependencies within the transport requests, scheduling transports to minimize disruption during peak usage times, and comprehensively testing in QA to reduce any potential issues in production.

Security is inherently embedded within the CTS, employing advanced user authentication, authorization checks, and comprehensive logging mechanisms. Transport requests undergo various levels of approval, ensuring that only authorized personnel execute sensitive changes, thus safeguarding the production environment's sanctity.

Importantly, SAP landscapes must adapt to **S/4HANA** and cloud environments, introducing complexities and requiring enhanced transport mechanisms. The suite optimizes for agility, requiring that traditional transport strategies be coupled with agile methodologies like DevOps, which can cause a transformational shift in logistics and strategic implementations in transport management.

1.5. UNDERSTANDING SAP LANDSCAPE AND TRANSPORT SYSTEM

A deep understanding of the SAP landscape and transport system is indispensable for any SAP professional tasked with maintaining the lifecycle, integrity, and efficiency of SAP applications. The strategic combination of environments and the disciplined process of managing transports are foundational to ensuring a seamless operation that supports the organization's business functions effectively. As technology evolves, the cloud's integration into this landscape is redefining paradigms, mandating an ongoing adaptation to these best practices and a readiness to embrace futuristic innovations.

Chapter 2

ABAP Syntax and Programming Fundamentals

This chapter delves into the core of ABAP programming, providing readers with a thorough understanding of its syntax and foundational constructs. Key topics include the basic structure of ABAP programs, the diverse range of data types and declarations used to define and manipulate variables, and essential statements and expressions that drive program logic. The chapter also covers fundamental techniques for string and numerical operations. Furthermore, the exploration of control flow structures, such as loops and conditional statements, equips readers with the skills needed to implement complex logic, while error handling and debugging techniques ensure robust program execution.

2.1 ABAP Program Structure

In understanding the structure of an ABAP program, one must thoroughly comprehend its essential components, starting from the basic elements such as headers, declaration parts, and procedural elements. This section provides an exposé into the anatomy of an ABAP program to ensure a solid grasp of its construction and operation.

Headers: At the top of every ABAP program, headers define the program's name and specify the type of program it is or any interfaces it implements. This section also includes pertinent metadata that can assist in program categorization and subsequent management. Header syntax commonly starts with REPORT, PROGRAM, or CLASS. While dealing with executable programs, you typically use the keyword REPORT.

```
REPORT ZMY_FIRST_PROGRAM.
```

Here, ZMY_FIRST_PROGRAM signifies the name of the ABAP program. It is customary to use a unique identifier beginning with a 'Z' or 'Y' to denote user-defined programs, distinguishing them from standard SAP applications.

Declarations: Following headers, the declaration section initializes all the variables and constants that the program will use. ABAP, being a strongly-typed language, compels explicit declaration of all variables before they can be utilized within the main procedural parts of the program. Declaration involves defining the type, size, and other attributes of the data objects.

Basic data types include CHAR, NUMC, INT, DEC, and FLOAT. Each serves a specific purpose within the program, depending on the nature and requirements of data manipulation. Here is a typical variable declaration:

```
DATA: gv_number TYPE INT4,
      gv_name TYPE CHAR20.
```

In the above code, gv_number is an integer variable of length 4, and gv_name is a fixed-length character string of length 20.

Constants are similar to variables but differ in that their values remain

2.1. ABAP PROGRAM STRUCTURE

unchanged once set. Application constants are declared using the keyword CONSTANTS, for instance:

```
CONSTANTS: gc_pi TYPE F VALUE '3.14159'.
```

This declaration sets up a constant with the fixed value of Pi. This practice ensures better code readability and maintainability, especially in scenarios demanding periodic changes to constant values across multiple usage points.

Procedural Elements: These elements form the core where the logic of the program is defined, typically including subroutine calls and the main logic execution flow. Procedural programming within ABAP employs modularization units such as subroutines (FORM and ENDFORM), function modules, and methods.

Form statements allow encapsulating specific functionalities for re-use within the program, thereby promoting modularity and enhancing understandability. Here is how one would conventionally define a subroutine in ABAP:

```
FORM calculate_interest.
  "Procedural code goes here
ENDFORM.
```

The advantage of subroutines emerges in their ability to modularize specific tasks like data validation, business logic processing, or interactions with database tables, followed by implementing complex routines through a strategic blend of subroutine and mainline code sections.

Comments and Documentation: Within programs, comments serve as crucial documentation for developers to describe the logic used, the purpose of code sections, and variable usage. ABAP permits both single-line and multi-line comments. Single-line comments begin with an asterisk (*) or double quotation marks ("). Multi-line comments utilize the * symbol at the beginning of each line.

```
* This is a single-line comment
" Another single-line comment example

* Multi-line comment
* explaining the function.
```

Such practice is indispensable for maintaining clarity in code reviews, team development scenarios, and future maintenance developments.

Control Statements: The procedural section also involves control statements that manipulate the order of execution of program instructions. These include conditional constructs like IF, CASE, DO, WHILE, and LOOP.

Utilizing an IF statement:

```
IF gv_number = 10.
  WRITE: / 'The number is ten.'.
ELSE.
  WRITE: / 'The number is not ten.'.
ENDIF.
```

This block controls the flow of the program based on the condition set, determining which subsequent code block will execute. Each type of control statement finds usage depending on specific logical requirements like setting conditions, iterating over datasets, or managing complex programmatic flows.

Program Flow and Execution: Within most ABAP environments, program execution grants an implicit advantage through various lifecycle methodologies such as event-handling and process chains. Although the macroscale event framework isn't always visualizable within a coded structure, appreciation for programming flow, especially while dealing with data-heavy operations in large enterprises, remains paramount.

An appreciation of dynamic failure handling structures via systematic trapping of exceptions and errors using TRY and CATCH blocks grants an additional layer of robustness.

```
TRY.
  "Attempt to open a file
CATCH CX_SY_IO_ERROR.
  WRITE: / 'File cannot be accessed.'.
ENDTRY.
```

This kind of proactive error catching allows the maintenance of program stability despite unforeseen runtime discrepancies. This capacity to seamlessly integrate error management into procedural logic emphasizes another critical layer of ABAP's robust programming environment.

In sum, the essence of competent ABAP programming resonates through meticulous adherence to organized program structuring, intuitive variable handling through appropriate data definitions, and cognitive flow control via logically sound procedural execution pathways. Each aspect, when mastered, offers compelling blueprints for effectively navigating the vast suite of applications inhospitably resident in SAP's landscape. As one advances, leveraging the predictable yet powerful building blocks of an ABAP program becomes second nature, paving the way for richer, scalable, and logically coherent enterprise solutions. The thoughtful meld of consistent naming conventions, modularization strategies, and deliberate documentation are what delineate a professional approach from mere code existence, creating a foundation for innovative aspirations within SAP's technological realm.

2.2 Data Types and Declarations

In ABAP, recognizing and efficiently utilizing various data types and understanding the proper declaration of variables and constants is crucial for success in developing programs. This section will explore the diverse spectrum of data types available in ABAP, their characteristics, and their usage. In addition, we will analyze the declaration procedures that form an integral part of any ABAP program to ensure organized and efficient data handling.

Primitive Data Types: At the core of ABAP's data handling capabilities are primitive data types that cater to diverse data manipulation needs. These include character types, numeric types, packed decimals, floating-point numbers, and more. Understanding each type's nuances is essential for selecting the correct type for your specific application requirements.

Character types form a basic building block for handling textual data. The primary character data type in ABAP is CHAR. It accommodates fixed-length strings, facilitating precise control over text data. Consider the following variable declaration:

```
DATA gv_customer_name TYPE CHAR20.
```

Here, gv_customer_name is a character variable that can store up to 20 characters. It's important to note that unused spaces in such fixed-length strings are space-padded, potentially affecting comparison operations.

In numeric types, INT1, INT2, and INT4 cater to small integers, while DEC and FLOAT accommodate decimal and floating-point numbers respectively. ABAP's NUMC type represents numeric character strings, emphasizing numerical digits as characters:

```
DATA gv_account_number TYPE NUMC10.
DATA gv_amount TYPE DECIMAL8.
```

The above examples show `gv_account_number` as a 10-digit numeric string and `gv_amount` as a decimal variable with a precision of eight digits, enabling precise numeric operations in financial computing scenarios.

Structured Data Types: For scenarios where data organization demands grouping multiple elements, structured data types such as STRUCTURE or similar techniques are indispensable. A structure is a composite data type composed of fields, each with its distinct data type and attribute. This definition is ushered by the keyword BEGIN OF and END OF, as indicated below:

```
TYPES: BEGIN OF ty_address,
         street TYPE CHAR25,
         city TYPE CHAR20,
         zipcode TYPE CHAR10,
       END OF ty_address.
```

Subsequently, a structured variable of type `ty_address` could be declared using:

```
DATA gv_home_address TYPE ty_address.
```

This feature facilitates the hierarchical data organization necessary for settings like address management, inventory controls, or encapsulating personal data records. Such abstraction allows simultaneous manipulation of related data elements using single structured data entity pointers.

Internal Tables: ABAP provides internal tables as an essential way to manage dynamic datasets. They provide flexibility that traditional arrays in other programming languages might lack, as their size can be dynamically adjusted during runtime, thus adeptly managing variable

2.2. DATA TYPES AND DECLARATIONS

amounts of homogenous data elements.

Internal tables instantiate using TABLE OF construct, such as:

```
DATA: lt_numbers TYPE TABLE OF i WITH EMPTY KEY.
```

The table lt_numbers can dynamically store integer values, manipulating them using internal table operations. It's critical for scenarios requiring batch data processing, aggregation, or multistage analysis where inline performance optimizations significantly affect execution efficiency.

References and Object Data Types: In modern ABAP, objects facilitate the encapsulation of functionality and data. Object-oriented techniques utilize reference types for classes and interfaces. A reference variable points to objects instantiated in memory, defined by a class, such as:

```
DATA lr_order TYPE REF TO zcl_order.
CREATE OBJECT lr_order.
```

This code segment initializes a reference lr_order for the custom class zcl_order, later creating an instance with CREATE OBJECT. Emphasizing encapsulation, polymorphism, and inheritance, this method evolves the development into adaptable and maintainable solutions, adding agility requisite to large systems.

Component Processing: Finer granularity in managing complex variables involves component processing through field symbol constructs. Field symbols allow dynamic field assignments at runtime, thereby facilitating flexible and often more efficient manipulation of data objects. Employ ASSIGN statements in combination with field symbols as follows:

```
FIELD-SYMBOLS <fs_component> TYPE ANY.
DATA gv_variable TYPE i.
ASSIGN gv_variable TO <fs_component>.
```

Using field symbols removes compile-time size restrictions or data object nature, leading to efficient data processing where dynamic property assignments play a significant role in computational logic.

Data Declaration Techniques: How a program declares its data significantly impacts readability, scalability, and integrity. Emphasis should lie on meaningful variable names, consistent naming conventions (like Hungarian notation), and grouped declarations for related logical components.

Collating declarations at the program's inception ensures straightforward access and modification, especially when integrating changes into legacy systems or handling large codebases. Minimize or appropriately manage hard-coded values through constants to ensure maintainable code evolution. Appropriately-used comments deepen comprehension, describing purposes or caveats of declaration details, empowering teams operatively to connect intents to actions.

Type Compatibility and Conversion: Conscientious developers remain attentive to type compatibility, especially when involving comparison or arithmetic operations across different data types. The ABAP runtime environment inherently supports data type conversion, allowing operations with disparate numerical representations.

For instance, converting a character type to numeric involves explicit conversions:

```
DATA gv_num_string TYPE CHAR10 VALUE '100'.
DATA gv_numeric_value TYPE i.

gv_numeric_value = gv_num_string.
```

ABAP manages type conversions aiming at logical type compatibility with occasional conversions requiring explicit approach to manage precision or range issues. Here, type conversion facilitates leveraging data integrity operations where operator operand mismatches obstruct execution pathways.

In sum, the mastery of data types and precise declarations crafts foundational knowledge for effectively engaging with ABAP's powerful data manipulation capabilities. Equipped with these insights, programmers can aptly structure their data declarations, choose proper types for intended operations, and advance into intricate programmatic patterns with assured command over data integrity and architectural brilliance. The deployment of structured and hierarchical organizational methods not only provides functional efficacy but also aligns closely with best practices central to delivering resilient technology solutions in SAP systems. This deep understanding of data-centric constructs thus underpins the transformative realization from conceptualizing an idea to implementing a robust, efficient, and sustainable enterprise-level application solstice.

2.3 ABAP Statements and Expressions

The capability to define logical constructions within a program benefits from a robust understanding of statements and expressions. In ABAP, these elements lay the groundwork for conveying logic, manipulating data, and controlling the flow of execution. This section delves into the syntax, usage, and intricacies of ABAP statements and expressions, highlighting their role in shaping an executable program.

Statements: At the heart of any ABAP program are the statements that perform operations as instructed. An ABAP statement typically consists of a keyword, often followed by a set of operands or parameters, executed at runtime to bring about desired actions or results. Statements can operate for data assignments, control flow alterations, calling functions, or interacting with databases.

A ubiquitous example in ABAP is the assignment statement, whereby a value is assigned to a variable using the = operator:

```
DATA gv_total TYPE i.
gv_total = 100.
```

Here, the numeric value 100 is assigned to the integer variable gv_total. The simplicity of an assignment is foundational, forming the rudimentary syntax that enables the operational utility of more complex logic.

Expressions: Expressions are evaluative codes returning a result, a connection of variables, operands, and operators yielding a singular output. These expressions possess syntactic flexibility, embedding within conditional statements or function calls. A straightforward arithmetic operation acts as a prototypical expression:

```
DATA: gv_sum TYPE i,
      gv_num1 TYPE i VALUE 200,
      gv_num2 TYPE i VALUE 150.

gv_sum = gv_num1 + gv_num2.
```

Here, gv_sum is the evaluative result of summing gv_num1 and gv_-num2. Such expressions facilitate operations with arithmetic operators (+, -, *, /) or relational comparisons (>, <, =).

Control Statements: Control statements are pivotal in defining program execution paths, utilizing conditions, and loops. The IF statement assesses whether certain criteria hold true, guiding subsequent operations based on this logical decision.

```
IF gv_total > 100.
  WRITE: / 'Total is greater than 100.'.
ELSE.
  WRITE: / 'Total is less than or equal to 100.'.
ENDIF.
```

Here, the logic bifurcates into different output paths based on whether gv_total exceeds 100, showcasing conditional logic's capability to react to evolving program states or data.

For more complex conditions involving multiple expressions, logical operators such as AND or OR facilitate cohesive conditional evaluation.

```
IF gv_total > 50 AND gv_total < 200.
  WRITE: / 'Total is between 51 and 199.'.
ENDIF.
```

Such logical aggregation facilitates expressing multifaceted conditions succinctly, crucial for intricate data-driven decisions.

Loop Constructs: Loop constructs enable repetitive execution of code blocks, often iterating over datasets or retrying processes until specified conditions manifest. The DO loop iterates for a defined number of times, whereas the WHILE loop operates until a condition alters.

```
DATA: gv_count TYPE i VALUE 1.
DO 5 TIMES.
  WRITE: / 'Iteration', gv_count.
  gv_count = gv_count + 1.
ENDDO.
```

This DO loop writes out five lines of "Iteration #", typifying controlled repetition essential for iterative calculations, batch processing, or cumulative summaries.

Furthermore, the LOOP AT command is indispensable in processing internal tables, providing a streamlined mechanism for handling each

2.3. ABAP STATEMENTS AND EXPRESSIONS

row:

```
DATA: lt_customers TYPE TABLE OF string.
APPEND 'Customer1' TO lt_customers.
APPEND 'Customer2' TO lt_customers.

LOOP AT lt_customers INTO DATA(lv_customer).
  WRITE: / lv_customer.
ENDLOOP.
```

Here, looping through lt_customers executes the WRITE for each entry, demonstrating ABAP's efficiency in batch record evaluations.

Case Differentiation: The CASE statement, analogous to a combination of multiple IF-ELSEIF conditions, orchestrates block selection based on variable value concordance with designated cases.

```
DATA gv_choice TYPE i VALUE 2.

CASE gv_choice.
  WHEN 1.
    WRITE: / 'Option 1 selected'.
  WHEN 2.
    WRITE: / 'Option 2 selected'.
  WHEN OTHERS.
    WRITE: / 'Other option selected'.
ENDCASE.
```

The use of CASE simplifies complex decision trees, particularly when value mappings are sequential or exclusive, guaranteeing clearer, more readable code execution pathways.

Function Calls and Expressions: Function modules, akin to function invocations, are pivotal in ABAP for encapsulating and re-utilizing logic outside the immediate context, modulated through parameters and results:

```
CALL FUNCTION 'CONVERT_TO_FOREIGN_CURRENCY'
  EXPORTING
    FOREIGN_CURRENCY = 'EUR'
    LOCAL_AMOUNT = 500
  IMPORTING
    FOREIGN_AMOUNT = gv_foreign_amount.
```

The preceding example designates a function call altering a local amount to a foreign currency, encapsulating a fiscal conversion's inherent complexity, and yielding processed data via gv_foreign_amount.

Functionally analogous statements like PERFORM invoke subroutines, conferring modularization within program sections:

```
PERFORM calculate_tax USING gv_income CHANGING gv_tax.
```

This encapsulation efficiently manages localized logic reutilization across disparate program segments, curtailing redundancy while amplifying maintainability.

By synthesizing ABAP statements and expressions, developers sculpting programmatic logic proficiently engage with problem-solving frameworks, infusing efficiency, clarity, and robustness within the broader SAP technological ecosystem. Advanced familiarity with paradigms like exceptions handling, chaining expressions, or integrating object-oriented approaches further escalates this landscape's efficacy into high-order, intricate system implementations on an enterprise-ready scale. The balanced mix of statements and expressions furnishes a medium through which actionable business intelligence and operational workflows find accurate, deterministic expression and value realization, reified through an effective coding syllabus marred by neither ambiguity nor inefficiency.

2.4 Working with Strings and Numbers

In ABAP programming, the manipulation of strings and numbers is a fundamental operation critical to data processing and reporting tasks. This section provides an expansive examination of the methods and functions used to handle strings and numbers efficiently in ABAP, offering insights into best practices for leveraging built-in capabilities to optimize these operations.

String Manipulation: Strings, or sequences of characters, are central to handling textual information. ABAP provides a variety of operations and built-in functions to manipulate them. The data type primarily used for strings is CHAR, though STRING is also available for dynamic text handling where length variability is essential.

Concatenation: A frequent requirement is to concatenate, or join, multiple strings into a single string. This is achieved using the CONCATENATE statement:

2.4. WORKING WITH STRINGS AND NUMBERS

```
DATA: lv_first_name TYPE CHAR10 VALUE 'John',
      lv_last_name TYPE CHAR15 VALUE 'Doe',
      lv_full_name TYPE STRING.

CONCATENATE lv_first_name lv_last_name INTO lv_full_name SEPARATED BY
    space.
```

Here, lv_full_name results from combining lv_first_name and lv_last_name, separated by a space. This operation is pivotal when formatting strings for display or constructing key identifiers dynamically.

Substrings and Length: Extracting specific parts of a string or determining its length is crucial for data parsing tasks. The statement OFFSET with LENGTH is often used to retrieve substrings.

```
DATA: lv_substring TYPE CHAR10.

lv_substring = lv_full_name+0(4). "Extracts 'John'
WRITE lv_substring.
```

The operation above extracts a substring starting from position 0 with a length of 4. Similarly, computing the length of a string is facilitated via the STRLEN function:

```
DATA: lv_length TYPE i.

lv_length = STRLEN( lv_full_name ).
WRITE: / 'Length of full name:', lv_length.
```

Understanding these operations is essential in situations where validation of input, processing dynamic text fields, or trimming and formatting strings for output is required.

Pattern Matching and Replacement: ABAP supports pattern recognition and replacement within strings via functions like FIND and REPLACE, which are instrumental for data sanitization, validation, or transformation.

```
FIND FIRST OCCURRENCE OF 'Doe' IN lv_full_name.

REPLACE 'Doe' WITH 'Smith' INTO lv_full_name.
WRITE lv_full_name. "Outputs 'John Smith'
```

These operations heavily benefit task-specific manipulations, such as reconfiguring data sourced from texts, emails, or documents for integration into databases or standardized forms, crucial in ETL processes.

CHAPTER 2. ABAP SYNTAX AND PROGRAMMING FUNDAMENTALS

Numeric Operations: Handling numerical values involves various operations including arithmetic, rounding, and number formatting. ABAP provides a comprehensive set of operators for executing arithmetic calculations such as addition, subtraction, multiplication, and division, suitable for both integer and floating-point values.

```
DATA: gv_result TYPE i,
      gv_add TYPE i VALUE 5,
      gv_multiply TYPE i VALUE 10.

gv_result = gv_add + gv_multiply * 2.
WRITE: / 'Calculation Result:', gv_result.
```

The precedence and associativity rules standardize arithmetic expressions evaluation, observing natural mathematical hierarchy without need for explicit parentheses unless necessary for displacement.

Rounding and Conversion: Rounding decimal numbers to the nearest integer or a specific decimal place is performed through ROUND function calls:

```
DATA gv_rounded TYPE p DECIMALS 2.

gv_rounded = ROUND( 123.456, 'DECIMALS=2' ).
WRITE: / 'Rounded Value:', gv_rounded.
```

Furthermore, conversion between different numeric types and textual representation (e.g., from NUMC to numerical types) is frequently leveraged when working on form inputs or file exports.

Formatting Numbers: For displaying numerical values in a formatted output, the usage of conversion exits or formatted output statements adjusts the representation style. ABAP's WRITE statement allows formatted outputs with addition options:

```
WRITE: / lv_total NO-ZERO,
       / lv_total UNDER '_____'.
```

Such nuances in formatting make ABAP versatile for generating user-friendly tabular displays, invoices, or standardized reports.

Dynamic Numeric and String Handling: Efficiency in processing large datasets or performing fluid transformations dynamically is facilitated by internal tables and auxiliary variables, often capitalizing on collected techniques for indexing, traversing, or conditionally modifying entries.

Consider dynamically adjusting string values in an internal table:

```
DATA: lt_names TYPE TABLE OF CHAR25.

APPEND 'Johnathon' TO lt_names.
APPEND 'Mike' TO lt_names.

LOOP AT lt_names INTO DATA(lv_name).
  IF STRLEN( lv_name ) > 6.
    WRITE: / lv_name.
  ENDIF.
ENDLOOP.
```

This code highlights string evaluation within a loop, conditionally writing those exceeding a defined character threshold.

Efficiency and Performance Considerations: When dealing significantly with strings or numerical computations, considerations towards buffer management, memory usage, and performance become critical. Effective practices involve utilizing localized variables, minimizing data format changes, and aligning logic flow to minimize redundant computations or extensive runtime checks.

Internal table optimizations on large data populations, retracting unnecessary reads/writes, unequivocally enhance throughput, especially when bolstered by database indexing or optimized SQL integrations for large datasets.

An adept comprehension of string and numeric handling translates into assured capabilities in creating sophisticated data-centric solutions attuned to corporate analytics, report generation, or service interfaces. Collective operational mastery ensures ABAP professionals distinguish themselves with qualitatively superior coding practices, accommodating scalability, precision, and project deliverables alignment, defining them as assets in SAP environments.

2.5 Control Flow in ABAP

Control flow structures are fundamental components that guide the execution sequence of a program. In ABAP, effective implementation of these structures facilitates decision making, repetition, and conditional operations which are foundational for more complex procedural logic. This section elaborates on the various control flow techniques available in ABAP, illustrating their usage through detailed examples and emphasizing their importance in developing robust and efficient programs.

Conditional Statements: At the heart of decision-making in programming, conditional statements enable the execution of code based on Boolean evaluations. ABAP offers the IF statement to execute code blocks when conditions evaluate to true.

```
DATA: gv_balance TYPE p DECIMALS 2 VALUE 200.00,
      gv_threshold TYPE p DECIMALS 2 VALUE 100.00.

IF gv_balance > gv_threshold.
   WRITE: / 'Balance is above the threshold.'.
ELSE.
   WRITE: / 'Balance is below the threshold.'.
ENDIF.
```

Here, the code block inside the IF statement will execute if gv_balance exceeds gv_threshold; otherwise, the ELSE block is executed. This bifurcation in logic is crucial when dealing with user-driven inputs or real-time data processing scenarios.

Nested IF Statements: ABAP also supports nested IF statements, allowing further branched logic which is indispensable in processing multiple conditions that interdepend sequentially.

```
DATA: gv_status TYPE CHAR10 VALUE 'ACTIVE'.

IF gv_balance > gv_threshold.
   IF gv_status = 'ACTIVE'.
      WRITE: / 'Account active and balance exceeds threshold.'.
   ELSE.
      WRITE: / 'Account inactive, but balance exceeds threshold.'.
   ENDIF.
ELSE.
   WRITE: / 'Balance is below the threshold.'.
ENDIF.
```

Here, nested conditions allow us to further evaluate gv_status only when the balance threshold condition is fulfilled, paving the way for streamlined and hierarchical decision making.

CASE Statement: An alternative to multiple IF-ELSEIF constructs, the CASE statement provides a cleaner structure for evaluating a variable against a set of discrete values.

```
DATA gv_role TYPE CHAR10 VALUE 'USER'.
```

2.5. CONTROL FLOW IN ABAP

```
CASE gv_role.
  WHEN 'ADMIN'.
    WRITE: / 'Access level: Admin'.
  WHEN 'USER'.
    WRITE: / 'Access level: User'.
  WHEN 'GUEST'.
    WRITE: / 'Access level: Guest'.
  WHEN OTHERS.
    WRITE: / 'Access level: Undefined'.
ENDCASE.
```

The CASE statement's utility is apparent in situations like role-based access control, where a variable may equal precisely one of several predetermined values, enhancing readability while maintaining performance by eliminating redundant condition evaluations once a match is identified.

Loop Constructs: Repetitive execution is often necessary for data processing, whether traversing datasets, performing iterative calculations, or facilitating regular operations until specific criteria clarify. The DO loop in ABAP is straightforward for fixed repetition:

```
DATA: gv_count TYPE i VALUE 1.

DO 5 TIMES.
  WRITE: / 'Iteration ', gv_count.
  gv_count = gv_count + 1.
ENDDO.
```

This loop executes the inner block five times, incrementing and displaying the count with each iteration. Its simplicity is ideal for consistent, predetermined iterations, like initializing rows or running setup operations.

For more flexible iterations based on conditions, the WHILE loop provides adaptability:

```
DATA gv_result TYPE i VALUE 1.

WHILE gv_result <= 5.
  WRITE: / 'Result:', gv_result.
  gv_result = gv_result + 1.
ENDWHILE.
```

Here, the loop continues executing while gv_result remains below or equal to five, showcasing a data-driven flexibility requisite for runtime evaluations or operations framed around dynamically determined thresholds.

Looping Through Internal Tables: ABAP's LOOP AT construct is optimized for processing internal tables. It simplifies extracting, displaying, or modifying table rows iteratively:

```
DATA: lt_orders TYPE TABLE OF STRING,
      lv_order TYPE STRING.

APPEND 'Order1' TO lt_orders.
APPEND 'Order2' TO lt_orders.

LOOP AT lt_orders INTO lv_order.
   WRITE: / 'Processing', lv_order.
ENDLOOP.
```

This loop structure processes each entry in lt_orders, essential for business applications housing datasets in internal tables requiring consecutive evaluations or manipulations, like processing orders or transactions.

Exit and Continue Statements: Within loops, it may sometimes be necessary to either prematurely exit the current loop iteration or bypass specific conditions for continued processing. The EXIT statement halts an ongoing loop entirely, while CONTINUE skips to the next cycle, maintaining efficiency and control over logic execution purview:

```
LOOP AT lt_orders INTO lv_order.
   IF lv_order = 'Order50'.
      EXIT. "Loop termination condition
   ENDIF.

   IF lv_order = 'Order10'.
      CONTINUE. "Skip processing for Order10
   ENDIF.
   WRITE: / 'Order:', lv_order.
ENDLOOP.
```

Using these strategically mitigates unnecessary evaluations or enters a premature completion path, vital for circumventing unwarranted operations, notably in resource-intensive or integrity-critical contexts.

Error Handling and Control Transfer: Robust control flows integrate exception handling mechanisms to safeguard against runtime errors, ensuring resilient error capture and message dissemination. ABAP utilizes TRY and CATCH blocks for such exception handling:

```
TRY.
   CALL METHOD unsafe_method.
CATCH cx_sy_arithmetics.
   WRITE: / 'Arithmetic error encountered.'.
```

```
CATCH cx_sy_no_handler.
  WRITE: / 'Unhandled general error.'.
ENDTRY.
```

The inclusion of such handling constructs provides reliable fail-safes for critical computations, often encountering potential hazards during arithmetic operations, memory allocations, or external system interactions.

In mastering ABAP's control flow structures, developers elevate their ability to build logically coherent, efficient, and error-resistant programs. These elements, intertwined with conventional processes, provide a comprehensive toolkit conducive to robust solution engineering in SAP environments, fortifying applications against the unpredictability of enterprise-level computational demands and state fluidity inherent to complex system operations. Mastering these constructs consequently charts a path toward consistent technical dexterity, enabling businesses and organizations alike in transforming procedural paradigms into sustainably realized success.

2.6 Error Handling and Debugging Techniques

In ABAP programming, error handling and debugging are pivotal for creating resilient, error-free enterprise applications. Mastery of these techniques ensures robust code execution and seamless user experiences while mitigating potential system failures. This section delves into the methodologies and tools available in ABAP for error handling and debugging, emphasizing their critical role in software development.

Error Handling Frameworks: ABAP provides structured mechanisms to anticipate, manage, and recover from errors that can arise during program execution. Such mechanisms are crucial for ensuring program stability and reliability, especially when interfacing with external systems or handling large datasets. Central to this is the concept of exception handling, which relates to capturing and managing errors within a program's flow.

Exceptions and Exception Classes: Exceptions in ABAP can be categorized as system or application-specific. System exceptions are low-level errors generated by the runtime environment, such as division by zero or memory allocation issues. In contrast, application-specific exceptions are user-defined, encapsulating business or logic-related errors.

To manage these exceptions, ABAP employs exception classes, forming the cornerstone of robust error management. Built upon the base exception class CX_ROOT, SAP offers specific subclasses like CX_SY_ARITHMETIC_ERR or custom user-defined classes for tailored scenarios:

```
CLASS lcx_my_exception DEFINITION INHERITING FROM cx_static_check.
ENDCLASS.

CLASS lcx_my_exception IMPLEMENTATION.
ENDCLASS.
```

Exception classes like lcx_my_exception facilitate specialized handling scenarios by extending upon existing exceptions, offering a mechanism to raise and handle errors gracefully within applications.

TRY...CATCH Constructs: The TRY...CATCH block provides a controlled environment to encapsulate potentially erroneous code, processing exceptions effectively:

```
TRY.
  "Potentially risky operation
  CALL METHOD some_dangerous_method.
  CATCH cx_sy_dyn_call_illegal_type.
    WRITE: / 'Illegal type during dynamic call.'.
  CATCH cx_sy_no_handler.
    WRITE: / 'Unhandled error occurred.'.
ENDTRY.
```

Here, errors occurring within the TRY block are captured by matching CATCH statements, allowing remedial action or logging. Employing these structures enhances program robustness by directing unpredictable flows into known response sequences.

PROPAGATE and RAISE Exception Keywords: ABAP's control over error scenarios extends through PROPAGATE and RAISE keywords. PROPAGATE forwards exceptions to a parent context, while RAISE explicitly triggers defined exceptions, signaling an inherently problematic state:

2.6. ERROR HANDLING AND DEBUGGING TECHNIQUES

```
METHOD compute_area.
  IF lv_length <= 0 OR lv_width <= 0.
    RAISE lcx_invalid_dimension.
  ENDIF.
ENDMETHOD.
```

By judiciously utilizing these constructs, developers can architect applications that are neither blind to nor ignorant of execution anomalies, instead actively managing all tiers of operational capacity.

Logging and Monitoring: Logging plays a crucial role in enhancing the maintainability of an ABAP system. Effective logging captures pertinent information about program execution, facilitating troubleshooting and audit opportunities:

```
LOG-POINT ID 'program_flow' SUBKEY 'calculation'.
```

Utilizing LOG-POINT statements provides locational insight into program flow, crucial for retrospective analyses when investigating executed sequences. This capability, in tandem with external monitoring tools like SAP Solution Manager, delivers a comprehensive system tracking mechanism.

ABAP Debugger: When programmatic errors are elusive or deeply entrenched, the ABAP Debugger becomes indispensable. As an interactive diagnostic tool, it meticulously traces program execution, offering real-time insights into variables, field symbols, and other runtime constructs.

The Debugger can set breakpoints on specific lines or conditional breakpoints triggered by criteria:

```
BREAK-POINT ID sy-uname.
```

The above statement introduces a user-specific breakpoint, halting execution when reached, and offering a sandbox environment to dissect program flow, root out misconceptions, and validate assumptions underlying logic formulations.

Advanced techniques within the Debugger include variable watches, stack displays, and memory analyses to identify misalignments or anomalies, empowering developers to pinpoint and surgically correct intricate bugs.

ST22 and ST05 Transactions: SAP additionally equips developers with specialized transactions for error analysis—ST22 for ABAP runtime errors and ST05 for performance tracing:

- **ST22 (Dump Analysis):** Offers a detailed display of runtime errors, capturing stack traces, variable states, and error contexts essential for post-mortem debugging efforts.

- **ST05 (Performance Trace):** Focuses on identifying performance bottlenecks, assessing SQL execution paths, and revealing costly operations impacting system efficiency.

Unit Testing Frameworks: Proactive error prevention integrates into developmental workflows through automated testing via ABAP Unit or Test Sequences. These methodologies favor a test-driven approach by formally validating code behavior against prescriptive assertions, safeguarding against regressions or unintentional modifications.

```
CLASS lt_example_test DEFINITION FOR TESTING RISK LEVEL CRITICAL
    DURATION SHORT.
  PRIVATE SECTION.
    METHODS test_calculate_area FOR TESTING.
ENDCLASS.

CLASS lt_example_test IMPLEMENTATION.
  METHOD test_calculate_area.
    DATA: lv_area TYPE i VALUE 0.
    CALL METHOD under_test=>calculate_area
      EXPORTING iv_length = 3 iv_width = 4
      RECEIVING rv_area = lv_area.
    cl_abap_unit_assert=>assert_equals( act = lv_area exp = 12 ).
  ENDMETHOD.
ENDCLASS.
```

Unit tests, shrewdly designed, constitute an integral pillar upholding resilient, high-quality code outputs amidst iterative enhancement cycles.

By embracing these error handling and debugging techniques, ABAP developers shape systems distinguished by precision, robustness, and adaptability, adeptly navigating the complexities of business logic implementations within SAP's technological universe. The converged deployment of these strategies underscores a methodological commitment that transcends mere functionality, delivering scalable, sustainable solutions that inspire trust and collaboration amidst even the most challenging problem spaces encountered in the digital enterprise sphere.

Chapter 3

Working with Data: Internal Tables and Data Dictionary

This chapter focuses on the pivotal components of data handling in ABAP: internal tables and the Data Dictionary. It offers an in-depth exploration of the Data Dictionary's role in structuring and organizing data within SAP, including creating and managing transparent tables. Readers will gain insights into the definition and efficient use of internal tables for data manipulation, along with operations such as sorting and aggregating data. The chapter also covers optimizing data access through keys and indexes and provides guidance on using SAP tools to manage Data Dictionary objects, ensuring efficient and effective data management in ABAP applications.

3.1 Understanding the Data Dictionary

The SAP Data Dictionary is an integral component in SAP systems, serving as a centralized repository for metadata and a cornerstone for data management. It is responsible for defining the structure and organization of data within the system. This section delves into the intricacies of the SAP Data Dictionary, focusing on its components such as tables, views, data elements, and domains, which are essential for efficient data handling. Understanding these elements is crucial for any developer or data analyst working within the SAP environment.

At its core, the SAP Data Dictionary provides several key functionalities: it maintains data definitions consisting of tables and indexes, logically groups database tables, and provides descriptions for fields, data types, and domain values. By offering a structured environment, it enables consistent handling of data across different SAP applications.

Tables

In the SAP Data Dictionary, tables are the primary structures for storing data. They are used to model real-world entities and relationships within the SAP environment. Each table in the SAP system is linked to a structure in the underlying database, allowing data to be stored persistently.

Tables in SAP are categorized into different types, each serving specific purposes:

- *Transparent tables:* These tables maintain a direct relationship with the database tables. They are used to store application data that can be accessed directly by the underlying database management system (DBMS). Every transparent table in SAP corresponds to an identical table in the database, ensuring data consistency.

- *Pooled tables:* Pooled tables are used to group several tables logically. They do not exist directly in the database. Instead, the data of several small tables is stored together in a single table, known as a table pool. This type of table structure is particularly useful for small data that is accessed infrequently.

- *Cluster tables:* Similar to pooled tables, cluster tables store data

3.1. UNDERSTANDING THE DATA DICTIONARY

from multiple tables in a clustered manner. However, cluster tables differ in storing highly related tables together in large volumes for efficient access.

Views

Views in the SAP Data Dictionary are logical representations of one or more tables. They do not store data themselves but provide a mechanism to present data dynamically from multiple tables based on specific criteria, without the need for redundant data storage. There are several types of views in SAP:

- *Database views:* Directly correspond to SQL views in the database, providing a way to join and display data from multiple database tables.
- *Projection views:* Allow selection of certain fields from a table without copying the data, reducing unnecessary data processing.
- *Maintenance views:* Designed for maintaining data across several tables using a single transaction.
- *Help views:* Provide search help for data fields, enhancing user interaction by offering a list of possible input values.

Data Elements

A data element in the SAP Data Dictionary defines the semantic meaning of a table field or a structure field. It represents the metadata related to a particular field, such as the field label, search help, and any documentation associated with it. Data elements describe the type of data that a field can hold, which could be a textual description, numerical value, or another form of data.

Data elements also serve an important role in ensuring consistency across the system. By defining a field's type and any associated validation criteria, data elements maximize data integrity by ensuring that data input adheres to predefined parameters.

Domains

Domains define the technical characteristics of a data element, including its data type, length, and value ranges (also known as fixed values).

They are the technical foundation for specifying how data is stored, displayed, and processed.

Whenever a data element is created, it is associated with a corresponding domain, which provides the underlying data type and formatting rules. For example, a domain might specify that a particular field is an integer with a certain number of digits, a string of a certain length, or a date in a specific format.

The use of domains ensures that data fields sharing similar properties are handled consistently across the database, guaranteeing standardized treatment of data within SAP applications.

Example: Creating a Transparent Table

Creating a transparent table using ABAP involves several steps, requiring SAP's development tools to ensure the table's properties and relationships are properly defined.

```
CREATE TABLES my_table (
    KeyField INT NOT NULL PRIMARY KEY,
    NameField NVARCHAR(50),
    DateField DATE
);

INSERT INTO my_table (KeyField, NameField, DateField)
VALUES (1, 'John Doe', '2023-10-10');
```

The above code snippet uses ABAP syntax to define a table called my_table. It includes a primary key, KeyField, ensuring uniqueness, as well as additional fields NameField and DateField, which accommodate varying data types.

Working with Views

Consider the practical example of creating a database view to join data from multiple tables for reporting purposes:

```
CREATE VIEW employee_view AS
SELECT e.EmployeeID, e.FirstName, e.LastName, d.DepartmentName
FROM Employees e
JOIN Departments d ON e.DepartmentID = d.DepartmentID;
```

This view, employee_view, fetches and combines data from the Employees and Departments tables by joining them on a common attribute DepartmentID. It allows users to retrieve comprehensive employee data including department information without redundancy in data storage.

Ensuring Data Integrity with Data Elements and Domains

The SAP Data Dictionary plays a crucial role in maintaining data integrity. Through data elements and domains, it establishes a consistent framework for validating data inputs, enforcing data constraints, and providing informative error messaging in the event of inconsistencies.

For instance, imagine defining a domain called WeightDomain with constraints that a value must be a positive decimal number up to a maximum of 99.99. This domain can then be linked to any data element needing similar validation, ensuring all fields using this domain will inherently respect these restrictions.

By harmonizing data definitions through a common dictionary, SAP achieves congruity in data handling, reducing the risk of data redundancy or inconsistencies that can occur in decentralized systems.

Summary of Data Dictionary Uses

The SAP Data Dictionary is not just a storage mechanism; it is a guidepost and validator ensuring all data within a SAP system conforms to a unified schema. By centralizing definitions, SAP simplifies application maintenance, supports rapid development, and provides robust data management essential for business operations.

Developers leveraging the SAP Data Dictionary must grasp the benefits and methodologies encapsulated in these features to effectively manage data systems within SAP projects. This clarity brings about enhanced data precision and coherence throughout the application's lifecycle, allowing for scalable and adaptable software architectures in ever-evolving organizational landscapes.

Mastering the SAP Data Dictionary is indispensable for developers tasked with the responsibility of building reliable and efficient data-driven applications on the SAP platform.

3.2 Creating and Managing Transparent Tables

Transparent tables in SAP serve as the foundational structure for storing application data in a way that is both accessible and modifiable by the underlying relational database management system (RDBMS). They reflect a significant aspect of the SAP Data Dictionary, and their proper creation and management are crucial for ensuring efficient data storage and retrieval within the SAP environment.

Understanding Transparent Tables

A transparent table in SAP is a database table that has a one-to-one relationship with the table in the database. It is called "transparent" because it is directly reflected in the database. This one-to-one mapping ensures that data stored in transparent tables can be accessed and manipulated using standard SQL queries, providing flexibility and performance benefits.

Transparent tables are used extensively to store application data, configuration settings, and operational records. When a new table is needed for an SAP application, it is often created as a transparent table to allow seamless access by both the SAP system and external database applications.

Steps to Create Transparent Tables

Creating a transparent table involves several key steps, ensuring that the table meets the application's data requirements and conforms to best practices for database design.

1. **Define Table Properties:**

The first step is to define the name and basic properties of the table, such as delivery class and data class. SAP provides various delivery classes that define the changeability of the table and its contents.

- **Application Table (A):** Table used to store data relevant to applications.
- **Customizing Table (C):** Default data for customizing.
- **Organizational Table (O):** Configuration related tables and

objects.

2. Specify Field Definitions:

Each table is composed of fields, and each field has a specific type and length. The fields are typically created based on predefined data elements and domains to maintain consistency.

```
DATA: BEGIN OF it_my_data OCCURS 0,
    field1 TYPE c LENGTH 10,
    field2 TYPE i,
    END OF it_my_data.
```

3. Set Primary Key:

Every transparent table must have a primary key. This key uniquely identifies each record within the table and is crucial for ensuring data integrity and supporting efficient query performance.

```
CREATE TABLE my_table (
    id INT PRIMARY KEY,
    name VARCHAR(50),
    age INT
);
```

4. Activate the Table:

Once all properties and fields have been defined, the table must be activated. Activation checks ensure the table definitions meet all structural requirements and enable the table to be generated in the database.

5. Define Technical Settings:

After activation, technical settings such as buffering options and logging can be configured. Buffering enhances performance by reducing database access for read operations, whereas logging ensures changes are traceable.

```
TECHNICAL SETTINGS:
BUFFERING: SINGLE RECORD
LOGGING: YES
```

Managing Transparent Tables

Efficient management of transparent tables is crucial for maintaining optimal performance and ensuring data integrity over the lifecycle of an application.

1. **Data Maintenance:**

Transparent tables allow direct SQL operations for inserting, updating, and deleting records. Integrating these tables into transaction codes (TCODES) enables users to interact with data directly from SAP's interface.

```
INSERT INTO my_table (id, name, age) VALUES (1, 'Alice', 30);
UPDATE my_table SET age = 31 WHERE id = 1;
DELETE FROM my_table WHERE id = 1;
```

2. **Index Creation:**

To enhance data retrieval, secondary indexes can be defined on non-primary key fields. While the primary key ensures uniqueness, secondary indexes optimize query operations for specific search criteria.

```
CREATE INDEX age_index ON my_table(age);
```

3. **Buffer Management:**

Managing the buffering of tables is crucial in systems with high-volume transaction processing. SAP provides buffering settings that must be fine-tuned based on the table's access patterns.

4. **Monitoring and Performance:**

SAP provides several utilities to monitor table performance, such as database transaction statistics and SQL performance analysis tools. These help in identifying bottlenecks and optimizing table usage.

Practical Example of Creating Transparent Table

Consider the scenario where a developer needs to create a simple employee table to store basic employee information within an SAP system.

1. **Determining Requirements:**

The table should capture details like Employee ID, Name, Department, and Date of Joining. Employee ID will serve as the primary key.

2. **Defining the Table:**

```
CREATE TABLE emp_table (
    emp_id INT NOT NULL PRIMARY KEY,
    emp_name VARCHAR(100),
    department VARCHAR(50),
    date_of_joining DATE
);
```

3.2. CREATING AND MANAGING TRANSPARENT TABLES

3. **Database Operations:**

The table can now effectively be queried, updated, and managed using standard SQL and ABAP routines.

4. **Efficient Query Example:**

```
SELECT * FROM emp_table WHERE department = 'HR';
```

5. **Transaction Code Creation:**

A custom TCODE can be generated to facilitate real-time interaction with the new employee table, enabling data input and reporting directly from SAP's GUI.

Advanced Management Considerations

Transparent tables can also support advanced configurations tailored to organizational and data model requirements:

- **Partitioning:** For larger tables, partitioning can enhance performance and manageability by splitting the table into smaller, more manageable parts stored across different database instances.

- **Archiving:** Regular data archiving strategies can prevent performance degradation due to excessive table size while maintaining historical data.

- **Data Replication:** Synchronize table contents across multiple environments to ensure robust disaster recovery and backup solutions.

Transparent tables are pivotal in SAP's ecosystem, providing the necessary framework for application data storage and retrieval. Mastery of creation and management techniques for transparent tables equips developers with critical skills to optimize data handling in SAP applications, achieving streamlined operations, robust data integrity, and superior database performance. This section has laid out a comprehensive guide for crafting effective and well-optimized transparent tables, paving the way for proficient database management in the complex landscape of SAP software systems.

3.3 Internal Tables: Definition and Usage

Internal tables in ABAP are one of the fundamental structures used for processing and manipulating data within the SAP system. They provide a flexible mechanism for handling collections of data in memory, allowing developers to perform complex data operations efficiently without affecting the database. Understanding the definition, typology, and practical usage of internal tables is crucial for crafting effective ABAP programs.

Definition of Internal Tables

An internal table is a temporary table created in the memory of the application server during program runtime. Internal tables are used to store a sequence of records, which can then be processed using various ABAP statements. They provide a dynamic way to process data read from database tables or datasets, making them indispensable tools in application development.

Internal tables are particularly suited for tasks that involve:

- Aggregating data from multiple sources
- Manipulating datasets for reporting
- Sorting, filtering, and searching data in memory
- Staging data before applying operations that modify the database

The lifecycle of an internal table is limited to the program execution that creates it, and they are automatically destroyed upon completion of the process, ensuring that memory is efficiently managed.

Structure of Internal Tables

Internal tables consist of rows, each of which follows a consistent data structure defined by line types. Line types can be a structure, table, or a single data field type. ABAP supports three types of internal tables: standard tables, sorted tables, and hashed tables.

1. **Standard Tables:**

3.3. INTERNAL TABLES: DEFINITION AND USAGE

Standard tables are the most flexible type of internal table. They do not impose any restrictions on the order of entries or key uniqueness, and operations like appending new entries or performing sequential searches are straightforward.

```
DATA: lt_stand TYPE TABLE OF STRUCTURE,
      lw_st TYPE STRUCTURE.
```

The APPEND statement is typically used to add new entries:

```
APPEND lw_st TO lt_stand.
```

Standard tables are ideal when a sequence of operations doesn't require the data to be ordered, as they maintain the order of insertion.

2. Sorted Tables:

Unlike standard tables, sorted tables maintain entries in a defined order according to a specified criterion and enforce uniqueness based on specified keys.

```
DATA: lt_sort TYPE SORTED TABLE OF STRUCTURE WITH UNIQUE KEY
      field.
```

This structure reduces the computational cost of operations like searching and inserting, as the sorting order is maintained automatically.

3. Hashed Tables:

Hashed tables provide efficient key-based access, similar to a hash map in other programming languages. The unique key requirement optimizes the retrieval of individual records.

```
DATA: lt_hash TYPE HASHED TABLE OF STRUCTURE WITH UNIQUE KEY
      field.
```

Hashed tables deliver constant-time complexity for retrieval, making them optimal for scenarios where specific lookup operations dominate.

Defining and Populating Internal Tables

The creation of an internal table typically involves defining its type, followed by the process of populating it with data. Defining an internal table requires specifying the line type, which could be a reference to a defined structure or an explicit field list.

Let's demonstrate creating, populating, and processing an internal table:

1. **Define Line Structure:**

```
TYPES: BEGIN OF ty_employee,
       emp_id TYPE i,
       emp_name TYPE c LENGTH 50,
       dept_id TYPE i,
       END OF ty_employee.
```

A structure is defined here named ty_employee, consisting of fields such as emp_id, emp_name, and dept_id.

2. **Declare Internal Table:**

```
DATA: lt_employees TYPE TABLE OF ty_employee.
```

This statement declares an internal table lt_employees based on the structure ty_employee.

3. **Populate the Table:**

```
DATA: ls_employee TYPE ty_employee.
ls_employee-emp_id = 101.
ls_employee-emp_name = 'John Smith'.
ls_employee-dept_id = 10.
APPEND ls_employee TO lt_employees.

ls_employee-emp_id = 102.
ls_employee-emp_name = 'Jane Doe'.
ls_employee-dept_id = 20.
APPEND ls_employee TO lt_employees.
```

Two records are added to the table using the APPEND keyword, populating it with employee details.

Common Operations on Internal Tables

Once an internal table is populated, a variety of operations can be performed to analyze and modify the data as needed.

- *Reading Data:*

The READ TABLE statement retrieves entries, typically using criteria such as index or key:

```
READ TABLE lt_employees INTO ls_employee WITH KEY emp_id = 101.
IF sy-subrc = 0.
  WRITE: / ls_employee-emp_name, ls_employee-dept_id.
ENDIF.
```

3.3. INTERNAL TABLES: DEFINITION AND USAGE

The sy-subrc system variable indicates whether the operation was successful.

- Modifying Data:

To change specific data, locate the entry, then use the MODIFY keyword:

```
READ TABLE lt_employees INTO ls_employee WITH KEY emp_id = 102.
IF sy-subrc = 0.
  ls_employee-emp_name = 'Jane D. Doe'.
  MODIFY TABLE lt_employees FROM ls_employee.
ENDIF.
```

This code modifies the name of the employee with ID 102.

- Deleting Entries:

Remove entries using DELETE according to various logical criteria:

```
DELETE lt_employees WHERE dept_id = 20.
```

Here, all employees in department 20 are removed from the internal table.

Advanced Usage Scenarios

Internal tables support numerous advanced patterns that enhance their versatility:

- Nested Tables: Internal tables can also accommodate other tables as line types, facilitating the management of complex, hierarchical data.

- Critical Data Processing: They can be leveraged to efficiently execute operations on datasets retrieved from databases, reducing the number of database calls needed and enhancing performance.

- Parallel Processing: Internal tables can be processed in parallel by dividing the workload into smaller tasks, making them ideal for computations requiring higher throughput.

- Memoization: Frequently accessed results can be stored in internal tables to reduce repeated calculations, boosting performance for computationally expensive operations.

Performance Considerations

Memory usage and processing speed are pertinent when handling substantial data volumes:

- *Table Type Choice:* Choosing the right table type aligned with use-case—standard, sorted, or hashed—directly influences the speed of search, insert, and modify operations.

- *Index-Based Access:* For standard tables, preferring index-based access can expedite operations, though for sorted and hashed tables, key-based access remains optimal.

Internal tables are a powerful toolset for developers indicated by their efficiency in data handling and manipulation within an ABAP program. The focus on different types and operations enriches understanding and application, enabling versatile data processing. Emphasis on efficient memory and resource usage ensures that developers can harness the full potential of internal tables while maintaining system integrity and performance. Understanding the subtleties of their use empowers developers to create more dynamic, responsive, and scalable SAP applications that meet complex business requirements effectively. Through thorough comprehension and strategic implementation of internal tables, developers can address broad-ranging data operations essential in today's data-intensive environments.

3.4 Operations on Internal Tables

Internal tables are a vital element of the ABAP programming language, providing an efficient way to handle collections of records temporarily within memory for various processing needs. Understanding and mastering the operations that can be performed on internal tables is crucial for managing data dynamically and efficiently within SAP applications. This section covers a gamut of operations like inserting, deleting, modifying, and reading data in internal tables, along with strategies and techniques for optimizing these operations.

Inserting Data into Internal Tables

The insertion of data into internal tables is one of the primary operations and can be achieved using the APPEND, INSERT, and COLLECT statements, each serving different purposes and use cases.

- *APPEND:* The APPEND statement is the most straightforward way to add a new line to the end of an internal table. It is com-

3.4. OPERATIONS ON INTERNAL TABLES

monly used for standard tables where order is not critical.

```
DATA: lt_students TYPE TABLE OF string,
      lv_student TYPE string.

lv_student = 'Alice'.
APPEND lv_student TO lt_students.

lv_student = 'Bob'.
APPEND lv_student TO lt_students.
```

- **INSERT:** This operation allows inserting data either at a specific index or adhering to a sorting order in sorted tables. For hashed tables, INSERT adds entries as defined by their unique keys.

```
INSERT 'Charlie' INTO lt_students INDEX 2.
```

This inserts 'Charlie' at the second position in lt_students in a standard table.

- **COLLECT:** Specifically designed for accumulating values into tables with numerical fields, COLLECT ensures that duplicate keys accumulate values instead of creating repeated entries.

```
TYPES: BEGIN OF ty_sale,
         product TYPE string,
         quantity TYPE i,
       END OF ty_sale.

DATA: lt_sales TYPE TABLE OF ty_sale,
      ls_sale TYPE ty_sale.

ls_sale-product = 'Book'.
ls_sale-quantity = 10.
COLLECT ls_sale INTO lt_sales.

ls_sale-product = 'Book'.
ls_sale-quantity = 5.
COLLECT ls_sale INTO lt_sales.
```

Here, the quantity for 'Book' is accumulated, combining similar keys.

Modifying Data in Internal Tables

Modification involves altering existing records' data within an internal table, which can be efficiently achieved using the MODIFY statement. Modifications are commonly executed when adjustments or updates to already processed data are necessary.

```
READ TABLE lt_students INTO lv_student INDEX 1.
IF sy-subrc = 0.
   lv_student = 'Alice Johnson'.
   MODIFY lt_students FROM lv_student INDEX 1.
ENDIF.
```

This example reads the first entry and modifies it if the read operation is successful. The system field sy-subrc indicates the outcome of the operation, confirming whether a modification can proceed.

Modifications can also be performed with a key reference, particularly useful for sorted and hashed tables:

```
MODIFY lt_sales FROM ls_sale INDEX sy-tabix TRANSPORTING quantity.
```

Using the TRANSPORTING addition allows modifying specific fields only, optimizing resource use and ensuring performance efficiency.

Deleting Data from Internal Tables

Deleting records from internal tables involves determining the condition for removal and then executing the removal. The DELETE statement handles this operation precisely.

- *Delete by Condition:* Removes rows meeting specified conditions.

  ```
  DELETE lt_students WHERE lv_student = 'Bob'.
  ```

  This removes all entries where the value equals 'Bob'.

- *Delete at Index:* Executes deletion at a specific table index.

  ```
  DELETE lt_students INDEX 2.
  ```

  Such operation directly targets specific positions within standard tables.

- *Freeing Memory:* Post-deletion, referencing FREE releases memory, which has become redundant, an imperative action in extensive datasets to manage memory allocations efficiently.

  ```
  FREE lt_students.
  ```

  By using FREE, the table memory is deallocated, although it doesn't impact the data within it until called.

3.4. OPERATIONS ON INTERNAL TABLES

Reading and Retrieving Data

Extracting data from internal tables involves locating desired records based on index positions or row keys.

- *Index-based Access:* Reads specific positions directly. It's a straightforward method beneficial to standard tables when positions are predetermined.

  ```
  READ TABLE lt_students INTO lv_student INDEX 1.
  IF sy-subrc = 0.
    WRITE: / 'First entry:', lv_student.
  ENDIF.
  ```

- *Key-based Access:* For both sorted and hashed tables, aligns with keys enhancing efficiency.

  ```
  READ TABLE lt_sales INTO ls_sale WITH KEY product = 'Book'.
  IF sy-subrc = 0.
    WRITE: / 'Product:', ls_sale-product, 'Quantity:', ls_sale-quantity.
  ENDIF.
  ```

- *Looping Structures:* Processing entire tables or subsets of rows with iterative loops (e.g., LOOP ...ENDLOOP) allow developers to apply operations seamlessly across records.

  ```
  LOOP AT lt_students INTO lv_student.
    WRITE: / 'Student:', lv_student.
  ENDLOOP.
  ```

Advanced Operations and Optimization Techniques

When handling more extensive datasets and requiring rapid executions or greater computational accuracy, advanced techniques in internal table operations are invaluable.

- *Binary Search:* Having sorted data allows using binary search, a switch (BINARY SEARCH) included with the READ TABLE statement ensures quick retrieval by halving search iterations recursively.

  ```
  SORT lt_sales BY product.
  READ TABLE lt_sales INTO ls_sale WITH KEY product = 'Book'
      BINARY SEARCH.
  IF sy-subrc = 0.
  ```

```
WRITE: / 'Product found:', ls_sale-product.
ENDIF.
```

- *Field-symbols and Data References:* Efficiently manipulating or accessing larger volumes of data through aliases can boost processing efficiency.

```
FIELD-SYMBOLS: <fs_student> TYPE ty_student.
LOOP AT lt_students ASSIGNING <fs_student>.
  <fs_student>-emp_name = 'Updated ' && <fs_student>-emp_name.
ENDLOOP.
```

Using field-symbols, entries are accessed and updated seamlessly without formal data transport overhead.

- *Table Expressions:* Simplified access via inline expressions allows compact code and reduces processing repetitions.

```
lv_student_name = lt_students[ 1 ]-emp_name.
```

Strategic Considerations in Designing Operations

Maximizing efficiency while handling operations on internal tables benefits significantly from conscious design choices and architectural strategies:

- *Prioritize Correct Table Type:* Align table types to usage patterns; use standard tables for flexibility, sorted tables for searches needing order, and hashed tables for direct key-based lookups.

- *Memory Management Cues:* Efficiently devise memory usage strategies, including table initialization routines that consider the typical size and estimation for INITIAL SIZE declaration.

```
DATA: lt_large_table TYPE TABLE OF ty_large INITIAL SIZE 1000.
```

- *Profiling and Monitoring Performance:* Ensuring continuous performance benchmarking through tools like SQL Trace (ST05) and Runtime Analysis (SAT) affirms operational efficiency and identifies bottlenecks to be addressed promptly.

The ability to perform various operations on internal tables is fundamental for dynamic data management in any SAP environment. Through precise execution and strategic understanding, such operations do not merely endow adaptability to programs but create paradigms of efficiency, contributing actively to the robustness of SAP solutions. This comprehensive exposition of internal table operations lays the groundwork for developers to perform sophisticated data manipulations to meet complex business requirements.

3.5 Advanced Internal Table Techniques

In ABAP programming, internal tables serve as dynamic arrays for processing datasets within memory. As developers seek to achieve more sophisticated data manipulations and enhance program efficiency, advanced techniques on internal tables become indispensable. This section explores a selection of these advanced techniques, focusing on sorting, searching, aggregating data, and the utilization of innovative expressions and constructs, bringing a deeper level of dynamism and performance optimization to ABAP applications.

Sorting Data in Internal Tables

Sorting is a universal requirement across data handling applications, aimed at organizing data sequences for more streamlined processing or presentation. ABAP offers robust sorting functionalities, customizing the order based on single or multiple fields.

- *Basic Sorting:* For a fundamental sort, the SORT statement orders an internal table by specified fields, defaulting to ascending order.

  ```
  SORT lt_data BY field1 field2.
  ```

  Here, lt_data is classified primarily by field1 and secondarily by field2, ensuring orderly sequence across specified fields.

- *Descending Order Sort:* The inclusion of DESCENDING keyword enables reverse ordering when data priorities demand such arrangements.

```
SORT lt_data BY field1 DESCENDING field2 ASCENDING.
```

This will place field1 entries in descending sequence while maintaining field2 in ascending order.

- *Sort with Comparison Rule:* For more complex sorting logic, developers might define comparison operators explicitly:

```
SORT lt_employees BY salary DESCENDING NAME.
```

This advanced sort prioritizes data on the basis of numeric constraints, enriching business scenarios like ranking employees by salary before alphabetic arrangement by name.

- *Sort Within Control Level:* Frequently used with control break statements like ATEND OF, this ensures specific aggregates are calculated correctly during reporting structures.

```
SORT lt_sales BY dept_id.
```

This allows data to be grouped for detailed summations within departments, highlighted during control break processing.

Searching Data in Internal Tables

Efficient search techniques can substantially enhance performance by rapid identification of required data records. The choice of search method must align with table type and criteria requisites.

- *Linear Search:* For standard tables lacking intrinsic order, linear search (LOOP or READ without addition) reflects a fundamental but exhaustive method.

```
LOOP AT lt_students INTO ls_student WHERE student_name = 'John
    Doe'.
    WRITE: / 'ID:', ls_student-student_id, 'Age:', ls_student-age.
ENDLOOP.
```

- *Binary Search:* Especially for sorted tables, binary searches expedite lookups in logarithmic time complexity by halving the search space iteratively.

```
SORT lt_books BY title.
```

3.5. ADVANCED INTERNAL TABLE TECHNIQUES

```
READ TABLE lt_books INTO ls_book WITH KEY title = 'ABAP
    Fundamentals' BINARY SEARCH.
IF sy-subrc = 0.
    WRITE: / 'Found:', ls_book-title.
ENDIF.
```

This code exemplifies how pre-sorting data allows more effective explorations, unlocking quicker results.

- *Advanced Search Using Expressions:* Recently introduced expressions streamline searches through concise syntaxes, aiding clarity and lowering execution overhead.

```
ls_value = lt_employees[ ID = 101 ]-name.
```

Leveraging table expressions abstracts complexity and introduces straightforward, index-free accesses, especially in nested operations.

Aggregating Data in Internal Tables

Aggregation condenses datasets to yield insightful metrics or succinct summaries, crucial for analytics and reports.

- *Summation and Averages:* Standard aggregated calculations can be performed efficiently using loop structures.

```
DATA(lv_total_salary) = 0.
LOOP AT lt_employees INTO ls_employee.
    lv_total_salary = lv_total_salary + ls_employee-salary.
ENDLOOP.

DATA(lv_avg_salary) = lv_total_salary / lines( lt_employees ).
```

Calculating total and averages across employee salaries demonstrates the utility of aggregating operations for actionable intelligence.

- *Control Break Processing:* This technique works in tandem with sorting to tally subgroup results, boosting informative outputs from within grouped queries.

```
SORT lt_sales BY dept_id.
LOOP AT lt_sales INTO ls_sale.
    AT END OF dept_id.
        SUM.
```

```
            WRITE: / 'Total for Department:', ls_sale-dept_id, 'Amount:',
                  lv_total.
          ENDAT.
        ENDLOOP.
```

As indicated, this pattern reads control breaks in sales data, providing aggregated totals at departmental junctions, enriching insights effortlessly.

Using Table Expressions and Functional Methods

Modern ABAP provides versatile expressions that transform programming styles towards greater efficiency and legibility.

- *Table Expressions:* These include inline access and simple usage formats to advance ease and flexibility.

```
lv_student_name = lt_students[ 1 ]-student_name.
```

Skip traditional READ statements for singular operations and adopt direct access methods comprehensively.

- *Functional Method Calls:* Asserts cohesion by wrapping table operations in re-usable methods boosting modularity.

```
METHOD get_highest_salary.
  DATA(lv_max_salary) = 0.
  LOOP AT it_employees INTO DATA(ls_employee).
    IF ls_employee-salary > lv_max_salary.
      lv_max_salary = ls_employee-salary.
    ENDIF.
  ENDLOOP.
  RESULT = lv_max_salary.
ENDMETHOD.
```

Such method codification encapsulates operations progressing consistency and preventing redundancy.

Performance Optimization Techniques

Maximized performance demands not just optimized execution but also adherence to best-in-class programming customs.

- *Choosing Suitable Table Types:* Opt for table types that match functionality precisely; use hashed tables when distinct keys can be leveraged for swift retrievals, align sorted tables with ordered queries, and exercise standard tables where simple insertions are frequent.

- *Memory Precautions:* Clarify memory reservations early using OCCURS (adds on deprecated methodologies) or INITIAL SIZE to anticipate allocations.

```
DATA: lt_comprehensive TYPE TABLE OF ty_line INITIAL SIZE 500.
```

Defining initial sizes based on anticipated usage endeavors better memory management.

- *Parallel Processing:* Adapt internal table operations for parallel execution where feasible, resulting in high-concurrency solutions that reduce serial processing bottlenecks.

- *Profiling and Diagnostics:* Commit to regular profiling using SAP's built-in analysis tools (e.g., SQL Trace (ST05), Runtime Analysis (SAT)) for methodical diagnostics that pinpoint inefficiencies.

Creating advanced data workflows with internal tables elevates ABAP programs' ability to analyze, manipulate, and dedicate resources effectively in diverse settings. By immersing in these advanced techniques, developers attain superior insights, refine applications, and streamline operations, underpinning business processes with elevated capabilities that tackle aggregate challenges while remaining nimble and responsive. Embracing innovation through up-to-date techniques and performance paradigms fortifies ABAP solutions, putting them squarely amidst the cutting edge of enterprise resource planning tools.

3.6 Using Secondary Indexes and Keys

In SAP and ABAP programming, the efficiency of data retrieval and manipulation is pivotal to application performance and scalability, especially in database interactions. Secondary indexes and keys play a critical role in optimizing these interactions. Understanding how to utilize these elements effectively is essential for robust SAP development.

This section explores the nuances of primary and secondary keys, the creation and utilization of secondary indexes, and strategies for leveraging these tools to enhance database performance.

Understanding Primary and Secondary Keys

In database design, keys are mechanisms that enable unique identification of rows within a table, thereby facilitating efficient access, updates, and integrity constraints.

- *Primary Keys:* This is a unique identifier for table records. Each table must have a primary key, ensuring no duplicate rows exist. It affirms entity integrity and is integral to relational databases' foundational design.

  For example, in a table with student records, student_id might serve as the primary key:

  ```
  CREATE TABLE students (
      student_id INT PRIMARY KEY,
      first_name VARCHAR(50),
      last_name VARCHAR(50)
  );
  ```

  In this schema, student_id uniquely identifies each record.

- *Secondary Keys:* Unlike primary keys, secondary keys (or non-primary keys) do not require uniqueness and are used to enhance search performance on non-unique columns. These keys facilitate faster searches by maintaining additional indexes for quick lookups.

Creating and Using Secondary Indexes

While primary keys determine the primary method for row retrieval, secondary indexes allow additional paths, enabling more flexible and efficient data access.

- *Purpose and Benefits:* Secondary indexes are used to speed up query retrieval times, especially in cases with large datasets where searches involve non-key columns. They maintain a separate entity in the database, providing a quick lookup table for indexed columns without scanning the entire table.

3.6. USING SECONDARY INDEXES AND KEYS

- *Creating Secondary Indexes:* Secondary indexes are defined at the database level. When queries reference these indexed columns, databases use the index instead of scanning the entire table, significantly reducing access times.

  For instance, consider adding an index on the last_name column:

  ```
  CREATE INDEX idx_last_name ON students(last_name);
  ```

  This command establishes a secondary index, optimizing any searches based on the last_name attribute.

- *Utilization in Queries:* The addition of a secondary index means that queries involving indexed columns become markedly more efficient:

  ```
  SELECT * FROM students WHERE last_name = 'Smith';
  ```

  Such a query uses the defined index for last_name, which speeds retrieval by swiftly locating required records.

Considerations for Index Usage

While secondary indexes provide notable benefits in querying performance, they must be employed judiciously.

- *Storage Overhead:* Each additional index carries a storage cost and may increase the complexity of data modifications, as indexes must be updated alongside data.

- *Write Performance Impact:* Secondary indexes can slow down insert, update, and delete operations. Every change to the table necessitates corresponding updates to each secondary index.

- *Selective Indexing:* Indexes should target columns frequently used in search conditions or join operations but not those constantly updated, which may negate performance benefits.

- *Frequency of Use:* Assess query usage patterns to ensure that secondary indexes are applied to frequently queried columns, delivering optimal performance gains.

Enhancing Performance with Composite Keys and Indexes

In many scenarios, single-column keys or indexes might not suffice. Composite keys or compound indexes, built on multiple columns, are deployed for such cases.

- *Composite Keys:* A composite key involves multiple columns creating a unique identity for table rows, essential when no single column is sufficient.

  ```
  CREATE TABLE enrollments (
      student_id INT,
      course_id INT,
      enrollment_date DATE,
      PRIMARY KEY(student_id, course_id)
  );
  ```

  With student_id and course_id combined, a composite key uniquely identifies enrollment records.

- *Composite Indexes:* Similar to composite keys, composite indexes improve retrieval for queries involving multiple columns:

  ```
  CREATE INDEX idx_student_course ON enrollments(student_id,
      course_id);
  ```

  This composite index supports queries filtering by both student_id and course_id simultaneously, accelerating performance in complex joins or search conditions.

Practical Implementation and Example Scenarios

Consider how secondary indexes and composite keys might be effectively utilized in realistic database management scenarios. Suppose a library system needs rapid access to book records by author and title for both borrowing and inventory management.

- **Table Definition:**

  ```
  CREATE TABLE books (
      book_id INT PRIMARY KEY,
      title VARCHAR(100),
      author VARCHAR(100),
      published_year INT
  );
  ```

- **Create Secondary Indexes:**

```
CREATE INDEX idx_author ON books(author);
CREATE INDEX idx_title ON books(title);
```

- **Execute Optimized Query:**

    The library can now efficiently execute refined book search operations:

    ```
    SELECT * FROM books WHERE author = 'George Orwell' AND title
        LIKE '1984%';
    ```

    By leveraging both idx_author and idx_title, the database navigates swiftly, delivering the requisite information seamlessly.

- **Use Composite Index for Multi-Faceted Searches:**

    To cater to multi-column searches, composite indexing provides a cohesive solution:

    ```
    CREATE INDEX idx_author_title ON books(author, title);
    ```

    Queries employing both elements exhibit faster retrieval due to consolidated index use, enhancing efficiency:

    ```
    SELECT * FROM books WHERE author = 'George Orwell' AND title =
        '1984';
    ```

Balancing Trade-offs and Strategic Indexing

Effective index utilization mandates a comprehensive understanding of the balance between benefit and overhead involved in database optimization.

- *Monitoring and Analysis:* Systematic analysis using database monitoring and profiling tools to discern which columns substantiate indices by gaining essential insight into application logics.

- *Maintenance Scheduling:* Regularly assess index relevance and performance, archiving or eliminating those outdated or offering lesser value in current use cases.

- *Dynamic Workloads Adaptation:* Adjust index strategies in alignment with evolving business workloads, iterating over setup to consistently match operational context shifts.

By thoughtfully implementing and managing primary and secondary keys and indexes, developers ensure that databases remain responsive, scalable, and optimized for rapid data retrieval, accommodating the ever-increasing dynamics of modern enterprise environments. Understanding these mechanisms forms a cornerstone of proficient database management in SAP systems, affording unparalleled insights and adaptability in pursuing comprehensive and dynamic data strategies.

3.7 Data Dictionary Tools in SAP

The SAP Data Dictionary is a pivotal component within SAP systems, providing the framework for data storage, integrity, and consistency. It encapsulates the metadata required to maintain and structure data across various applications. Certain tools within SAP facilitate myriad operations associated with the Data Dictionary, from definition and manipulation of tables, views, and indexes, to ensuring data integrity and enforcing business rules. Understanding these tools is essential for developers and data stewards who seek to maximize the efficiency and reliability of SAP implementations. This section delves into key Data Dictionary tools and utilities, elaborating on their functionalities and applications within SAP environments.

Overview of Data Dictionary Tools

The SAP environment features several robust tools that make managing Data Dictionary objects intuitive and efficient. Key among these are:

1. **Transaction SE11 - Data Dictionary Maintenance:** SE11 is a core transaction code that allows users to view and edit database objects, including tables, views, data elements, domains, search helps, and lock objects.

- **Creating Tables:** Using SE11, developers can define the structure of custom tables, decide primary keys, set technical attributes, and enforce data integrity rules through checks and constraints.

```
To create a new table:
1. Open transaction SE11.
2. Select 'Database table' and enter a new table name.
```

3.7. DATA DICTIONARY TOOLS IN SAP

> 3. Define fields, keys, and data types.
> 4. Save and activate the table.

- **Modifying Data Elements:** Data elements associate a domain with fields, specifying their field labels, search help, and documentation. They ensure consistent data typing across tables.

> To modify a data element:
> 1. Open SE11, choose 'Data element'.
> 2. Enter the name and click 'Change'.
> 3. Update domain or field labels as needed.
> 4. Save and activate changes.

- **Creating Views:** Views are virtual tables representing datasets from one or more tables. They do not store data physically but render data dynamically based on query criteria.

> To create a view:
> 1. Access SE11, select 'View'.
> 2. Define view type (Database, Projection, Maintenance, or Help View).
> 3. Add tables and join conditions.
> 4. Specify output fields, save, and activate.

2. **Transaction SE14 - Database Utility:** This tool facilitates operations that go beyond typical table creation, such as reorganization, deletion, and resizing. SE14 empowers users to maintain the physical storage and performance of database tables.

- **Table Reorganization:** Reorganization is essential for optimizing database storage, such as after mass deletions or structural alterations, helping ensure no fragmentation and optimal data retrieval times.

> To reorganize a table:
> 1. Open SE14, enter the table name.
> 2. Choose 'Reorganize'.
> 3. Follow prompts to execute reorganization.

- **Table Conversion:** In cases of structural changes like new keys or field alterations, conversion adjusts physical storage without data loss.

> To convert a table:
> 1. Access SE14, input the table.
> 2. Select 'Convert to conversion routine'.
> 3. Execute the conversion protocol.

3. **Transaction SE80 - Object Navigator:** SE80 serves as an integrated development environment for all SAP objects, including those

CHAPTER 3. WORKING WITH DATA: INTERNAL TABLES AND DATA DICTIONARY

in the Data Dictionary. This navigator organizes viewing and editing of not only data elements but also associated programs, UI components, and interfaces.

- **Synchronizing Definitions:** Facilitates consistent development framework across different SAP modules through synchronized object deployments using generated code templates or workspace configurations.

> To open Data Dictionary in SE80:
> 1. Navigate to SE80.
> 2. Select 'Repository Browser'.
> 3. Browse to the Dictionary Object for edits or synchronization.

- **Extending and Managing Associations:** To visualize and navigate to objects linked with Data Dictionary elements, ensuring coherent integration within application landscapes.

> VIEW: Look-up associations within SE80 interface.
> EDIT: Perform structured updates respecting object dependencies.

Best Practices for Utilizing Data Dictionary Tools

While the SAP Data Dictionary tools offer robust capabilities, their effectiveness is amplified when practitioners adhere to certain best practices:

- **Comprehensive Documentation:** Maintain clear documentation for every Data Dictionary change or creation process. Use naming conventions that are descriptive and consistent with organizational policies.

- **Version Control and Backups:** Implement version control practices and create backups before executing significant alterations. This permits rollback to previous implementations if needed.

- **Change Impact Analysis:** Before executing changes such as altering database structures or converting data types, perform thorough analysis to predict downstream effects or service disruptions.

- **Regular Maintenance Checks:** Practice routine checking using SE14 to detect and rectify fragmentation or inefficiencies in data storage usage, maintaining streamlined operational performance.

Advanced Techniques and Considerations

3.7. DATA DICTIONARY TOOLS IN SAP

Harnessing Data Dictionary tools transcends fundamental use, encompassing advanced methodologies enabling nuanced and tailored solutions:

- **Performance Analysis via Indexes:** With SE11, indexes can be designed by evaluating query performance metrics, thereby tailoring data storage structurally to align with dominant access patterns. For instance, frequently queried columns should receive index enhancements, optimizing retrieval.

- **Utilization of Data Class and Size Category:** Accurately determine data class association to dictate physical storage allocation strategies and align size categories with expected data volumes. This pre-emptive understanding supports scalability and sustained performance.

```
When creating tables, specify:
  - Data Class (Master, Transaction, Organization)
  - Size Category (Small, Medium, Large)
```

- **Reorganizing Database Structures:** Regular SE14 engagement for reorganizing tables after heavy modifications assures operational efficiency and minimizes data access latencies.

```
Reorganization benefits:
  - Eliminates table fragmentation
  - Optimizes database space usage
  - Improves data retrieval times
```

- **Dynamic Data Element and Domain Definitions:** Strategically create domain-definitions conveying data constraints and enable system-consistency with cohesive data element management to encapsulate varied data interaction rules.

```
DEFINE domain and constraints:
  - Data type declaration
  - Value ranges/validation criteria
```

Leveraging Search Helps and Lock Objects

Beyond direct data manipulations, two vital categories in the Data Dictionary tools facilitate advanced data consistency and ease-of-use:

- **Search Helps:** Intended to refine user experiences by rendering intuitive selection dialogs that streamline data entry processes. Developers utilizing these attributes link seamless data browsing to backend search capabilities.

To create search help: 1. Open SE11, choose 'Search Help'. 2. Define parameters and search logic. 3. Guide users through data form selection.

- **Lock Objects:** Critical for concurrent data access management, lock objects enforce consistency by restricting data entry while updates are pending, safeguarding concurrent transactions from overwriting unsynchronized data changes.

To define a lock object: 1. Launch SE11, select 'Lock Object'. 2. Set parameters specifying lock behaviors. 3. Integrate with application transactions.

By weaving these dynamic capabilities into regular SAP programming and maintenance routines, developers and data users can fashion a more intuitive, reliable, and inherently agile SAP environment. The SAP Data Dictionary includes a comprehensive suite of management tools integral to effective data governance, ensuring enterprise-grade applications sustain robust data fidelity and superior usability standards. These elements provide a foundational pillar in a wide array of SAP system deployments, fortifying systemic integrity across the tableau of advanced business-process automation solutions.

Chapter 4

Advanced Data Handling and Processing Techniques

This chapter explores sophisticated strategies for managing and processing data within ABAP applications, crucial for tackling complex business challenges. It introduces tools like the ABAP List Viewer (ALV) for creating dynamic reports and discusses methods for efficiently handling large data sets to optimize memory usage and performance. Key topics include dynamic programming techniques, utilizing field symbols and data references for flexible data manipulation, and optimizing data access with strategic selection methods. Additionally, advanced error handling ensures program reliability, while parallel processing techniques are highlighted to enhance performance in data-intensive tasks, providing a comprehensive toolkit for advanced ABAP data handling.

CHAPTER 4. ADVANCED DATA HANDLING AND PROCESSING TECHNIQUES

4.1 Working with ALV Grid Display

The ABAP List Viewer (ALV) is an essential tool in SAP systems for displaying data in a flexible and interactive manner. ALV grid display enables developers to create sophisticated reports, allowing users to manipulate data visually without requiring extensive programming knowledge. This section delves into the core functionalities of the ALV grid and demonstrates how it can be effectively utilized for dynamic data presentation in ABAP applications.

ALV offers various views such as simple lists, hierarchical sequential lists, and full-screen grids, each catering to different reporting needs. The ALV grid display, in particular, provides a robust interface that supports real-time data interaction, making it preferable for complex data presentations.

Setting Up the ALV Grid Display

To initiate an ALV grid display, the function module REUSE_ALV_-GRID_DISPLAY is commonly leveraged. This function module is supplemented by specific internal tables and field catalog configurations that determine the structure and appearance of the displayed data. The increased acceptance and reliance on ALV stem from its ability to produce reports that are comprehensive, visually intuitive, and customizable in lesser development time compared to traditional ALV List reports.

The initial step in setting up an ALV grid involves declaring internal tables to hold the data and the field catalog. The field catalog acts as a blueprint for how data fields from internal tables are rendered in the grid display.

```
DATA: lt_fieldcat TYPE TABLE OF lvc_s_fcat WITH HEADER LINE,
      lt_data TYPE TABLE OF <data_type>.

" Preparing Data: Filling in lt_data with relevant entries

" Preparing Field Catalog: Customize each layout attribute
CALL FUNCTION 'LVC_FIELDCATALOG_MERGE'
  EXPORTING
    i_structure_name = '<data_type>'
  CHANGING
    ct_fieldcat = lt_fieldcat.
```

Above, the field catalog is generated using LVC_FIELDCATALOG_-

4.1. WORKING WITH ALV GRID DISPLAY

MERGE, which automatically maps the structure's fields to an ALV grid configuration. However, manual additions and modifications to the field catalog can enhance the final output by controlling parameters like column headings, visibility, alignment, and data formatting.

Customizing the Grid Display

Customization in ALV involves setting properties that adjust the grid's behavior and presentation to align with user requirements. These configurations impact interaction elements like sort order, filter capabilities, editable status, and aggregation methods such as sum, average, or count. For instance, hiding or grouping particular fields may streamline data analysis.

```
LOOP AT lt_fieldcat INTO DATA(ls_fieldcat).
  CASE ls_fieldcat-fieldname.
    WHEN 'CUSTOMER_NAME'.
      ls_fieldcat-seltext_l = 'Customer';
      ls_fieldcat-outputlen = 30.
    WHEN 'ORDER_VALUE'.
      ls_fieldcat-no_zero = 'X'.
      ls_fieldcat-col_pos = 3.
  ENDCASE.
  MODIFY lt_fieldcat FROM ls_fieldcat.
ENDLOOP.
```

In the example above, field catalog entries are customized so that the column label for CUSTOMER_NAME is shortened and the ORDER_VALUE column is restricted to non-zero entries and placed explicitly in the third column position. This detail-oriented approach empowers users to focus on pertinent data.

Display Options and Layout Variations

Beyond simple data organization and display, ALV grid permits multiple presentation formats and layouts. These formats include hierarchical views and cross tabulations, which organize complex datasets into manageable sections. Additionally, multi-level sorting and filtering can be applied for enhanced data analysis, making the ALV grid a dynamic data manipulation tool.

```
DATA: l_grid_layout TYPE lvc_s_layo.
l_grid_layout-colwidth_optimize = 'X'.
l_grid_layout-zebra = 'X'.
l_grid_layout-sel_mode = 'A'.

CALL FUNCTION 'REUSE_ALV_GRID_DISPLAY'
  EXPORTING
```

```
    is_layout = l_grid_layout
TABLES
    t_outtab = lt_data
    t_fieldcat = lt_fieldcat.
```

In the above example, layout features such as optimized column width and zebra patterning for rows are applied. These enrich the user interface, highlighting data differentiation and aiding quick visual processing.

Event Handling in ALV

The ALV grid design incorporates event handling, which enables responsive interaction models. By subscribing to specific ALV events, developers provide users with a dynamic, controlled interaction experience, allowing for context-sensitive actions such as detailed drilling, row selection, and subtotal aggregation based on user interactions.

```
DATA: lt_events TYPE slis_t_event,
      ls_event TYPE LINE OF slis_t_event.

" Register user commands event
ls_event-name = 'USER_COMMAND'.
ls_event-form = 'HANDLE_USER_COMMAND'.
APPEND ls_event TO lt_events.

" Event handling routine
FORM handle_user_command USING r_ucomm LIKE sy-ucomm
                               rs_selfield TYPE slis_selfield.
    CASE r_ucomm.
        WHEN '&DETAIL'.
            PERFORM display_detailed_view USING rs_selfield-tabindex.
    ENDCASE.
ENDFORM.
```

The event handling mechanism involves defining callback routines to intercept and process user actions like button clicks or field double-clicks. It allows the transformation of these interactions into logical operations, such as displaying further detailed views or related data dialogues, without generating heavy server-side processes.

Performance Optimization of ALV Reports

Despite its flexibility, ALV grid's interactive capabilities can introduce performance concerns, especially with large datasets. Optimization strategies include minimizing data volume to essential records using filters and leveraging backend optimizations to reduce on-screen data transformation overhead.

Indexing, database-side filtering, and summarization before data retrieval are among the techniques employed to enhance performance. The integration of ALV interfaces with optimized data flow further refines the user experience, eliminating potential latency and ensuring data integrity.

Equally important, incremental data loading or server-side pagination methods can manage memory usage effectively when dealing with vast data volumes, only loading viewable data with each client request.

Advanced ALV Capabilities and User-Driven Enhancements

One advanced ALV feature is the integration of custom controls to improve the user experience further. Programmers can enrich reports through embedded charts, additional dialog functionalities, or even context-based modifications that make use of Custom Controls by implementing the CL_GUI_ALV_GRID class for custom screen modifications.

```
DATA: grid_control TYPE REF TO cl_gui_alv_grid,
      custom_container TYPE REF TO cl_gui_custom_container.

CREATE OBJECT custom_container
  EXPORTING
    container_name = g_custom_container.

CREATE OBJECT grid_control
  EXPORTING
    i_parent = custom_container.

grid_control->set_table_for_first_display(
  EXPORTING
    is_layout = l_grid_layout
  CHANGING
    it_outtab = lt_data
    it_fieldcatalog = lt_fieldcat ).
```

This method provides full control over ALV behaviors by manipulating grid properties and events directly through custom programming logic. Such flexibility promotes tailored user interfaces that align closely with organizational needs and reporting standards.

Conclusion and Best Practices

The ALV grid display in SAP serves as a versatile tool for data visualization and user interaction. By integrating event-driven programming, layout customization, and strategic data management, ALV grids provide an intuitive interface to developers and end-users alike. Best practices include attentive field catalog management, layout refinements, planned event handles, and backend optimization techniques to maximize report efficiency.

These tools collectively form an integral part of the advanced data handling toolkit for ABAP developers, meeting contemporary business intelligence needs with precision and flexibility while setting a foundation for exploring even more advanced data presentation solutions.

4.2 Handling Large Data Sets Efficiently

Efficiently handling large data sets is crucial in modern ABAP applications due to the expansive databases and complex processing required by contemporary business systems. Managing voluminous data effectively involves minimizing memory usage, optimizing performance, and ensuring data integrity. This section outlines techniques and strategies for handling large data sets efficiently within the ABAP environment, delving into methods like buffering strategies, optimized data selection, parallel processing, and efficient data aggregation.

Buffering Strategies

One technique for improving performance with large data sets is the use of buffering. Buffering involves temporarily storing frequently accessed data in memory to reduce database read operations. There are primarily two types of buffering strategies employed in ABAP: full buffering, which stores the entire table in the buffer, and single record buffering, which stores only specific records.

The choice of buffering strategy depends on several factors, such as the size of the table, the nature of the read operations, and the frequency of data changes. When implementing buffering, a careful analysis of access patterns is essential to determine the most suitable approach.

```
SELECT FROM scustom
  FIELDS id, field1, field2
  INTO TABLE @DATA(lt_buffered_data)
  WHERE id IN @lt_ids.
```

In the above example, buffering is manually mimicked by selecting a subset of data into an internal table for further processing. This aids in

4.2. HANDLING LARGE DATA SETS EFFICIENTLY

reducing repeated database access, though relying on ABAP's explicit table buffering settings in the data dictionary can further optimize performance.

Optimized Data Selection

The efficiency of data selection directly impacts the performance of operations on large datasets. Optimized data retrieval is achieved through selective querying techniques such as utilizing indexes, minimizing the dataset in the SELECT clause, and leveraging parallel cursor processing.

Indexing speeds up query operations by providing a direct lookup mechanism. Using suitable indexes ensures that the database search is constrained to relevant rows, reducing the workload.

```
" Make sure to leverage available database indexes
INDEX BY primary_key_index
SELECT single_field, aggregate_field
   INTO @DATA(single_row)
   FROM data_table
   WHERE filter_field = @filter_value.

" Using binary search to quickly locate data in internal tables
READ TABLE internal_table
  WITH KEY filter_criteria
  BINARY SEARCH.
```

The above code snippets illustrate the use of indexing for database retrieval and binary search in internal tables, both critical for fast and efficient data operations.

Parallel Processing

Parallel processing is a significant technique to exploit system resources to handle extensive data. By distributing tasks across multiple processing units, applications achieve improved performance and throughput. In ABAP, parallel processing can be implemented using asynchronous RFC calls or background jobs for batch data processing.

```
CALL FUNCTION 'RFC_FUNCTION_NAME'
   STARTING NEW TASK 'TASK#'
   DESTINATION 'DEST'
   AS SEPARATE UNIT
   EXPORTING
      parameter = value
   EXCEPTIONS
      communication_failure = 1
      system_failure = 2.
```

CHAPTER 4. ADVANCED DATA HANDLING AND PROCESSING TECHNIQUES

Here, an asynchronous RFC (Remote Function Call) is employed to distribute workload between multiple processes, enhancing processing speed by concurrent task execution. Careful synchronization of tasks is necessary to handle dependent operations and ensure data consistency.

Efficient Data Aggregation

Handling large data volumes often requires processing data aggregations efficiently. The goal is to summarize meaningful information without processing overhead. Efficient aggregation can be achieved by using built-in database functions when possible, instead of calculating aggregates in ABAP code post-retrieval.

```
" Direct aggregation in database
SELECT SUM(total_value)
  UP TO 1 ROWS
  INTO @DATA(total_sum)
  FROM large_data_table
  WHERE sale_date BETWEEN @start_date AND @end_date.
```

Using direct aggregation functions in SQL queries offloads processing work to the database, which often manages aggregation more effectively than processing within the ABAP environment.

Streaming and Incremental Data Processing

Streaming data processing is a technique employed to handle real-time data flows efficiently. It processes data continuously as it arrives, reducing memory constraints and processing latency. Incremental loading processes data in small, manageable chunks, which is crucial for data transformation operations on large datasets.

```
DATA: lv_count TYPE i,
      lt_chunk TYPE TABLE OF data_type WITH EMPTY KEY.

SELECT field1, field2
  FROM large_table
  INTO TABLE lt_chunk
  PACKAGE SIZE 1000.
  lv_count = lv_count + lines(lt_chunk).

  " Process current chunk
  PERFORM process_data CHANGING lt_chunk.
ENDSELECT.
```

In the above code, 'PACKAGE SIZE' in a SELECT query is used to fetch and process chunks of data iteratively, reducing memory use in work-

4.2. HANDLING LARGE DATA SETS EFFICIENTLY

loads involving substantial datasets.

Memory Management Techniques

Efficient memory management involves strategies that minimize memory use, avoiding performance degradation. Techniques include leveraging ABAP's capacity for streaming, optimized internal table usage, and dynamic data deletion.

ABAP offers memory management instructions like freeing up memory that is no longer needed, avoiding unnecessary internal table extensions, and proper dataset size estimation.

```
" Free up memory by clearing temporary data when done
CLEAR: my_var, itab.

" Delete processed entries to free memory
DELETE lt_data WHERE processed = 'X'.
```

Prudent allocation and deallocation of memory resources significantly enhance application performance when processing extensive datasets.

Data Cohesion and Compression

Data cohesion refers to maintaining data integrity and relevance through homogeneity and meaningful organization. Organizing data efficiently includes utilizing ABAP's range of data compression techniques, such as unique keys for join operations and data-type specific compression.

Combining appropriate join operations with optimized indexing and condition-based fetches maintains data integrity while supporting data processing performance.

```
SELECT field1, field2, COUNT(*)
  INTO TABLE @DATA(lt_data)
  FROM table1
  INNER JOIN table2 ON table1.key = table2.key
  GROUP BY field1, field2.
```

Such SQL joins efficiently correlate data across tables while performing aggregation, demonstrating cohesion through uniform data handling.

Tools for Performance Analysis

SAP provides various performance analysis tools for system workload monitoring, such as the ST05 SQL trace, ST12 analysis, and the SAT runtime analysis tool. These tools help identify inefficient code, potential bottlenecks in data access, and recommend optimizations.

ST05 captures SQL statements executed by ABAP programs, enabling real-time database interaction analysis, while ST12 combines SQL and performance tracing functionalities for comprehensive data handling insights.

Integrating these tools into the development cycle fosters continual performance assessments and incremental improvements, leading to well-tuned applications that can handle large data sets confidently and expediently.

The methods described above form a comprehensive framework for efficiently managing large data volumes within SAP's ABAP environment. By applying these techniques, developers can confidently design systems that maximize processing efficiency while controlling resource usage, ensuring robust application performance and reliability.

4.3 Dynamic Programming Techniques

Dynamic programming techniques in ABAP are a pivotal approach for developers seeking flexibility and adaptability within their applications. These techniques allow for the execution of operations where the data structures, function calls, or table interactions can be determined at runtime rather than compile time. This section explores various dynamic programming methodologies, such as dynamic data types, dynamic function calls, and runtime field creation, providing a robust toolkit for handling scenarios that demand on-the-fly processing capabilities.

Dynamic Data Types

Dynamic data types allow programmers to define and manipulate data structures during runtime. These are particularly useful when dealing with data whose structure cannot be determined at design-time. The primary mechanism for creating such structures in ABAP is through the use of field symbols and data references.

Field symbols in ABAP serve as placeholders or pointers to other data objects. Unlike static references, they present the flexibility to attach to diverse data structures dynamically.

4.3. DYNAMIC PROGRAMMING TECHNIQUES

```
DATA: lv_value TYPE i VALUE 5,
      field_symbol TYPE REF TO data,
      data_ref TYPE REF TO i.

" Assign reference dynamically
CREATE DATA data_ref.
field_symbol ?= data_ref.
ASSIGN field_symbol→* TO <fs_variable>.

IF <fs_variable> IS ASSIGNED.
   <fs_variable> = lv_value.
ENDIF.
```

In this example, a field symbol <fs_variable> dynamically references an integer. This capability is integral for applications requiring fragmentary data processing or transformation according to runtime data structure needs.

Dynamic Internal Tables

Internal tables in ABAP can be declared dynamically, which is essential when the table type or structure is only known at runtime. These tables are vital in situations needing flexible data operations, such as user-defined reports.

```
DATA: dynamic_table TYPE REF TO data,
      dynamic_line TYPE REF TO data.

FIELD-SYMBOLS: <table> TYPE STANDARD TABLE,
               <line> TYPE any.

TYPES: BEGIN OF line_type,
         field1 TYPE c LENGTH 10,
         field2 TYPE i,
       END OF line_type.

CREATE DATA dynamic_table TYPE TABLE OF line_type.
ASSIGN dynamic_table→* TO <table>.
CREATE DATA dynamic_line LIKE LINE OF <table>.
ASSIGN dynamic_line→* TO <line>.

" Adding entry
<line>-field1 = 'Test'.
<line>-field2 = 100.
APPEND <line> TO <table>.
```

Here, the internal table is dynamically created based on a structure defined at runtime. The ability to dynamically form internal tables is well-suited for applications where the structure is built depending on variable user inputs or parameters determined during program execution.

Dynamic Function Calls

Dynamic function modules or method calls permit invoking functions at runtime based on certain conditions or inputs. This runtime flexibility supports various application layers and interaction scenarios, catering to decoupled architectures and plugin systems.

```
DATA: lv_func_name TYPE funcname VALUE 'DEMO_FUNCTION',
      lv_return TYPE any.

CALL FUNCTION (lv_func_name)
  EXPORTING
    input_param = lv_value
  IMPORTING
    return_param = lv_return.
```

This example showcases a dynamic function call where the function name is stored in a variable and invoked using parentheses. Such capabilities allow ABAP systems to dispatch function calls from a pool of predefined functions according to specific operational requirements or configurations.

Dynamic SQL Execution

Dynamic SQL execution in ABAP is powerful for constructing SQL statements where queries cannot be fully determined at design-time. While dynamic SQL should be used cautiously for considerations like security (e.g., SQL injection risk), it provides significant flexibility for mutable data-retrieval operations.

```
DATA: lv_table TYPE string VALUE 'sflight',
      lv_where TYPE string VALUE 'carrid = "LH"',
      lt_result TYPE TABLE OF sflight.

FIELD-SYMBOLS: <dynamic_table> TYPE STANDARD TABLE.

CONCATENATE 'SELECT * FROM' lv_table
            'WHERE' lv_where INTO @lv_query.

EXEC SQL.
  OPEN lv_query.
  FETCH NEXT CURSOR INTO :lt_result.
END EXEC.
```

Dynamic SQL allows the construction of queries based on user specifications or other dynamic conditions, closing the capability gap for universally applicable data-fetch operations. However, diligent valida-

4.3. DYNAMIC PROGRAMMING TECHNIQUES

tion and security practices are imperative when using dynamic SQL.

Dynamic Object Creation

Dynamic object creation in ABAP leverages the concept of RTTI (Runtime Type Identification), enabling the generation and manipulation of object instances based on their types determined at runtime. This proves useful in generic applications or frameworks where object types vary subjectively.

```
DATA: lv_class_name TYPE seoclsname VALUE 'CL_EXAMPLE',
      lv_obj_ref TYPE REF TO object.
CREATE OBJECT lv_obj_ref TYPE (lv_class_name) EXPORTING parameter = 1.
```

The example dynamically instantiates an object as defined by the class name stored in a variable. This pattern is widely applied in plugin systems, object factories, and interfaces accommodating numerous implementations.

Use Cases for Dynamic Programming

Numerous scenarios justify the use of dynamic programming in ABAP. These include user-defined report generators, adaptable front-end-to-back-end communication layers, data warehousing operations that require variable dataset configurations, and middleware systems for API adaptability.

Dynamic programming's application extends to integration scenarios involving external services where data structures and procedural logic may need configuration on the fly. Through employing dynamic programming principles, such ecosystems gain significant robustness, supporting varied operational demands with refined versatility.

Considerations and Best Practices

While dynamic programming provides exceptional flexibility, it also imposes challenges in terms of readability, maintainability, and performance. The interpretative nature of operations implies performance trade-offs as actions must be resolved during runtime, which may introduce latency.

Best practices involve balancing dynamic constructs with static, type-safe constructs, especially for core operations within the application. Also, encapsulating dynamic functionalities into modular, well-documented procedural units aids maintainability and understanding.

Security considerations must be paramount when implementing dynamic programming, especially concerning dynamic SQL and function calls, ensuring user inputs are sanitized and predefined constraints like whitelisting frameworks are enforced to mitigate security risks.

Dynamic programming techniques empower ABAP developers with versatile tools to adapt and morph application structures efficiently according to contextual requirements. Utilizing these methods thoughtfully and strategically brings out the intrinsic value of ABAP systems in managing complex, changing, real-world business applications and demands, ultimately cementing their position as dynamic transactional platforms.

4.4 Field Symbols and Data References

Field symbols and data references are imperative constructs in the ABAP programming language employed to enhance data handling flexibility and drive performance improvements. These constructs present core capabilities for working with heterogeneous data structures dynamically, supporting operations that require reference-based data manipulation without duplicating memory usage. This section examines their mechanisms, applications, benefits, and best practices, providing comprehensive insights into leveraging these powerful tools within ABAP development.

Understanding Field Symbols

Field symbols in ABAP function similarly to pointers in other programming languages. They act as symbolic placeholders or references to various data objects, allowing developers to perform operations on referred data seamlessly and efficiently.

Field symbols are declared using the 'FIELD-SYMBOLS' statement and are assigned to specific data objects using the 'ASSIGN' statement. Once assigned, field symbols can be used to manipulate the data without physically duplicating it, thereby conserving memory.

```
DATA: lv_value1 TYPE i VALUE 10,
```

4.4. FIELD SYMBOLS AND DATA REFERENCES

```
      lv_value2 TYPE i VALUE 20.
FIELD-SYMBOLS: <fs_any> TYPE any.

" Dynamically assign field symbol
ASSIGN lv_value1 TO <fs_any>.
IF <fs_any> IS ASSIGNED.
  WRITE: / 'Value of fs_any:' , <fs_any>.
ENDIF.

" Reassign to another variable
ASSIGN lv_value2 TO <fs_any>.
IF <fs_any> IS ASSIGNED.
  <fs_any> = <fs_any> * 2.
  WRITE: / 'Updated value of fs_any:' , <fs_any>.
ENDIF.
```

As illustrated above, the field symbol <fs_any> is dynamically assigned to different data objects, facilitating operations that modify these objects' values efficiently.

Applying Field Symbols to Internal Tables

Field symbols exhibit significant utility when manipulating internal tables—a common data structure in ABAP. They allow developers to process individual rows within a loop without copying data, thereby ensuring efficient data handling, especially for large datasets.

```
DATA: it_numbers TYPE TABLE OF i WITH EMPTY KEY,
      lv_sum TYPE i.
FIELD-SYMBOLS: <fs_row> TYPE i.

" Populating the internal table
APPEND 100 TO it_numbers.
APPEND 200 TO it_numbers.

LOOP AT it_numbers ASSIGNING <fs_row>.
  lv_sum = lv_sum + <fs_row>.
ENDLOOP.
WRITE: / 'Sum of numbers:', lv_sum.
```

Here, the field symbol <fs_row> directly points to the rows of the internal table it_numbers, enabling efficient iteration with updates reflecting instantaneously on the original data structure.

Introduction to Data References

Data references in ABAP facilitate dynamic memory allocation, enabling the creation and manipulation of data objects at runtime. Leveraging data references becomes essential when working with indeterminate data structures or complex, dynamic object instantiation patterns.

The 'CREATE DATA' statement in ABAP enables data object creation on the heap, with references maintained through variables declared using the 'TYPE REF TO' clause.

```
DATA: lr_data_ref TYPE REF TO i.
FIELD-SYMBOLS: <fs_dynamic> TYPE i.

" Create data object dynamically
CREATE DATA lr_data_ref.
ASSIGN lr_data_ref->* TO <fs_dynamic>.
<fs_dynamic> = 42.
WRITE: / 'Value in dynamic reference:', <fs_dynamic>.
```

In this demonstration, a data reference lr_data_ref points to an integer, dynamically instantiated at runtime. The assignment of the data reference to a field symbol <fs_dynamic> allows the value to be directly manipulated.

Using Data References with Dynamic Type Definitions

Data references are indispensable when handling scenarios requiring dynamic type determination and creation. This capability allows developers to define and instantiate data types not known until runtime, supporting diverse application needs efficiently.

```
DATA: lr_dynamic_tab TYPE REF TO data,
      lr_dynamic_line TYPE REF TO data.
FIELD-SYMBOLS: <fs_table> TYPE STANDARD TABLE,
               <fs_line> TYPE any.

TYPES: BEGIN OF ty_example,
         id TYPE c LENGTH 5,
         name TYPE c LENGTH 20,
       END OF ty_example.

CREATE DATA lr_dynamic_tab TYPE TABLE OF ty_example.
ASSIGN lr_dynamic_tab->* TO <fs_table>.

CREATE DATA lr_dynamic_line LIKE LINE OF <fs_table>.
ASSIGN lr_dynamic_line->* TO <fs_line>.

" Populating dynamic table
<fs_line>-id = '0001'.
<fs_line>-name = 'Sample'.
APPEND <fs_line> TO <fs_table>.
```

The above example represents dynamic table definition and manipulation. Using this approach facilitates the creation of data structures at runtime, accommodating systems where the structure evolves based on incoming parameters or predefined conditions.

4.4. FIELD SYMBOLS AND DATA REFERENCES

Advanced Applications and Use Cases

Field symbols and data references together enhance ABAP's capability in various advanced applications:

- **Report Generation**: Adaptable reporting systems that require runtime-constructed datasets based on user input or secondary data system results benefit significantly from field symbols and data references, enabling flexible data consolidation and manipulation.

- **Frameworks and Plug-ins**: Modular framework designs utilizing polymorphic behavior to interact with diverse components or plug-ins at runtime find these dynamic constructs invaluable due to their flexible interaction and integration capabilities.

- **Complex Data Migrations**: Migrating datasets from legacy or changing systems often demands runtime adaptability, particularly those involving structurally heterogeneous records. Field symbols and data references provide the necessary dynamic processing abilities for seamless migrations or transformations.

- **User Interface Development**: ABAP programs driving SAP GUI or Web Dynpro interfaces frequently rely on runtime personalization, needing adaptable data structures detoured through field symbols or data references to conserve memory and enhance UI responsiveness.

Performance Considerations and Best Practices

While the flexibility offered by field symbols and data references is significant, developers should exercise caution to ensure performance efficiency and maintainability. Performance implications arise when excessive dynamic references or field symbol operations generate overhead or obfuscate code flow.

Some best practice recommendations include:

- **Efficient Memory Use**: Employ data references judiciously to prevent excessive memory allocation on the heap. Regularly deallocate unneeded heap memory to keep resource utilization optimal.

- **Readable Code**: Maintain clarity by combining inline documentation and naming conventions for field symbols and data references, assisting not only immediate insight but also long-term maintainability.

- **Consistency and Validation**: Leverage type-checking and validation, ensuring data references and field symbols always point to expected and valid data structures, minimizing runtime errors.

- **Performance Profiling**: Use SAP performance tools, such as ST12 trace or SAT runtime analysis, to identify bottlenecks introduced by dynamic programming constructs, followed by targeted optimization and code refactoring strategies.

Field symbols and data references are instrumental in unlocking ABAP's dynamic processing capabilities. By wielding these tools efficiently within application frameworks, ABAP developers produce flexible and high-performance solutions aligned with modern enterprise's dynamic data processing needs, reinforcing robust application design and seamless data operations. Maximizing their utility necessitates strategic integration balanced with attentive resource management, safeguarding coherent and effective SAP environments.

4.5 Data Selection and Access Optimization

Optimizing data selection and access is a cornerstone of efficient SAP performance management, directly affecting application response times and system resource utilization. The ABAP language provides a suite of tools and techniques designed to optimize the retrieval and manipulation of data from relational databases, reflecting significant improvements when applied correctly. This section explores effective data selection strategies, indexing imperatives, modern techniques like CDS views, access optimizations, and performance monitoring methods that collectively enhance data handling efficacy in ABAP systems.

Optimized Data Selection

- **Minimizing Dataset Retrieval:** The initial step in optimizing data selection is to ensure that only relevant data is fetched from the database. This involves techniques like reducing the number of columns in SELECT lists, precise WHERE clause conditions, and utilizing logical partitioning.

```
DATA: lt_customers TYPE TABLE OF scustom.

SELECT name, city, country
  INTO TABLE lt_customers
  FROM scustom
  WHERE country = 'US'
  AND status = 'ACTIVE'.
```

In this example, the selection is limited to specific columns and filtered by exact conditions, reducing the data transfer overhead and enhancing processing efficiency.

- **Using Joins Effectively:** Employing SQL JOIN operations appositely is crucial for efficient data retrieval when dealing with multiple related tables. Instead of retrieving data separately and correlating it in ABAP, JOIN statements draw cohesive data sets directly, benefiting from relational database optimization strategies.

```
SELECT a.name, b.description
  FROM scustom AS a
  INNER JOIN sflight AS b
  ON a.id = b.customer_id
  INTO TABLE @DATA(lt_result).
```

Utilizing inner joins directly in SQL reduces application-level computations, producing expedited data retrieval with coherent alignment directly from the database.

Leveraging Indexes in Database Access

Indexes greatly expedite data access by allowing quicker search and retrieval operations within database tables. Well-designed indexes can improve query performance multifold, primarily when utilized in conditions within a WHERE clause or JOIN operations.

- **Creating Effective Indexes:** Designing indexes demands a keen understanding of data access patterns. Developers should focus on indexed fields that frequently appear in WHERE clauses or are actively involved in JOIN conditions. An important consideration is balancing index benefits against the performance overhead introduced during DML operations like INSERT or UPDATE.

```
CREATE INDEX idx_customer_status
  ON scustom (country, status).
```

Creating a composite index on the 'country' and 'status' fields enhances performance for query conditions filtering these columns, as demonstrated previously.

- **Assessing Index Impact:** ABAP and database administrators should continually assess index utility using tools such as the database explain plans or SAP's native performance monitoring tools to ensure indexes contribute positively toward query execution.

Harnessing Views for Data Selection

CDS (Core Data Services) views represent an advanced approach to managing data retrieval in SAP environments, offering abstraction, reuse, and centralized logic management over traditional database views.

- **Defining Consistent Logic:** CDS views allow defining complex logic directly at the data model layer, realizing a single source of truth for application data retrieval without redundant code replication across different application layers.

```
@AbapCatalog.sqlViewName: 'SCUSTOMVIEW'
define view SCUSTOM_DETAILED as select from scustom
  left join sbook on sbook.clientid = scustom.id
{
  scustom.name,
  sbook.bookid,
  sbook.fare
}
where sbook.status = 'CONFIRMED'
```

This CDS view unifies customer and booking details, providing a consistent abstraction of business entities suitable for reuse across multiple application components.

4.5. DATA SELECTION AND ACCESS OPTIMIZATION

- **Access Efficiency:** With performance optimization features built into the HANA database, CDS views benefit naturally from these enhancements, accelerating query execution times compared to analogous handcrafted SQL within ABAP programs.

Technical Optimization Techniques

- **Buffering Strategies:** Data buffering strategies within SAP can offer significant enhancements regarding access times, especially for static and infrequently changing data. By minimizing database accesses for repeated queries through buffer utilization, overall transaction performance can improve greatly.

```
SELECT * FROM SCUSTOM
  INTO TABLE @lt_customer
  BUFFER all CLIENT specified.
```

Activating buffering for the 'SCUSTOM' table in the above example mitigates repetitive database fetching by storing data locally within the buffer.

- **Efficient Loop Handling:** In scenarios mandating data iteration, efficient loop constructs can drastically reduce overhead. Favorable tactics include using field symbols or parallel cursor processing and avoiding nested loops that contribute to performance penalties.

```
LOOP AT lt_customers ASSIGNING <fs_customer>.
  " Efficient processing logic here
ENDLOOP.
```

Field symbols, exemplified here, provide direct access to rows, streamlining iterations over large datasets directly in memory without delta reassignments.

Monitoring and Optimizing Performance

Performance optimization in SAP systems involves ongoing monitoring and refinement. Key to this are tools like:

- **SQL Performance Trace (ST05):** This tool is indispensable for dissecting SQL queries executed in the system, identifying slow operations, and tracing SQL engagement specifics.

- **ABAP Runtime Analysis (SAT):** Utilized for understanding the performance characteristics of ABAP logic, enabling developers to pinpoint bottlenecks and inefficiencies within their code.

The integration of regular performance diagnostics and optimizations ensures that data selections remain efficient, particularly vital as workloads scale or data access patterns evolve.

Best Practices for Data Access Optimization

- **Regular Index Review:** Continuously review and tune database indexes as data access profiles or volume change. Adopt automation for periodic performance assessments, adjusting indexing strategies to align with contemporary access demands.

- **Batch Processing:** Use batch processing for large-scale data manipulations where feasible, employing techniques such as 'PACKAGE SIZE' for iterative processing to better manage memory and resource usage.

```
SELECT *
  FROM scustom
  INTO TABLE lt_customers
  PACKAGE SIZE 1000.
  " Perform data operation
ENDSELECT.
```

This emulation of batch processing enables applications to handle large datasets more gracefully, mitigating excessive memory consumption by processing subsets incrementally.

- **Decoding with Care:** Use detailed and in-depth plans for decoding and deconstruction of data in buffer and memory, ensuring that any dynamic data manipulation reflects efficient logic paths and minimal computation overhead.

In summary, data selection and access optimization in ABAP systems warrants a deliberate application of foundational strategies complemented with modern advancements like CDS views and HANA-centric performance characteristics. By adhering to these guiding principles, developers establish and maintain highly performant, scalable, and responsive SAP applications that align seamlessly with evolving enterprise data management requisites.

4.6 Handling Exceptions and Errors

Handling exceptions and errors effectively is essential in ABAP programming to ensure robust applications and seamless user experiences. As business processes increasingly depend on complex data-driven applications, providing mechanisms to manage unexpected events becomes crucial in maintaining system stability and integrity. This section explores advanced techniques in handling exceptions and errors in ABAP, discussing standard exception classes, exception handling mechanisms, in-depth error analysis, and best practice methodologies for ensuring application resilience.

Understanding Exceptions in ABAP

Exceptions in ABAP are categorized into classical exceptions, which belong to procedural programming that predominantly employs return codes, and object-oriented exceptions, which utilize classes for richer error handling and debugging capabilities.

Classical exceptions operate through SY-SUBRC, which often requires specific checks post-function or method execution to determine success states or failure modes.

```
CALL FUNCTION 'READ_TEXT'
  EXPORTING
    id = 'ST'
    language = sy-langu
  IMPORTING
    textline = lv_textline
  EXCEPTIONS
    not_found = 1
    others = 2.
IF sy-subrc <> 0.
  WRITE: / 'Error reading text! Return code:', sy-subrc.
ENDIF.
```

Here, the return code SY-SUBRC manages conventional errors, with comparisons to integer values denoting specific exceptions.

In contrast, object-oriented exceptions exploit exception classes, providing a more detailed and structured approach to error handling.

Object-Oriented Exception Handling

ABAP facilitates object-oriented exception handling through exception classes, which encapsulate error details and allow hierarchies of exception handling to be implemented. This approach involves calling error-handling logic encapsulated in TRY...ENDTRY blocks.

```
TRY.
    " Potentially hazardous code
    lv_result = divide_numbers( lv_numerator, lv_denominator ).

  CATCH cx_sy_divide_by_zero INTO DATA(lx_zero_division).
    WRITE: / 'Division by zero exception occurred:', lx_zero_division→get_text().

  CATCH cx_root INTO DATA(lx_general).
    WRITE: / 'General exception occurred:', lx_general→get_text().
ENDTRY.
```

The TRY...CATCH construct catches specific exception instances like cx_sy_divide_by_zero for division errors or broader cx_root for generic errors, permitting detailed error-specific responses.

Custom Exception Classes

Developers often define custom exception classes that extend standard exception classes to address unique application requirements. This mechanism allows encapsulating application-specific error context and generating finely-tuned handling strategies suitable for unique business logic.

```
CLASS cx_custom_error DEFINITION INHERITING FROM cx_static_check
      CREATE PUBLIC.
  PUBLIC SECTION.
    DATA mv_error_code TYPE i READ-ONLY.
    METHODS constructor IMPORTING iv_code TYPE i.
ENDCLASS.

CLASS cx_custom_error IMPLEMENTATION.
  METHOD constructor.
    mv_error_code = iv_code.
  ENDMETHOD.
ENDCLASS.
```

By deriving from cx_static_check, custom exception cx_custom_error inherits exception handling functionalities while incorporating additional details (like mv_error_code) relevant to application contexts, enriching error handling with more quantifiable data.

4.6. HANDLING EXCEPTIONS AND ERRORS

Error Handling Best Practices

Effective exception and error handling is strengthened through adherence to best practices that emphasize both preventive and reactive strategies:

- **Error Prevention through Validation**: Incorporate input validation and precondition verification at critical points within application logic to deflect errors through earlier detection and user feedback.

```
IF lv_input_value IS INITIAL OR lv_input_value > lv_max_allowed.
  RAISE EXCEPTION TYPE cx_invalid_parameter
    EXPORTING
      error_message = 'Invalid input value'.
ENDIF.
```

- **Exception Filtering**: Implement granular and fine-filtered exception handling designs that segment handling strategies based on exception attributes, such as severity, source, or occurrence context.

- **Ensure Clean-Up Routines**: Combine error handling with resource clean-up using comprehensive FINALLY sections in TRY...ENDTRY constructs to assure that resource allocations are systematically released.

```
TRY.
  " Execute operations
CLEANUP.
  " Reset allocated resources
  clear_temp_data( ).
ENDTRY.
```

Logging and Monitoring Errors

Incorporating comprehensive error logging mechanisms facilitates subsequent debugging and analysis. Consistent logs preserve error details like timestamps, severity levels, and affected modules, essential for identifying recurrence patterns and system vulnerability.

```
TRY.
  " Block with potential error
CATCH cx_root INTO DATA(lx_error).
  WRITE: / 'Logged error:', lx_error→get_text( ).
  perform_log_error( lx_error→get_text( ) ).
ENDTRY.
```

When coupled with monitoring frameworks and alert systems, real-time error tracking ensures swift diagnostics and resolution protocols are triggered.

Analyzing and Debugging Errors

Advanced debugging tools in SAP systems, such as the ST22 dump analysis or ABAP Debugger, are leveraged to scrutinize exception details meticulously. These tools offer insights into call stacks, variable states, and object lifecycles during execution, contributing to error alleviation.

- **ST22 Transaction**: This transaction pinpoints runtime errors, presenting detailed error logs with insights into program states at the time of fault occurrence.

- **ABAP Debugger**: Through breakpoints, watchpoints, and runtime state inspections, developers dissect error mechanisms and system interactions leading up to the event, allowing targeted fixes.

Error Handling in Advanced Scenarios

Complexities inherent in concurrent processing, distributed systems, and transactional integrity introduce advanced error handling requirements. Exception handling in these environments demands:

- **Concurrent Execution**: Satisfactory execution flows should incorporate retry mechanisms, conflict resolution (e.g., deadlock resolution), and cancellation logic to preserve transaction homogeneity amidst errors.

```
TRY.
  " Asynchronous call
CATCH cx_rfc_exception.
  " Retry operation or log temporary error
ENDTRY.
```

- **Distributed Systems**: Network latency or transaction propagation errors necessitate implementing transactional integrity checks (Two-Phase Commit) with compensation algorithms that counterbalance transaction fragments on failures.

Handling exceptions and errors aptly is not just about resolution but involves designing systems to be as error-resilient as possible. In collaborative environments driven by reliable processing and integration needs, robust error handling ambitiously minimizes downtime, averts data inconsistency, and upholds organizational operations' continuity. Consequently, these strategies embed resilience across applications, meriting select attention throughout the development lifecycle.

4.7 Parallel Processing in ABAP

Parallel processing in ABAP leverages multiple processing units to execute computational tasks simultaneously. This approach is integral in optimizing performance for data-intensive applications by effectively utilizing available resources, thus reducing execution time and enhancing throughput. This section explores the methodologies underpinning parallel processing within ABAP, including asynchronous RFC calls, background jobs, parallel cursor processing, and leveraging modern SAP architectures such as the HANA database for concurrency optimization.

The Fundamental Concept of Parallel Processing

Parallel processing divides a large computational task into multiple smaller sub-tasks that can be executed concurrently across several processors. These tasks communicate with each other through shared resources and synchronize their operations to maintain data integrity.

This concept is crucial for ABAP environments supporting large-volume data manipulations or complex calculations, where sequential processing could significantly impede application performance.

Asynchronous RFC for Parallel Execution

The Asynchronous Remote Function Call (aRFC) is a primary tool in ABAP to achieve parallel processing. It allows multiple function modules to execute simultaneously in separate work processes, facilitating parallel data processing across distributed systems.

```
DATA: lt_destination TYPE TABLE OF rfcdest,
      lv_itab_strings TYPE TABLE OF string.

LOOP AT lt_data_parts INTO DATA(ls_data_part).
```

CHAPTER 4. ADVANCED DATA HANDLING AND PROCESSING TECHNIQUES

```
CALL FUNCTION 'PROCESS_DATA_PART'
  STARTING NEW TASK 'TASK'
  DESTINATION IN GROUP lt_destination
  EXPORTING
    data_part = ls_data_part
  EXCEPTIONS
    communication_failure = 1
    system_failure = 2.
ENDLOOP.

WAIT UNTIL flag_condition.
```

In this code, each data part is processed in parallel using aRFC, initiated through multiple tasks. The 'WAIT UNTIL' clause synchronizes the processing, ensuring all tasks are complete before proceeding.

Utilizing Background Jobs for Parallel Processing

Background jobs are an effective method in SAP's batch processing environment to execute long-running data operations in parallel, suitable for tasks that are not time-sensitive and do not need immediate user feedback.

```
SUBMIT report_name
  WITH p_param = value
  AND RETURN.
```

Here, the 'SUBMIT' command is used to initiate separate reports as background jobs, distributing workload across various system batches and freeing the online environment for immediate transactional requirements.

Parallel Cursor Technique

The parallel cursor technique ameliorates inefficiencies of nested loops over large datasets by incrementally synchronizing cursor positions across tables. It achieves a notable reduction in resource consumption by optimizing read operations on aligned datasets.

```
SORT it_table1 BY key_field.
SORT it_table2 BY key_field.

LOOP AT it_table1 INTO DATA(wa_table1).
  READ TABLE it_table2 WITH KEY key_field = wa_table1-key_field BINARY
      SEARCH INTO DATA(wa_table2).
  IF sy-subrc = 0.
    " Process matched pairs
  ENDIF.
ENDLOOP.
```

4.7. PARALLEL PROCESSING IN ABAP

This example illustrates efficient dataset synchronization using binary searches rather than exhaustive iterations, significantly optimizing time-complex operations on large tables.

Leveraging In-Memory Capabilities of SAP HANA

SAP HANA's in-memory database architecture complements parallel processing through its multi-core processing capabilities and advanced data processing algorithms. By executing complex calculations close to the data, HANA reduces data movement overhead and enhances parallel execution efficiency.

- **Columnar Storage**: HANA's columnar data layout facilitates parallel access and compressed storage techniques, optimizing bandwidth when executing concurrent analytical queries.

- **Pushdown Mechanisms**: Logic and computations are pushed down to the HANA database level, leveraging its intrinsic parallel CPU operations for processing within the database, minimizing data retrieval and transformation overhead in the application layer.

```
@AbapCatalog.sqlViewName: 'DAILY_SALES_VIEW'
define view DAILY_SALES as select from sales_table
{
  sales_date,
  sum(sales_amount) as total_sales
}
group by sales_date
```

In this CDS (Core Data Services) view example, the aggregation is offloaded to the HANA database, taking advantage of its built-in parallel query execution capabilities.

Ensuring Data Consistency in Parallel Processing

Parallel execution inherently risks overlapping operations on shared data, leading to data anomalies. Safeguarding consistency involves:

- **Locking Mechanisms**: Implement read/write locks to control concurrent access to shared resources. ABAP's 'ENQUEUE' and 'DEQUEUE' function modules enable transaction locks on affected tables, preserving sequential integrity.

```
CALL FUNCTION 'ENQUEUE_E_TABLE'
  EXPORTING
    mode_table = 'E'
    mandt = sy-mandt
    primary_key = ls_record-key
  EXCEPTIONS
    foreign_lock = 1.
```

- **Atomic Operations**: Design transactions as atomic units of work to ensure that concurrent processes maintain complete operation sequences without partial updates.

- **Conflict Resolution Strategies**: Develop sophisticated resolution protocols that handle conflicts, prioritizing data consistency over concurrency when conflicts arise, such as implementing compensation transactions to revert partial changes.

Monitoring and Tuning for Performance Optimization

Continuous monitoring through SAP's transaction codes 'ST06' (workload statistics) and 'SM66' (global work process overview) provides insights into parallel processing efficiency and system resource utilization.

- **Performance Tuning**: Fine-tune parameters like background processing priorities, work process distribution, and execution intervals to maintain optimal system resource balance, maximizing parallel processing benefits without overwhelming available CPU and memory capacities.

Conclusion and Best Practices

Parallel processing in ABAP is cardinal for advancing application performance in data-centric environments. Implementations, however, require meticulous planning and design consideration:

- **Assessment of Task Parallelizability**: Identify independent units of work that can be safely parallelized, preserving data integrity while maximizing concurrency benefits.

- **Efficient Resource Utilization**: Balance parallel workload distribution across system capacity without contrived depletion of shared processing resources, fostering a harmonious interchange of parallel processing efficiency against system stability.

- **Ongoing Evaluations**: Continuously employ performance diagnostics and benchmarks to align parallel processing executions with evolving workloads and system configurations, enabling adaptive modifications that enhance future operations.

By employing these techniques, ABAP developers harness parallel processing as a formidable instrument for sustainable high-performance implementations, manifesting scalable, robust systems supporting growing enterprise demands.

Chapter 5

Modularization Techniques: Includes, Function Modules, and Methods

This chapter delves into the essential modularization techniques in ABAP, focusing on enhancing code maintainability and reusability. It covers the use of INCLUDE programs and subroutines to organize and segregate code logically. The creation and application of function modules are discussed, highlighting how to encapsulate functionality and facilitate parameter passing. Object-oriented methods within classes are explored, illustrating the implementation of modular and flexible coding practices. In addition, strategies for effective exception handling within these modular components are presented, along with guidance on using packages and adhering to naming conventions to streamline the development process and enhance code clarity.

5.1 Understanding Modularization in ABAP

Modularization in ABAP is a fundamental concept that significantly enhances the maintainability and reusability of the code. Understanding modularization is crucial for any ABAP programmer aiming to develop efficient, scalable, and well-organized solutions. At its core, modularization in ABAP involves breaking down large and complex programs into smaller, manageable units or modules, each responsible for a specific task. This approach not only facilitates easier debugging and testing but also promotes code reuse across different programs, reducing redundancy and improving consistency.

One of the primary motivations for modularization in programming, and specifically in ABAP, is to handle the growing complexity of software systems. As projects expand, the lines of code increase, leading to challenges in managing and maintaining the codebase. Modularization addresses these challenges by allowing developers to create discrete modules that encapsulate specific functionalities. These modules can then be independently developed and managed, simplifying the development process.

In ABAP, modularization can be achieved through several mechanisms, such as INCLUDE programs, subroutines, function modules, and object-oriented approaches using classes and methods. Each technique offers unique benefits and can be employed in different scenarios to achieve optimal results.

To understand the significance of modularization, consider a real-world analogy where a large task is divided into smaller, manageable parts, each handled by different specialists. Similarly, modular programming decomposes a large program into distinct modules, enabling multiple developers to work concurrently on separate parts of the application. This parallel development can significantly reduce the time to deliver software and improve the quality by leveraging the expertise of individuals responsible for specific modules.

```
REPORT zmodular_example.

INCLUDE zcalculate_tax.
INCLUDE zgenerate_invoice.
```

5.1. UNDERSTANDING MODULARIZATION IN ABAP

```
START-OF-SELECTION.
  PERFORM calculate_tax.
  PERFORM generate_invoice.
```

In the above example, a report is modularized using INCLUDE programs to separate different functionalities such as tax calculation and invoice generation. Each INCLUDE program encapsulates a specific logic block, maintaining the main program in a clean and concise manner.

One of the primary benefits of modularization is the reusability of code. Reusability refers to the ability to use existing code modules in different programs without the need to rewrite logic, reducing development time and ensuring consistency across applications. In ABAP, this reusability is exemplified through the use of INCLUDE programs, subroutines, and especially function modules. Function modules encapsulate a particular logic and can be called from multiple programs, promoting code uniformity and reducing errors.

```
FUNCTION calculate_total.
* Importing parameters
  IMPORTING value1 TYPE i
            value2 TYPE i.
* Exporting parameter
  EXPORTING result TYPE i.

  result = value1 + value2.
ENDFUNCTION.

* Calling the function module in a report program
DATA: sum_result TYPE i.
CALL FUNCTION 'CALCULATE_TOTAL'
  EXPORTING
    value1 = 10
    value2 = 20
  IMPORTING
    result = sum_result.
WRITE: / 'The sum is:', sum_result.
```

In the above ABAP example, the function module calculate_total is defined to compute the sum of two numbers, demonstrating how function modules can stream functionality to different parts of a software application.

Another significant advantage of modularization is improved maintainability. By organizing code into separate modules, developers can quickly locate and update specific parts of the software without fear of causing unintended side effects in other parts. This clarity is critical when changes or enhancements are required, particularly in large and complex systems. Furthermore, maintaining a well-documented and clearly defined interface for each module ensures that developers using these modules understand their purpose and how to integrate them effectively.

Modularization also aids in enhancing the readability and understandability of the code. When code is well-structured and segmented into self-contained modules, it's easier for developers to read and comprehend, particularly those who are new to the project or involved in code review. With a clear structure, code reviews become more efficient as each module can be reviewed in isolation.

Incorporating modular techniques results in naturally occurring documentation, as each module's name and parameter list inherently describe its functionality. This documentation is beneficial not only for developers but also for project managers and stakeholders who may need to understand the software's structure at a higher level.

Moreover, modularization plays a vital role in facilitating testing. Individual modules can be tested independently before integrating them into the broader application, allowing for early detection of defects. Unit tests can be developed for individual modules to ensure that each piece works as expected, facilitating a robust test-driven development process.

Apart from functional benefits, modularization also introduces the concept of information hiding, which is central to software engineering principles. By limiting the exposure of implementation details to only what is necessary for the module's use, modularization minimizes dependencies and the impact of changes, offering a more robust and flexible application design.

The significance of modularization extends beyond the technical advantages; it also influences project management and team dynamics. With a modular approach, teams can work in parallel on different modules, accelerating development cycles and improving team collaboration and communication.

A structured modularization strategy necessitates careful consideration of program design, especially in aligning interfaces between modules to ensure smooth integration. This requires a comprehensive understanding of the overall architecture and careful planning during the initial design phases. It also emphasizes the need for a consistent naming convention and a well-organized hierarchy of packages, as these elements play a crucial role in locating and using modules efficiently.

In summary, understanding and implementing modularization in ABAP is essential for developing maintainable, reusable, and efficient software applications. By structuring programs into logical, self-contained modules, developers can overcome the complexities associated with large codebases, leading to faster development cycles, improved code quality, and easier maintenance.

5.2 Includes and Subroutines

In ABAP, the use of includes and subroutines forms an integral part of modularization techniques, enabling developers to create more organized, reusable, and maintainable code. Both constructs help break down complex programs into manageable parts, facilitating better understanding and reduced error propagation. In this section, we delve into these constructs, providing insights into their functionality, use cases, and implementation within ABAP.

The concept of an INCLUDE program refers to a placeholder for code that can be used in multiple programs by including it within them. This inclusion ensures that any changes made to the INCLUDE file are automatically reflected in every program that includes it. The key advantage of using INCLUDE programs is the promotion of code reusability and consistency. They allow for logical segregation of code into separate files based on functionality, which can be shared among multiple applications, thus avoiding code duplication.

An INCLUDE program can contain ABAP code blocks such as subroutines, data declarations, or even full program sections. The use of includes fosters a collaborative development environment where different team members can work on different components without interference.

```
REPORT zinclude_example.
```

CHAPTER 5. MODULARIZATION TECHNIQUES: INCLUDES, FUNCTION MODULES, AND METHODS

```
INCLUDE zcompute_sales.
INCLUDE zprint_report.

START-OF-SELECTION.
  PERFORM init_data.
  PERFORM compute_totals.
  PERFORM print_data.

INCLUDE zinit_utilities.
```

In the above example, the report includes different functionalities encapsulated within separate INCLUDES. The code within each IN-CLUDE such as zcompute_sales, zprint_report, and zinit_utilities may define particular functions that can be used interchangeably in other reports, showcasing the flexibility and reusability offered by INCLUDES.

Subroutines, on the other hand, are defined within a program and consist of a sequence of ABAP statements that perform a specific task. They are known as Form routines or internal subroutines and are defined using the FORM and ENDFORM statements. A subroutine can be used multiple times within a program or in other programs if properly linked using INCLUDEs.

Subroutines enhance modularity by encapsulating specific logic within a FORM block, allowing for separation of concerns within the program. This encapsulation not only improves readability and maintenance by narrowing down where specific pieces of logic are handled, but also aligns with the DRY (Don't Repeat Yourself) principle.

The following is an example of simple subroutine usage in ABAP:

```
FORM calculate_discount USING p_price TYPE i
                              p_discount TYPE i
                        CHANGING p_final_price TYPE i.

  p_final_price = p_price - ( p_price * p_discount / 100 ).

ENDFORM.

DATA: total_price TYPE i VALUE 1000,
      discount TYPE i VALUE 10,
      final_price TYPE i.

START-OF-SELECTION.
  PERFORM calculate_discount USING total_price
                                   discount
                             CHANGING final_price.
  WRITE: / 'Total price after discount:', final_price.
```

5.2. INCLUDES AND SUBROUTINES

In this example, the subroutine calculate_discount is invoked to apply a discount to a price. The use of USING and CHANGING parameters demonstrates how data is passed into the subroutine and how results can be returned or modified directly, facilitating flexible data handling and enablement of reusable procedures across various use contexts within the same program.

One more advanced feature of subroutines is their ability to include local interface structures, allowing parameter passing by value or reference, depending on the requirements of the subroutine. This offers a high level of flexibility in terms of how data is utilized, ensuring optimal performance and minimizing data handling constraints.

For instance, pass-by-value copies the actual data, whereas pass-by-reference only passes the reference to the data location, minimizing memory usage. Choosing the proper method depends on the computational context and data integrity needs. In ABAP, subroutine parameters default to pass-by-reference to enhance efficiency, but this can be overridden using VALUE to specify pass-by-value when needed.

Moreover, both INCLUDE programs and subroutines support a structured development workflow, allowing multiple developers to collaborate effectively by working on separate INCLUDE files or subroutines, which are then integrated into larger programs. This approach facilitates modular upgrades and debugging as each component can be tested and enhanced independently.

It is essential to document these components properly, describing their purpose, expected inputs, and outputs, making it easier for others to understand and use them effectively.

Includes and subroutines play a critical role in maintaining a balance between performance and organizational clarity. While there is some overhead in function calls when utilizing subroutines, the modular benefits often outweigh the performance costs in practice, particularly in complex applications where clarity and reusability become key developmental factors.

When utilizing INCLUDES and subroutines, consideration must be given to how these components interact with the broader program environment. Care needs to be taken with shared variables and side effects, as these could lead to unexpected behaviors if not properly managed or isolated using other modularization techniques such as function modules.

To conclude, includes and subroutines are powerful methodologies in ABAP that promote a clean, organized approach to programming. By leveraging these techniques, developers can ensure that their code is not only efficient but also maintainable and scalable, aligning with best practices in modern software development.

5.3 Creating and Using Function Modules

Function modules in ABAP are a vital feature that exemplifies the modular programming paradigm within the SAP environment. They allow for the encapsulation of specific functionality into reusable and independently executable units. This section explores the creation, management, and utilization of function modules, providing comprehensive insights into their architecture and practical applications.

A function module is a self-contained subprogram that executes a particular task. It is created within the Function Builder environment, which is part of the SAP system. These modules are globally available across the system, meaning that they can be invoked from any ABAP program, providing a flexible mechanism to promote code reuse and maintain a consistent codebase throughout the enterprise system.

The creation process of function modules involves several essential steps, starting with defining a function group. A function group acts as a container for function modules, managing them collectively and sharing global data. Using function groups is advantageous, as it allows developers to organize function modules logically, aligning them with specific business processes or functionalities.

To create a function module, the developer needs to navigate to the Function Builder with transaction code SE37. Here, the creation process begins with defining the function module's metadata, such as name, description, and associated function group.

Additionally, specifying the interface of the function module is crucial. The interface includes formal parameters classified into importing, ex-

5.3. CREATING AND USING FUNCTION MODULES

porting, changing, and tables parameters. Each parameter type serves a distinct purpose:

- Importing parameters: Allow data to be passed to the function module upon invocation but are not intended to be altered.
- Exporting parameters: Provide output from the function module after execution.
- Changing parameters: Combine importing and exporting functionalities, allowing values to be passed in and altered upon execution.
- Tables parameters: Facilitate the transfer of table-like structures to and from the function module, optimizing data manipulation tasks.

Consider the following ABAP example demonstrating the creation of a simple function module intended to calculate a discount on transaction values based on a given percentage:

```
FUNCTION y_calculate_discount.
*"----------------------------------------------------------------------
*"*"Local interface:
*"  IMPORTING
*"     VALUE(original_price) TYPE p DECIMALS 2
*"     VALUE(discount_rate) TYPE p DECIMALS 2
*"  EXPORTING
*"     VALUE(final_price) TYPE p DECIMALS 2
*"----------------------------------------------------------------------
  final_price = original_price * ( 1 - discount_rate / 100 ).
ENDFUNCTION.
```

In this function module, y_calculate_discount, the parameters original_price and discount_rate are imported, while final_price is exported as the computed result. This simple example highlights how function modules are structured, with a focus on clarity and encapsulation.

The logic encapsulated within function modules can significantly vary in complexity, from simple mathematical operations to elaborate database queries or data processing tasks involving multiple business entities. Regardless of complexity, the primary goal is to offer a clearly defined, testable, and reusable block of logic that aligns with business objectives.

One remarkable attribute of function modules is exception handling, providing built-in mechanisms to capture and manage runtime anomalies seamlessly. Exception handling in function modules involves defining potential exceptions within the module's metadata and specifying how they should be addressed during execution. These responses can range from ignoring an anomaly to terminating execution or specifying a custom processing pathway.

When invoking function modules in an ABAP program, developers use the CALL FUNCTION statement, which executes the module and handles parameter passing appropriately:

```
DATA: lv_original_price TYPE p DECIMALS 2 VALUE 1000,
      lv_discount_rate TYPE p DECIMALS 2 VALUE 10,
      lv_final_price TYPE p DECIMALS 2.

CALL FUNCTION 'Y_CALCULATE_DISCOUNT'
  EXPORTING
    original_price = lv_original_price
    discount_rate = lv_discount_rate
  IMPORTING
    final_price = lv_final_price.

WRITE: / 'The final price after discount is:', lv_final_price.
```

The above example illustrates how to pass parameters when calling a function module and how structured data flows between the calling program and the function module ensuring operations deliver expected results.

Function modules are versatile and can interact with various components within the SAP system. For instance, they can process data from databases using Open SQL, integrate with external systems via RFC (Remote Function Call), and interact with SAP UI elements for dynamic interface development.

A sophisticated capability of function modules is the ability to invoke them remotely using Remote Function Call (RFC). RFCs enable function modules to be executed on different servers or instances, facilitating distributed system architectures and cross-system communication. To support RFC, function modules must be explicitly declared with the 'Remote-Enabled Module' attribute, and suitable authorizations need to be configured.

Function modules can also interface with SAP internal events and workflows, ensuring they align seamlessly with enterprise-grade business process automation goals. Structuring business logic within function modules benefits not only system integrators but also business users who depend on these functions to provide reliable data-driven insights and actions.

Moreover, function modules emphasize encapsulation and information hiding, abiding by crucial software engineering principles, promoting maintainability, and minimizing long-term technical debt. In ABAP developments, leveraging function modules is a strategic decision that aligns code maintenance efforts with evolving business demands.

Advanced use of function modules might involve creating function groups containing related function modules to handle unit testing, making developments more quality-assured. Testing function modules separately before integrating them into applications saves significant troubleshooting resources.

In summary, function modules offer a profound mechanism to encapsulate discrete functionalities into modular, reusable components that can be effortlessly invoked across different contexts within an enterprise SAP environment. As developers and architects proficiently implement and integrate function modules, they ensure that enterprise solutions remain scalable, maintainable, and aligned with business operations.

5.4 Parameter Passing Techniques

In ABAP programming, parameter passing is a fundamental aspect of modularization, allowing for data exchange between different components such as procedures, function modules, and methods. Understanding the various parameter passing techniques and their implications is crucial for designing efficient and effective ABAP programs. This section explores the core parameter passing mechanisms in ABAP, delving into their usage patterns, benefits, potential pitfalls, and practical implementation examples.

Parameter passing serves to provide input data to a procedure or function and to return results back to the calling program. In ABAP, this is facilitated through explicitly defined sets of parameters known as the subroutine, function module, or method interfaces. The key parameter types in ABAP include:

- **Importing**: Parameters used to pass data into a subroutine, function module, or method. These are typically read-only within the called module.

- **Exporting**: Parameters used to return data from the called module back to the caller, effectively functioning as output parameters.

- **Changing**: Parameters that act as both importing and exporting, allowing data to pass into the module, be modified, and returned.

- **Tables**: Primarily used in function modules, these parameters handle internal tables, allowing for complex data exchanges.

The method of parameter passing can significantly affect the performance, clarity, and reliability of the code. ABAP supports two principal parameter passing methods: pass-by-value and pass-by-reference.

Pass-by-Value

In pass-by-value, a copy of the actual argument's value is passed to the called procedure. This transaction implies that any modification made to the parameter within the procedure does not affect the original argument. Pass-by-value is suitable in scenarios where the original data should remain unchanged or when dealing with simple data types where duplication overhead is minimal.

Here is a simple illustration of pass-by-value using a subroutine in ABAP:

```
REPORT zs_parm_value.

FORM calculate_square VALUE(val) TYPE i
  USING return_val TYPE i.

  return_val = val ** 2.

ENDFORM.

DATA: num TYPE i VALUE 4,
      square TYPE i.

START-OF-SELECTION.
```

5.4. PARAMETER PASSING TECHNIQUES

```
PERFORM calculate_square USING num
                CHANGING square.
WRITE: / 'Original number:', num,
         'Square of the number:', square.
```

In the example, the parameter 'val' is passed by value (using the VALUE keyword), ensuring that 'num' remains unaltered after the subroutine execution, with the computation isolated within the subroutine boundary.

Pass-by-Reference

Pass-by-reference involves passing a reference to the actual argument, allowing called procedures to directly access and modify the original data. This method is efficient for complex data structures or large datasets, minimizing the overhead of data duplication.

Consider the following example utilizing pass-by-reference in a subroutine:

```
REPORT zs_parm_ref.

FORM increment_value USING ref_value TYPE i.

  ref_value = ref_value + 1.

ENDFORM.

DATA: counter TYPE i VALUE 5.

START-OF-SELECTION.
  PERFORM increment_value USING counter.
  WRITE: / 'Counter after increment:', counter.
```

Here, 'ref_value' is passed by reference without specifying the VALUE keyword, allowing the subroutine to modify 'counter' directly.

While pass-by-reference provides performance benefits, especially for large data structures, it necessitates careful handling to prevent unintended side effects. Developer awareness of how parameters can be affected throughout a program's execution is essential to maintaining code stability and readability.

Parameter Passing in Function Modules

Function modules extend parameter passing mechanisms to include tables parameters, which facilitate transferring entire table structures between the calling program and the function module. Given the potential size of tables, they are typically passed by reference by default, aligning with performance considerations.

An example of passing tables via a function module is shown below:

```
FUNCTION calculate_totals_for_orders.
*"----------------------------------------------------------------
*"*" CHANGING
*"  VALUE(order_table) TYPE TABLE.
*"----------------------------------------------------------------

  LOOP AT order_table TRANSPORTING NO FIELDS.

    APPEND INITIAL LINE TO order_table ASSIGNING FIELD-SYMBOL(<
        order_line>).
    ADD <order_line>-price TO <order_line>-total_with_tax.

  ENDLOOP.

ENDFUNCTION.
```

In a program, this function module is called as follows:

```
DATA: lt_orders TYPE TABLE OF zorder,
      ls_order LIKE LINE OF lt_orders.

CALL FUNCTION 'CALCULATE_TOTALS_FOR_ORDERS'
  CHANGING
    order_table = lt_orders.

LOOP AT lt_orders INTO ls_order.
  WRITE: / ls_order-total_with_tax.
ENDLOOP.
```

This example showcases a function module that adjusts prices within an order table by loop-processing each entry directly via reference, demonstrating its operational efficiency on potentially significant datasets.

Advanced Considerations

Beyond foundational techniques, developers must consider advanced practices to optimize the efficacy of parameter passing. These practices include:

- **Data Type Compatibility**: Ensuring that the types of parameters passed to subroutines or function modules match expected types within procedures. Mismatches often lead to runtime errors or incorrect results.

- **Default Values for Parameters**: Implementing default parameter values can provide flexibility in function/module calls, simplifying invocation interfaces and enhancing user experience.

- **Exception Handling during Parameter Passing**: Incorporating robust exception handling around parameter interactions can prevent unexpected program behaviors, increasing reliability.

Strategic calibration of parameter passing strategies forms an essential part of crafting well-organized, logical ABAP systems that excel in performance, clarity, and maintainability. Through a keen understanding of parameter behavior and decision-making that considers the dynamics of pass-by-value versus pass-by-reference, programmers ensure effective communication within and across ABAP constructs. This foresight, alongside leading practices like defining clear parameter interfaces and systematizing error management, underpins the delivery of maintainable, efficient ABAP applications.

5.5 Methods and Classes in ABAP

The adoption of object-oriented programming (OOP) principles in ABAP has transformed the way developers approach application design and functionality encapsulation. This section provides a comprehensive exploration of methods and classes in ABAP, emphasizing their role in streamlining code architecture, enhancing reusability, and promoting maintainability within SAP-based solutions.

In object-oriented ABAP, classes serve as blueprints for creating objects, combining data and behavior into a single, cohesive unit. A class encapsulates data in the form of attributes and logic via methods, effectively promoting an organized and modular approach to program development.

Methods, in essence, are functions defined within classes. They represent actions or behaviors that can be performed on or by the objects instantiated from the class. A method is the primary means by which objects manipulate data or initiate business logic based on encapsulated functionality.

The shift from procedural to object-oriented paradigms introduces several advantages, including:

- **Encapsulation**: By binding data and methods together, ABAP classes enforce a boundary, allowing controlled access to data and ensuring integrity.

- **Inheritance**: ABAP classes support inheritance, facilitating code reuse by allowing new classes to derive properties and behavior from existing classes.

- **Polymorphism**: Methods and classes support polymorphism, enabling uniform treatment of different objects through interfaces and superclasses.

- **Abstraction**: By abstracting complex processes into class and method structure, developers can simplify interface interactions and manage complexity effectively.

Developing a class in ABAP starts with defining its purpose and responsibilities. Using transaction SE24, developers can create classes and declare their attributes and methods. Consider the following example, which illustrates the definition of a simple class and associated methods for calculating employee salaries:

```
CLASS lcl_employee DEFINITION.
  PUBLIC SECTION.
    METHODS: set_details
      IMPORTING
        VALUE(name) TYPE string
        VALUE(base_salary) TYPE p DECIMALS 2.

    METHODS: calculate_salary
      IMPORTING
        VALUE(hours_worked) TYPE i.

    METHODS: get_salary
      RETURNING VALUE(result) TYPE p DECIMALS 2.

  PRIVATE SECTION.
    DATA: mv_name TYPE string,
          mv_base_salary TYPE p DECIMALS 2,
          mv_final_salary TYPE p DECIMALS 2.
ENDCLASS.

CLASS lcl_employee IMPLEMENTATION.
  METHOD set_details.
    mv_name = name.
```

5.5. METHODS AND CLASSES IN ABAP

```
    mv_base_salary = base_salary.
  ENDMETHOD.

  METHOD calculate_salary.
    mv_final_salary = mv_base_salary + ( hours_worked * 20 ).
  ENDMETHOD.

  METHOD get_salary.
    result = mv_final_salary.
  ENDMETHOD.

ENDCLASS.
```

The lcl_employee class demonstrates encapsulation by maintaining employee details as private attributes, while publicly accessible methods like set_details, calculate_salary, and get_salary manipulate and access the data. This separation of concerns allows for a clear delineation between internal data representation and external interfaces.

Once a class is defined and implemented, objects can be instantiated, and methods can be called. Instantiation involves creating an instance of a class that represents a single entity possessing the defined attributes and behaviors.

```
DATA: lo_employee TYPE REF TO lcl_employee,
      lv_hours_worked TYPE i VALUE 80,
      lv_salary TYPE p DECIMALS 2.

START-OF-SELECTION.
  CREATE OBJECT lo_employee.

  CALL METHOD lo_employee->set_details
    EXPORTING
      name = 'John Doe'
      base_salary = 2000.

  CALL METHOD lo_employee->calculate_salary
    EXPORTING
      hours_worked = lv_hours_worked.

  lv_salary = lo_employee->get_salary( ).

  WRITE: / 'Employee:', 'John Doe', 'Salary:', lv_salary.
```

In this example, the object lo_employee is created from the lcl_employee class, invoking methods to input details, calculate, and retrieve the salary. The use of method calls ensures encapsulation and minimizes external manipulation, safeguarding data integrity.

A crucial advantage of classes in ABAP is the ability to derive new classes from existing ones, inheriting attributes and methods. This not only reduces code duplication but also simplifies maintenance and enhancement by localizing behavior adjustments.

```
CLASS lcl_employee_salaried DEFINITION INHERITING FROM lcl_employee.
  PUBLIC SECTION.
    METHODS: calculate_bonus
      IMPORTING
        VALUE(bonus_percent) TYPE i.

  PRIVATE SECTION.
    DATA: mv_bonus TYPE p DECIMALS 2.
ENDCLASS.

CLASS lcl_employee_salaried IMPLEMENTATION.
  METHOD calculate_bonus.
    mv_bonus = ( mv_base_salary * bonus_percent ) / 100.
  ENDMETHOD.
ENDCLASS.
```

By extending lcl_employee, the derived class lcl_employee_salaried adds additional functionality for calculating bonuses, showcasing targeted enhancements while retaining core behavior.

Polymorphism in ABAP is achieved through abstract classes and interfaces, allowing different objects to be treated uniformly through shared interfaces. Interfaces define a contract that implementing classes must fulfill, thereby facilitating interchangeable components.

```
INTERFACE lif_employee.
  METHODS: get_final_salary RETURNING VALUE(salary) TYPE p DECIMALS 2.
ENDINTERFACE.

CLASS lcl_contract_employee DEFINITION.
  PUBLIC SECTION. INTERFACES lif_employee.
  PRIVATE SECTION.
    DATA mv_salary TYPE p DECIMALS 2.
ENDCLASS.

CLASS lcl_contract_employee IMPLEMENTATION.
  METHOD lif_employee~get_final_salary.
    salary = mv_salary + 500. " Contract bonus
  ENDMETHOD.
ENDCLASS.
```

In the example, contract employees implement lif_employee, allowing collections of employee types to be processed using shared methods.

Utilizing classes and methods effectively requires adhering to best practices aimed at maintaining code quality and readability:

- Clearly define class responsibilities and ensure that each class has a single responsibility where possible (Single Responsibility Principle).

- Use meaningful names for classes, methods, and attributes to enhance maintainability.

- Implement modularized, focused methods that perform a single well-defined task.

- Leverage inheritance consciously, being aware of complexities introduced by deep inheritance hierarchies.

- Document classes and methods with clear descriptions and expected parameter interfaces.

The incorporation of methods and classes into ABAP programming bridges traditional procedural paradigms to modern object-oriented methodologies, streamlining application architectures and enhancing the robustness of SAP applications. As programming shifts towards more intricate system designs, the effective use of methods and classes becomes quintessential in maintaining scalability, flexibility, and alignment with evolving business landscapes.

5.6 Handling Exceptions in Modular Components

Exception handling is a critical aspect of robust software development, aimed at managing and responding to errors and unexpected situations that arise during program execution. Effective exception handling ensures that programs react gracefully to anomalies, maintaining integrity and reliability across various components. This section delves into the techniques for handling exceptions within modular components in ABAP, focusing on function modules and classes with methods, providing a detailed understanding of how exceptions can be managed systematically and effectively.

Overview of Exception Handling in ABAP

In ABAP, exceptions can be raised when a program encounters a condition that it cannot handle normally. These conditions might include logical errors, resource constraints, data integrity issues, or unexpected inputs. Exception handling mechanisms allow developers to define response strategies to these conditions, mitigating potential disruptions to program flow.

An ABAP program can employ three main strategies for handling exceptions:

- **Class-based Exceptions**: Introduced with ABAP Objects, class-based exceptions allow for comprehensive exception management through inheritance and polymorphism. They provide a structured way to handle and anticipate multiple error conditions more elegantly.

- **Classic Exceptions**: These are older mechanisms, allowing exceptions to be declared for procedures like function modules using explicitly defined exception conditions.

- **Event-driven Approach**: Leveraging ABAP events and techniques such as using the event handler to manage special conditions as they occur.

Each approach has its distinct applications and benefits, and understanding when to use each is crucial for effective exception management.

Function Modules and Classic Exception Handling

When using function modules, especially in large systems, managing exceptions is essential. Exceptions in function modules are predefined and handled at the function call site. They allow the function to signal specific error conditions which the caller must process.

Consider an example function module that calculates the discount, with exceptions to handle abnormal conditions:

```
FUNCTION calculate_discount.
*"----------------------------------------------------------------------
*"*"Local interface:
*"  IMPORTING VALUE(price) TYPE p DECIMALS 2
*"  VALUE(discount_rate) TYPE p DECIMALS 2
*"  EXPORTING VALUE(discounted_price) TYPE p DECIMALS 2
```

5.6. HANDLING EXCEPTIONS IN MODULAR COMPONENTS

```
*" EXCEPTIONS invalid_discount_rate
*" calculation_error
*"------------------------------------------------------------

   IF discount_rate < 0 OR discount_rate > 100.
     RAISE invalid_discount_rate.
   ENDIF.

   discounted_price = price * ((100 - discount_rate) / 100).

   IF sy-subrc <> 0.
     RAISE calculation_error.
   ENDIF.

ENDFUNCTION.
```

In this example, two exceptions, 'invalid_discount_rate' and 'calculation_error', are defined. When invoking this function module, these exceptions must be handled:

```
DATA: lv_price TYPE p DECIMALS 2 VALUE 500,
      lv_discount_rate TYPE p DECIMALS 2 VALUE 150, " Invalid rate
      lv_final_price TYPE p DECIMALS 2.

TRY.
  CALL FUNCTION 'CALCULATE_DISCOUNT'
    EXPORTING
      price = lv_price
      discount_rate = lv_discount_rate
    IMPORTING
      discounted_price = lv_final_price.
  CATCH SYSTEM-EXCEPTIONS invalid_discount_rate = 1
                          calculation_error = 2.

    WRITE: / 'An error occurred while calculating discount'.
ENDTRY.

IF sy-subrc = 1.
  WRITE: / 'Invalid discount rate provided.'.
ELSEIF sy-subrc = 2.
  WRITE: / 'Error during calculation of discounted price.'.
ENDIF.
```

This example demonstrates trapping exceptions using the 'TRY'...'CATCH' block, which is a structured way to handle function module exceptions. If an exception is triggered, program control is transferred to the 'CATCH' clause where specific error handling logic can be implemented.

Class-based Exception Handling

ABAP classes and methods, part of the object-oriented paradigm, provide sophisticated mechanisms for exception handling through class-based exceptions. These exceptions are more structured and are inherited from standard exception classes, facilitating a polymorphic approach to handle related exceptions seamlessly.

Class-based exceptions involve creating exception classes, either inheriting from standard exceptions or custom definitions specific to application needs:

```
CLASS lcx_invalid_input DEFINITION INHERITING FROM cx_static_check.
  PUBLIC SECTION.
    METHODS: constructor IMPORTING iv_message TYPE string.
ENDCLASS.

CLASS lcx_invalid_input IMPLEMENTATION.
  METHOD constructor.
    super->constructor( iv_message = iv_message ).
  ENDMETHOD.
ENDCLASS.
```

Once defined, these exceptions can be used within method implementations:

```
CLASS lcl_order_processor DEFINITION.
  PUBLIC SECTION.
    METHODS: process_order
      IMPORTING iv_order_id TYPE string.
  PRIVATE SECTION.
ENDCLASS.

CLASS lcl_order_processor IMPLEMENTATION.
  METHOD process_order.
    IF iv_order_id IS INITIAL.
      RAISE EXCEPTION TYPE lcx_invalid_input
        EXPORTING
          iv_message = 'Order ID is missing or invalid.'.
    ENDIF.
    " Order processing logic
  ENDMETHOD.
ENDCLASS.
```

The method 'process_order' raises a class-based exception when the input condition (i.e., no order ID provided) is not met.

When invoking methods with potentially raised exceptions, handling is done through 'TRY'...'CATCH' blocks, ensuring that error conditions are handled correctly:

```
DATA(lo_order_processor) = NEW lcl_order_processor( ).
TRY.
```

5.6. HANDLING EXCEPTIONS IN MODULAR COMPONENTS

```
lo_order_processor->process_order( iv_order_id = '' ).
CATCH lcx_invalid_input INTO DATA(ex).
  WRITE: / 'Process failed:', ex->get_text( ).
ENDTRY.
```

In this example, the scenario catches and processes the 'lcx_invalid_input' exception, whereby the error message text is retrieved to make the error information consumable by the user or log it for further investigation.

Designing Robust Exception Mechanisms

Implementing exception handling requires careful consideration and design to effectively capture and report anomalous conditions without disrupting the user experience or data integrity. The following recommendations can guide developers:

- **Use Specific Exceptions**: Define specific exceptions that convey precise error conditions rather than generic exceptions.

- **Centralize Error Handling Logic**: Consider creating utility components capable of processing or logging exceptions consistently across an application.

- **Propagate Relevant Exceptions**: Ensure only relevant exceptions are propagated up the call stack, preserving context for end-users or peripheral systems.

- **Refactor Error-prone Areas**: Regularly review and refactor code associated with frequent exceptions for improved resilience.

By implementing structured and effective exception handling mechanisms within modular components, developers can enhance the robustness and reliability of ABAP applications. Properly managed exceptions maintain system integrity, prevent unexpected terminations or errors, and ultimately lead to better user experiences and operational continuity.

5.7 Packages and Naming Conventions

In ABAP development, the organization and clarity of code are paramount to creating maintainable, scalable, and easily navigable systems. Packages and naming conventions are integral components of this organizational paradigm. They provide the necessary structure and guidance for developers to efficiently manage the complexity inherent in large-scale enterprise software development within SAP environments. This section examines the significance of packages and the methodical application of naming conventions in ABAP, articulating their impact on project success and system coherence.

Understanding Packages in ABAP

Packages in ABAP serve as organizational units designed to group related development objects, such as programs, classes, function modules, and more. They are central to the hierarchical structuring of code, enabling logical segmentation based on functionality, application domains, or business processes. Packages facilitate clear and consistent grouping, which is crucial for efficient code navigation, maintenance, and reuse.

Key purposes of using packages include:

- **Encapsulation of Related Artifacts**: Packages encapsulate development artifacts, allowing for cleaner separation of different components, which enhances modularization and reduces complexity.

- **Namespace Management**: With packages, conflicts in naming can be minimized, as they promote the separation of concerns within an application's architecture.

- **Transport Layer Bindings**: Packages play a critical role in the SAP transport system, determining how objects are grouped and transported across different systems (e.g., from development to production environments).

- **Access Control**: By defining visibility and access rules within packages, ABAP provides mechanisms to limit the scope of use of certain components, enhancing data security and integrity.

5.7. PACKAGES AND NAMING CONVENTIONS

Creating and Managing Packages

Creating packages in ABAP is facilitated via the Object Navigator (transaction SE80). The process involves specifying package properties, such as descriptions and transport layer assignments, to establish a coherent grouping framework for development objects.

```
PACKAGE z_financials.
DESCRIPTION 'Financial Transactions Package'.

PCG_SECURE_VIA_ENCAPSULATION OF Z_UTIL FINANCIAL_CALCS.
    CREATE PROGRAM z_ledger_management.
    CREATE TABLE z_financial_entries.

ENDPACKAGE.
```

This example showcases the creation of a package z_financials, which organizes related programs and tables, thus serving as an entry point for the development and management of financial applications.

Developers can place objects within a package either at creation or by modifying their properties using the appropriate development workbench tools and transactions, ensuring alignment with organizational standards and expectations.

Importance of Naming Conventions

Naming conventions are structured guidelines that dictate the systematic approach to naming development objects like variables, functions, classes, and other entities within your ABAP programs. These conventions are critical for achieving consistency and clarity across the development landscape, aiding developers in understanding and navigating large codebases efficiently.

Enforcing consistent naming conventions yields several benefits:

- **Readability**: Names that follow a structured convention improve code readability, allowing new and existing team members to comprehend the purpose and function of various components quickly.

- **Maintainability**: Clear and consistent naming reduces the cognitive load required to maintain and modify code, decreasing the likelihood of introducing errors during updates.

- **Discoverability**: Adhering to naming conventions improves the ability to locate and use components, streamlining integration and reusability across projects.

Common naming convention practices in ABAP include:

- **Prefixes and Suffixes**: Using standardized prefixes or suffixes to denote object type, e.g., lv_ for local variables, gt_ for global tables, or z_ for custom developments.
- **CamelCase and underscore separation**: Applying CamelCase or underscores to separate words within identifying names, improving readability (CalculateDiscount, calculate_discount).
- **Meaningful Names**: Names should be descriptive of their purpose or function (e.g., CalculateDiscount for a method that computes a discount).

```
DATA: lv_total_amount TYPE p DECIMALS 2,
      lv_discount_rate TYPE p DECIMALS 2 VALUE 5.5,
      lv_final_amount TYPE p DECIMALS 2.

FIELD-SYMBOLS: <fs_record> TYPE ANY.

START-OF-SELECTION.
  PERFORM calculate_net_amount
    USING lv_total_amount
    CHANGING lv_final_amount.

WRITE: / 'Net amount after discount:', lv_final_amount.

FORM calculate_net_amount
  USING p_total_amount TYPE p
  CHANGING p_net_amount TYPE p.

  p_net_amount = p_total_amount - ( p_total_amount * lv_discount_rate / 100 ).

ENDFORM.
```

The above data set-up and procedural calls illustrate the use of structured naming strategies, helping delineate different types of variables and functions, thereby enhancing code comprehension.

Best Practices for Naming Conventions and Package Management

Establishing best practices for package management and naming conventions requires agreement among development teams and rigorous adherence through development life cycles. Recommendations include:

5.7. PACKAGES AND NAMING CONVENTIONS

- Define and Document Naming Conventions: Clearly document naming rules, guidelines, and examples, ensuring all developers utilize consistent styles.

- Use Package Naming to Reflect Functionality: Choose package names that align with business processes to aid logical grouping and accessibility.

- Organize Packages Hierarchically: Develop packages in a hierarchical structure to mirror business functions, facilitating the identification of related components.

- Leverage Naming Conventions for Automation: By adhering to conventions, automated tools can generate reports or metrics related to quality assurance and version control effectively.

- Regular Reviews and Audits: Regularly audit codebases to ensure adherence to established conventions and packages structures, enhancing long-term maintainability.

Through methodical naming conventions and strategic use of packages, ABAP development teams can enhance the quality, maintainability, and scalability of their software systems. These practices underpin effective collaboration and efficient development, ultimately leading to high-quality software solutions aligned with organizational and business objectives.

Chapter 6

Dialog Programming and SAP GUI

This chapter provides an in-depth examination of dialog programming within the SAP environment, focusing on enhancing user interaction through SAP GUI. It covers the design and structuring of screens using the Screen Painter and introduces key concepts of Dynpro programming. The chapter discusses managing various screen elements, implementing module pool programming, and techniques for capturing and validating user input. Additionally, it explores logic and navigation between screens, employing PBO and PAI events to ensure smooth user experience, and delves into integrating custom controls to augment standard SAP GUI functionality, ultimately aiming to optimize interface design and interaction.

6.1 SAP GUI and Screens Basics

The SAP Graphical User Interface (GUI) serves as the primary platform for user interaction within the SAP ecosystem. It is an integral aspect of SAP application environments, specifically designed to facilitate robust communication between users and the complex enterprise resource planning system underlying SAP. This section provides a detailed examination of the fundamental components and functionalities of the SAP GUI, alongside the processes involved in creating and organizing screens for efficient user interaction.

At its core, the SAP GUI is a client-side software application that provides a graphical interface for accessing SAP systems. The GUI enables users to interact with SAP transactions that manage business operations such as finance, logistics, and human resources. The design principles and structure of the SAP GUI allow for optimizing user roles, task completion, and data retrieval processes within an organization.

Components of SAP GUI

The SAP GUI comprises several key components that facilitate its operation. Each component plays a crucial role in the interface's ability to deliver seamless user experiences:

- **Navigation Area**: This component allows users to quickly access SAP menu items, user roles, favorites, and SAP transactions. It provides a well-organized structure of available operations that can be customized according to user requirements.

- **Menu Bar**: The menu bar provides access to application-specific functionalities. It contains options related to system commands, actions relevant to specific transactions, and utilities for supporting user tasks.

- **Standard Toolbar**: This toolbar consists of buttons for frequently used functions such as save, back, cancel, exit, and print. It enhances usability by reducing the number of clicks required to perform routine tasks.

- **Title Bar**: It displays the title of the currently active SAP screen or transaction.

- **Application Toolbar**: This contains buttons specifically designed for the transaction being executed. Its content changes dynamically according to the active transaction.

- **Status Bar**: Located at the bottom of the SAP GUI window, the status bar provides information on system messages, data processing status, and other context-specific insights critical to maintaining smooth interaction flows.

Creating and Organizing Screens

Screen creation and organization within the SAP GUI is a pivotal aspect of dialog programming. It involves using tools like the Screen Painter to design interaction layouts and manage screen flows. Screens form the nucleus of SAP transactions, representing the interface through which users perform their tasks and input data.

Screen Painter Tool

The Screen Painter is an SAP development tool that allows developers to design and modify screen layouts. It provides a drag-and-drop interface for placing and configuring a variety of UI elements, including input fields, text labels, radio buttons, checkboxes, and buttons. The Screen Painter is characterized by functionalities that support the following:

- **Field Arrangement**: Developers can arrange fields to create logical workflows and intuitive user experiences. It supports alignment, spacing control, and field grouping for enhanced clarity.

- **Field Attributes Configuration**: Each field can be configured with specific attributes such as length, input/output capacity, and visibility settings. This is crucial for tailoring screen elements to meet enterprise-specific requirements.

- **Element Properties**: Developers can assign properties to screen elements to control their behavior. For instance, adjusting field read-only status, setting default values, or defining mandatory fields.

- **Resolution and Layout Management**: The tool accommodates the design of screens suitable for various display resolutions, ensuring consistency and usability across different devices.

Managing Screens in Dialog Programming

Screens are managed within dialog programs through modules known as Dynpros (Dynamic Programs). These modules are part of the ABAP development environment, applied in building interactive SAP applications. Each Dynpro is associated with screen attributes, I/O fields, and processing logic, which collectively define user interaction with SAP applications.

- **Screen Attributes**: This includes parameters like screen number, screen title, and program name that define the screen's core characteristics.

- **Input/Output Fields**: Defined within screens, these fields capture user input and display system output. The synchronization between application logic and user interface is managed via field names and variable binding.

- **Flow Logic**: This defines the logical flow and response to events within the screen. SAP employs a two-part processing model, involving "Process Before Output" (PBO) for initializing screen elements, and "Process After Input" (PAI) for capturing user actions.

Example of a Simple Screen Design in Screen Painter

Let's consider an example of designing a simple user registration screen using the Screen Painter. The objective is to create a form where users can input their name, email, and phone number.

```
PROCESS BEFORE OUTPUT.
  MODULE set_title.

PROCESS AFTER INPUT.
  MODULE user_registration.

MODULE set_title OUTPUT.
  SET TITLEBAR 'REGISTRATION'.
ENDMODULE.

MODULE user_registration INPUT.
  SAVE USER INPUT.
  IF necessary_verifications.
    MODULE save_to_db.
  ELSE.
    MESSAGE 'Input not valid' TYPE 'E'.
  ENDIF.
ENDMODULE.
```

In this example, a screen consists of an output module to set the title of the interface, and an input module to process user registration. The

6.1. SAP GUI AND SCREENS BASICS

logic begins by setting the title of the screen via the set_title module, followed by collecting user inputs through fields defined in the Screen Painter. Proper verification processes ensure data integrity before storage, maintaining consistency in input methodologies.

Organizing Screen Flow

Organizing screens within the SAP GUI involves determining the sequence of screens users will interact with while engaged in a particular transaction. This process, known as screen flow design, is essential for ensuring seamless user experiences and efficient task completion.

- **Forward Navigation**: This refers to progressing from one screen to another, typically following the user input or task completion workflow. Forward navigation should be logical, reflecting the natural order of the transaction process.

- **Backward Navigation**: Often includes mechanisms allowing users to revisit previous screens, either to correct input errors or review information.

- **Dynamic Screen Modification**: In complex applications, certain conditions may require changing the screen layout or sequence in response to specific user actions or data states. This necessitates sophisticated logic within the SAP ABAP environment.

Example of Sequential Screen Navigation

Consider a business scenario where a billing clerk processes billing orders across multiple screens. The navigation follows a simple order and can be encapsulated using the screen flow logic:

```
MODULE screen_navigation INPUT.
  CASE current_screen.
    WHEN '100'.
      SET SCREEN '200'.
    WHEN '200'.
      SET SCREEN '300'.
    WHEN '300'.
      PERFORM finalize_process.
    WHEN OTHERS.
      MESSAGE 'Invalid screen number' TYPE 'E'.
  ENDCASE.
  LEAVE TO SCREEN 0.
ENDMODULE.
```

This example demonstrates the use of a CASE statement within an input module to control the sequence of screens based on the current processing state. By branching screens through the SET SCREEN command followed by LEAVE TO SCREEN, dynamic navigation paths can be efficiently managed.

Best Practices for Screen Design in SAP GUI

Effective screen design should adhere to a series of best practices ensuring maximum efficiency, usability, and user satisfaction:

- **Simplicity and Clarity**: Screens should provide users only with necessary information and input fields relevant to their tasks, minimizing clutter and cognitive load.

- **Consistency**: Maintain uniform design elements, such as font sizes, labels, and colors, to enhance familiarity and reduce user error.

- **Feedback and Error Handling**: Implement user-friendly messages and simple validation processes that guide users through correcting input errors without frustration.

- **Performance Considerations**: Optimize the number of screens and dialogues to prevent latency. Heavy screens should be broken down into manageable parts with efficient data retrieval mechanisms.

Through these practices, system usability can be significantly enhanced, encouraging user engagement with the SAP environment in a more efficient and satisfying manner. By combining meticulous GUI components and well-structured screens, SAP developers can create powerful applications that facilitate enterprise operations and support complex business processes effectively.

6.2 Screen Painter and Dynpro Programming

Screen Painter and Dynpro (Dynamic Program) programming are integral components of SAP dialog programming, forming the backbone of sophisticated user interaction designs within the SAP environment. These tools facilitate the creation and management of interactive user interfaces that ensure a seamless flow of user activities and data handling. This section delves into the functionalities of the Screen Painter tool and the intricacies of Dynpro programming, exploring methodologies, code implementations, and best practices that equip developers with the skills needed to design efficient SAP applications.

Screen Painter Tool - An Overview

The Screen Painter is a graphical design tool used within the ABAP Workbench to create and modify screen elements in SAP applications. It allows developers to design custom screens that align with business requirements, offering a range of functionalities for placing, configuring, and linking user interface components. The tool is a key enabler for realizing user requirements through visually appealing and functional layouts.

Key Features of the Screen Painter:

- **Graphical Interface**: Offers a drag-and-drop environment for creating screen elements, allowing developers to visually compose layouts with minimal coding.

- **Field Elements**: Provides a wide array of elements including input/output fields, text labels, radio buttons, and checkboxes, customizable through property attributes to suit transaction needs.

- **Layout Management**: Facilitates control over field positioning, size, alignment, and grouping, ensuring consistency in screen designs.

- **Attribute Configuration**: Supports the configuration of attributes for each screen element, such as labels, input restrictions, obligatory fields, and default values.

Creating a Basic Screen

Developing a basic screen using the Screen Painter requires an understanding of how to create screens and incorporate essential elements. Suppose there is a requirement to create a data entry form for capturing employee details such as Employee ID, Name, and Department.

In the Screen Painter:

1. **Create a New Screen**: Navigate to the desired module pool program and initiate a new screen number.

2. **Field Placement**: Utilize the tool's graphical interface to place elements on the screen canvas.

3. **Customize Field Properties**: Adjust field lengths, set labels, and configure data types according to expected user inputs.

Example Screen Layout:

- **Employee ID**: Numeric input field configured to accept integers only.
- **Name**: Text input field with a set maximum length.
- **Department**: Dropdown list field allowing selection from predefined department codes.

Dynpro Programming Fundamentals

Dynpro programming in SAP involves creating and managing dialog screens, known as Dynamic Programs or Dynpros. Each Dynpro consists of user interface elements, screen attributes, and processing logic that define how users interact with the application. Dynpro programming encompasses managing screen flow logic, integrating with backend ABAP logic, and handling user events.

Structure of a Dynpro

Each Dynpro is defined by:

- **Screen Number**: A unique identifier for each screen, typically within a module pool.
- **Screen Elements**: These include input/output fields, selection buttons, and action triggers that collect user inputs or display data.
- **Flow Logic**: Programming logic that manages screen rendering and user interaction processing. Flow logic includes PBO (Process Before Output) and PAI (Process After Input) events.

6.2. SCREEN PAINTER AND DYNPRO PROGRAMMING

Dynpro Processing Logic

Understanding and implementing Dynpro flow logic is critical for handling user interactions and ensuring data integrity. It involves programming the sequence and conditions under which user actions are processed.

- **PBO (Process Before Output)**: This event module is executed immediately before a screen is displayed. It is used to prepare the screen with necessary data from the database or application logic.

    − Example: Initializing field values, setting up dropdown list options, and modifying element visibility.

```
MODULE pbo_screen_initialization OUTPUT.
  INITIALIZE DROP-DOWN LISTS.
  FETCH DEFAULT VALUES.
ENDMODULE.
```

- **PAI (Process After Input)**: This event is triggered by user actions such as pressing a button. PAI modules process user inputs, perform validations, and update backend data if inputs are valid.

    − Example: Validating employee input data, checking for required fields, and committing data to the database.

```
MODULE pai_user_input_process INPUT.
  CHECK USER INPUT VALIDITY.
  IF VALID INPUT.
    UPDATE DATABASE RECORDS.
  ELSE.
    DISPLAY ERROR MESSAGE.
  ENDIF.
ENDMODULE.
```

Handling User Inputs and Events

Event handling within Dynpro programming ensures responsive and interactive SAP applications by capturing user inputs and translating them into actionable processes. Event handling involves monitoring user actions such as clicks, text entry, and navigation commands.

- **Input Validation**: Verifies user inputs for correctness and completeness. Effective validation includes checks against business rules, data format constraints, and field interdependencies.

- **Error Messaging**: Involves notifying users of input errors or system issues through consistent and informative messages.

- **Action Responses**: Defines system behavior in response to user inputs, such as navigating screens, updating data fields, or triggering business processes.

Best Practices in Dynpro Programming

Achieving robust and efficient SAP applications through Dynpro programming involves adhering to best practices that enhance code maintainability and user satisfaction.

- **Modular Design**: Structuring code into separate, reusable modules promotes clarity and reduces redundant coding efforts. This approach simplifies debugging and future enhancements.

- **Consistent UI Design**: Ensures uniformity in the presentation and behavior of screens across the application, enhancing usability.

- **Performance Optimization**: Minimizes response times by efficiently handling data loads, reducing I/O operations and optimizing database queries.

- **User-Centric Feedback**: Implements clear, context-sensitive messages that guide users regarding system states, expected inputs, and error resolutions.

Advanced Examples and Techniques

As the complexity of business processes increases, the need for advanced Dynpro techniques becomes evident. These techniques allow for richer user experiences and more dynamic screen interactions.

- **Subscreen Implementation**: Enables nesting of screens within other screens, facilitating modular UI designs for complex tasks.

```
MODULE include_subscreens OUTPUT.
  CALL SUBSCREEN subscreen_areas INCLUDING sub_screen_program
     sub_screen_number.
ENDMODULE.
```

- **User-Driven Dynamic Content**: Manipulating screen contents in real-time based on user interactions—for example, dynamically populating related fields based on user selection.

- **Lifecycle Management**: Employing mechanisms for transaction lifecycle management to maintain application state, including data consistency across sessions and interactions.

Screen Painter and Dynpro programming are core components of SAP dialog programming, empowering developers to create intuitive, efficient, and responsive user interfaces. By mastering the graphical design capabilities of Screen Painter and the logical underpinnings of Dynpro programming, developers can deliver tailored solutions that meet enterprise-specific needs while adhering to user-centric design principles. Best practices in these areas ensure applications that are not only functional and robust but also maintain efficient user interaction paradigms, leading to improved productivity and user satisfaction in SAP environments.

6.3 Working with Screen Elements

In SAP dialog programming, screen elements are the fundamental building blocks that form the graphical interface of an SAP application. These elements allow users to interact with the system by providing input and receiving feedback, thus playing a pivotal role in the user experience. This section explores the various types of screen elements available in SAP GUI, the methodologies for managing their properties and events, and best practices for utilizing them to create efficient and user-friendly interfaces. By understanding these elements, developers can construct detailed and functional SAP screens that enhance the overall effectiveness of SAP applications.

Types of Screen Elements

Screen elements in SAP GUI can be categorized based on their function and interaction capabilities. These elements are instrumental in crafting user interfaces that align with business processes and optimize workflow.

1. **Input/Output Fields**: These fields represent the most direct form of user interaction, allowing for data entry and display. Input fields capture data from users, while output fields present data from the system. Common attributes include length, data type, and visibility properties.

2. **Labels**: Used for identifying fields and providing context, labels are static text elements that help in understanding the purpose of adjacent input or output fields.

3. **Buttons**: Operational elements that trigger predefined actions in response to user clicks. Buttons are critical for executing commands, navigating between screens, and submitting data.

4. **Checkboxes and Radio Buttons**: Used for selecting options. Checkboxes typically allow for multiple selections, whereas radio buttons are used for exclusive selection within a defined group.

5. **Dropdown Lists (Combo Boxes)**: Provide a list of options from which users can select, thus saving screen space and ensuring standardized data entry.

6. **Tables and Grids**: Facilitate the display and manipulation of data in a tabular format, allowing users to view multiple records at once and perform collective operations.

7. **Text Areas**: Fields that allow for multiline text input, typically used for comments or descriptions.

8. **Tab Strip Controls**: These allow for organizing screen content within tabs, thereby enhancing structure and navigation without overwhelming users with too much information on a single screen.

Managing Screen Element Properties

6.3. WORKING WITH SCREEN ELEMENTS

Screen elements in SAP can be customized extensively by configuring their properties. Managing these properties effectively is essential for creating intuitive and responsive user interfaces.

- **Data Binding**: Each element can be bound to a specific data field within the underlying application. Proper data binding ensures the seamless flow of data between the user interface and application logic.

- **Attribute Configuration**: Developers can configure attributes such as default values, mandatory status, data type validation, visibility, and length constraints to suit business requirements.

- **Event Handlers**: Elements can be linked to event handlers that determine application behavior when user interactions occur. Event handlers facilitate executing logic when elements gain focus, when input changes, or when specific actions like button clicks occur.

- **Style and Presentation**: While SAP GUI is predominantly a functional interface, elements can still be styled to some degree using transportation status, icons, or font weight changes, helping emphasize key information.

Example: Creating a Customer Information Screen

Suppose there is a need to develop a customer information screen capturing and displaying details such as Customer Name, Contact Number, Address, and Preferred Contact Method.

```
SCREEN 100 FLOW LOGIC.
PROCESS BEFORE OUTPUT.
  MODULE prepare_screen_100.

PROCESS AFTER INPUT.
  MODULE process_user_entries.

* MODULES
MODULE prepare_screen_100 OUTPUT.
  CLEAR: customer_name, contact_number, address.
  LOOP AT it_method INTO wa_method.
    APPEND wa_method-method TO listbox_methods.
  ENDLOOP.
ENDMODULE.

MODULE process_user_entries INPUT.
```

```
CHECK customer_name IS NOT INITIAL.
CHECK contact_number IS NOT INITIAL.
IF preferred_contact_method IS INITIAL.
  MESSAGE 'Select a preferred contact method' TYPE 'E'.
ELSE.
  SAVE customer_name customer_details.
  MESSAGE 'Customer information saved successfully' TYPE 'S'.
ENDIF.
ENDMODULE.
```

In this scenario:

- **Input Fields**: Capture the Customer Name, Contact Number, and Address.

- **Dropdown List**: Present options for the Preferred Contact Method (e.g., Email, Phone), populated dynamically from an internal table.

The screen logic employs PBO to prepare the screen and fill the dropdown list, and PAI to validate inputs and capture events when a user submits the form.

Working with Dynamic Screen Content

Dynamic screen content management is crucial when creating interactive SAP applications, as it allows for responsive interfaces that adapt to user actions and data state.

- **Conditional Display**: Certain screen elements might only be relevant under specific conditions, such as displaying a discount section only if an order exceeds a predetermined amount. By dynamically toggling the visibility attribute, screens can alter content according to real-time conditions.

```
MODULE set_dynamic_attributes OUTPUT.
  IF order_value > 1000.
    discount_field-visible = 1.
  ELSE.
    discount_field-active = 0.
  ENDIF.
ENDMODULE.
```

- **Interactive Content Update**: Elements can be updated based on user interactions. For example, selecting a customer ID from a dropdown can trigger the display of customer-specific data in related fields.

- **Real-Time Input Feedback**: Implement immediate validation and user feedback as data is being entered to catch errors early and improve the user experience. Use the ON CHANGE event to detect changes in input and trigger logic accordingly.

Handling Screen Element Events

Handling events in SAP screen elements entails defining responses to user actions, thereby enabling interactive and cohesive applications. Critical aspects include:

- **Field Validation**: Ensures the integrity of data by checking individual field inputs for correctness and logical consistency. Validation can be implemented at the PAI event to gauge the accuracy of user inputs.

```
MODULE check_field_validity INPUT.
  CHECK email_field CO '@'.
  IF NOT valid_email_format(email_field).
    MESSAGE 'Invalid email format' TYPE 'E'.
  ENDIF.
ENDMODULE.
```

- **Chain Processes**: Grouping related fields in a CHAIN END-CHAIN construct allows for coordinated validation or processing, typically used when dependencies exist among fields.

- **Command Validation**: Ensures commands executed through buttons or keyboard shortcuts are appropriately processed, allowing command authorization and integrity checks.

Best Practices for Using Screen Elements

Several best practices can be followed when working with screen elements to construct effective user interfaces:

- **User-centric Design**: Prioritize the user's needs and tasks when designing screen layouts, ensuring elements are logically structured and intuitively accessed.

- **Optimization of Information Layout**: Avoid clutter and overwhelming users by deliberately structuring screens. Group related elements, utilize tabs or subscreens for extensive data, and prioritize the most critical information.

- **Minimal Required Inputs**: Ensure that required parameters are minimized to what is absolutely necessary, automating data retrieval where possible and reducing user input burden.

- **Responsive Error Handling**: Implement clear and helpful error messages that contextually guide users in correcting any input errors, fostering a more seamless user experience.

Summary and Conclusion

Working with screen elements in SAP GUI is foundational to crafting applications that are both powerful and intuitive. By effectively leveraging input/output fields, buttons, dropdown lists, and checkboxes, a developer can create interfaces that facilitate user tasks and drive operational efficiencies. Critical to this endeavor is understanding how to manage element properties, handle dynamic content, respond to events, and integrate best practices in user interface design. Through mastery of these elements and practices, SAP applications can be designed to achieve high levels of performance and user satisfaction, enhancing their role in modern business environments.

6.4 Module Pool Programming

Module Pool Programming, also known as dialog programming, is an advanced technique within the SAP environment that involves creating complex interactive applications. These applications utilize screens, or Dynpros, to interact with users, process transactions, and manage business logic. A module pool is a collection of screens and the associated flow logic, dedicated to a specific application or set of functionality within the SAP system. This section delves into the fundamentals of Module Pool Programming, its structure, benefits, and implementation methodologies, enriched with examples and best practices.

Understanding Module Pool Programming

6.4. MODULE POOL PROGRAMMING

Module Pool Programming is characterized by its focus on managing complex interactions and transactions within the SAP GUI. It allows developers to design interfaces where users can perform various operations, from data entry to transaction processing, within a cohesive application framework. The uniqueness of module pool programs is their tight integration with SAP's screen management system, allowing for dynamic and responsive user interfaces that cater to enterprise-specific needs.

Core Components of a Module Pool

A typical module pool application consists of the following core components:

- **ABAP Program**: The logical layer where business logic is implemented, including data processing, calculations, and validation processes.

- **Screens (Dynpros)**: Interfaces through which users interact with the application. Each screen comprises elements like input/output fields, buttons, and tables, alongside the flow logic that dictates screen behavior.

- **Flow Logic**: Consists of modules triggered by PBO (Process Before Output) and PAI (Process After Input) events that manage the transition between screens, data validations, and triggers for actions.

- **Subroutines and Function Modules**: May be used to encapsulate reusable logic, reduce redundancy, and enhance code maintainability.

Structure of a Module Pool Program

The structure of a module pool program is inherently modular to facilitate comprehensive screenings and logical transaction processing. It is organized around ABAP code and screen definitions, linked through flow logic that determines the interactions.

```
PROGRAM z_module_pool_example.

* Include necessary modules
INCLUDE: zmpo_screens,
```

```
        zmpo_status,
        zmpo_subroutines.

TABLES: smp_cust_data.

*----------------------------------------------------------------*
* Event: PBO (Process Before Output)
*----------------------------------------------------------------*
MODULE status_initialize OUTPUT.
  SET PF-STATUS 'MAIN100_STATUS'.
  SET TITLEBAR '100TITLE'.
  PERFORM initialize_screen_100.
ENDMODULE.

*----------------------------------------------------------------*
* Event: PAI (Process After Input)
*----------------------------------------------------------------*
MODULE user_commands INPUT.
  CASE ok_code.
    WHEN 'SAVE'.
      PERFORM save_data.
    WHEN 'BACK'.
      LEAVE TO SCREEN 0.
    WHEN 'EXIT'.
      LEAVE PROGRAM.
  ENDCASE.
ENDMODULE.
```

In this structure, screens and logical processing are defined, accompanied by event-specific modules for initializing display elements and managing user interactions.

Screen and Flow Logic Management

The management of Dynpro screens and flow logic is central to a module pool program's operational capacity. Each screen is designed to connect with the program's logic and deliver precise responses to user inputs.

- **Screen Design**: Screens define the user interface for the program. Their structure includes fields for user input and elements that direct the execution of transactions. The design process within the Screen Painter involves placing components such as buttons for navigation and processing control.

- **PBO and PAI Events**: Each screen in a module pool program has associated flow logic:

    - **PBO (Process Before Output)**: Prepares the screen before it is displayed. This includes setting field default values,

6.4. MODULE POOL PROGRAMMING

populating tables, and setting the screen status.

- **PAI (Process After Input)**: Covers input processing once the user has entered data and executed an action. This involves validation, command execution, and preparation for the next screen.

Executing Transactions in Module Pools

One of the main outcomes of module pool programming is the ability to execute complex transactions within a user-focused framework. The arrangement and functionality of screens facilitate the efficient capture and processing of transaction data, allowing for dynamic workflows.

Example: Customer Management Application

Consider a module pool application for managing customer data, where the primary operations are handling inputs for customer creation, modification, and deletion.

```
PROGRAM zcustomer_management.

TABLES: zcustomers.

* Screen Module for Adding New Customer
MODULE add_customer_screen_100 OUTPUT.
  IF NOT zcust_id IS INITIAL.
    SELECT SINGLE * FROM zcustomers INTO CORRESPONDING FIELDS OF
          wa_customer
      WHERE zcust_id = zcust_id.
    IF sy-subrc = 0.
      MOVE-CORRESPONDING wa_customer TO zm_screen_fields.
    ENDIF.
  ENDIF.
ENDMODULE.

* Processing Customer Data Input
MODULE process_customer_input INPUT.
  IF NOT zm_screen_fields-zcust_name IS INITIAL.
    MOVE-CORRESPONDING zm_screen_fields TO wa_customer.
    INSERT INTO zcustomers VALUES wa_customer.
    IF sy-subrc = 0.
      MESSAGE 'Data saved successfully' TYPE 'S'.
    ELSE.
      MESSAGE 'Error saving data' TYPE 'E'.
    ENDIF.
  ELSE.
    MESSAGE 'Customer name is required' TYPE 'E'.
  ENDIF.
ENDMODULE.
```

This example illustrates managing a customer data screen, where user inputs are validated and updated in the corresponding database table.

Advanced Techniques in Module Pool Programming

Advanced module pool techniques enhance the robustness and flexibility of SAP applications. These approaches include more complex data interaction, user navigation, and system integration.

- **Subscreens**: Enable segmenting a screen into smaller, reusable areas, which can be modularly integrated across multiple screens or transactions. This approach enhances reusability and structures complex user interactions.

- **Tabstrip Controls**: Facilitate organizing information within tabs on the same screen, allowing users to view and interact with data across multiple contexts without additional navigation.

- **Dynamic Screen Modification**: Adapt screen contents in real-time based on business logic or user inputs. Techniques such as hiding/showing fields or dynamically populating list boxes help tailor the user experience to current processing requirements.

Best Practices for Module Pool Programming

Efficiency and maintainability in module pool programming require adherence to best practices:

- **Streamlined Navigation**: Ensure logical screen navigation paths that follow user expectations and task flow, employing clear and consistent navigation controls.

- **Consistent Interface Design**: Strive for uniformity in screen layouts, including consistent use of field labels, button placements, and validation messages.

- **Encapsulation of Logic**: Employ subroutines, includes, and function modules to encapsulate complex logic, reducing redundancy and increasing code clarity and maintainability.

- **Performance Optimization**: Efficient database interaction and minimized screen load times are vital. Optimize queries and limit the amount of data loaded into each screen session to what is necessary for user tasks.

Module Pool Programming is an essential skill in SAP development, offering the means to create powerful, user-centric applications that facilitate business processes effectively. By mastering module pool components, flow logic, and advanced dialog techniques, developers can deliver tailored solutions that meet enterprise demands and enhance user experience. Through careful consideration of best practices and efficient design patterns, module pool programming enables the development of sophisticated, high-performance applications that support complex business requirements in the SAP environment.

6.5 Managing User Input and Validation

Managing user input and validation is a critical aspect of SAP dialog programming, ensuring data integrity, security, and consistency within applications. Effective handling of user input involves capturing data efficiently, validating user entries against business rules and constraints, and providing intuitive guidance and feedback to users. This section explores the underlying concepts and best practices for managing user input and validation in SAP GUI applications, enhanced by detailed examples and technical insights.

Essentials of User Input Management

User input management encompasses the structured collection, processing, and validation of data entered by users through SAP GUI interfaces. In dialog programming, user input is primarily received via screens, composed of various input fields, buttons, checkboxes, and other interactive elements designed using tools like the Screen Painter.

- **Input Collection**: Efficient input collection involves designing screens that facilitate easy and accurate data entry. This includes selecting appropriate field types, logical arrangement of fields, and providing clear instructions and labels.

- **Data Binding**: Each input field is typically bound to a data field in the backend, ensuring direct synchronization between the user's interaction and the application's data model.

- **Feedback Mechanisms**: Providing immediate and relevant feedback is essential for guiding users during data entry. Feedback can be in the form of input suggestions, default values, or real-time validation messages.

Principles of Input Validation

Input validation is an indispensable part of managing user input, safeguarding against incorrect or malicious data entries that could disrupt operations or compromise system security. Validation strategies ensure that data meets specific criteria before being processed or stored.

- **Field-Level Validation**: Ensures that individual field entries conform to expected formats, lengths, and logical constraints. This can prevent data corruption and enhance the accuracy of user entries.

- **Form-Level Validation**: Examines the relationships and dependencies between multiple fields, ensuring that the data across an entire form is logically consistent and complete.

- **Business Rule Validation**: Verifies that inputs align with business processes and rules. This level of validation is crucial for maintaining compliance and operational integrity.

Implementing Validation in SAP GUI

Implementing input validation in SAP GUI applications is generally achieved through ABAP programming within the PAI (Process After Input) modules. The logic checks for valid conditions and reacts accordingly, often using message handling to inform users of invalid entries or required corrections.

Example: Capturing and Validating Employee Information

Consider a screen designed for entering employee information, which includes fields for Employee ID, Name, Email, and Salary.

```
MODULE check_employee_data INPUT.
  FIELD employee_id
    MODULE check_id_validity.
```

6.5. MANAGING USER INPUT AND VALIDATION

```
FIELD name
  MODULE check_name_validity.

FIELD email
  MODULE check_email_format.

FIELD salary
  MODULE check_salary_limits.

CHAIN.
  FIELD: employee_id, email.
  MODULE verify_employee_email.
ENDCHAIN.

MODULE check_id_validity INPUT.
  IF employee_id IS INITIAL.
    MESSAGE 'Employee ID must not be empty' TYPE 'E'.
  ELSEIF NOT employee_id CO '0123456789'.
    MESSAGE 'Employee ID must be numeric' TYPE 'E'.
  ENDIF.
ENDMODULE.

MODULE check_name_validity INPUT.
  IF name IS INITIAL.
    MESSAGE 'Name must not be empty' TYPE 'E'.
  ENDIF.
ENDMODULE.

MODULE check_email_format INPUT.
  IF NOT email CO '@'.
    MESSAGE 'Enter a valid email address' TYPE 'E'.
  ENDIF.
ENDMODULE.

MODULE check_salary_limits INPUT.
  IF salary < 0.
    MESSAGE 'Salary must be a positive number' TYPE 'E'.
  ENDIF.
ENDMODULE.

MODULE verify_employee_email INPUT.
  IF employee_id EQ '123' AND email CN 'example@'.
    MESSAGE 'Invalid email for this Employee ID' TYPE 'E'.
  ENDIF.
ENDMODULE.
```

In this example, various modules perform field-level checks for each specific field using simplistic conditional logic, while a CHAIN-ENDCHAIN construct allows validations that depend on the values of multiple fields.

Dynamic Input Validation Techniques

Beyond basic validation, advanced techniques can dynamically adapt validation rules based on the context of input or previous user actions.

These strategies enhance flexibility and user experience.

- **Context-Sensitive Validation**: Adjusts validation criteria according to factors like user role, prior entries, or current data values. This promotes flexible systems responsive to diverse conditions.

- **Data-Driven Validation**: Uses data tables or external configuration settings to define validation rules. This approach enables easy updates to validation criteria without changing code, aiding maintainability.

Example: Context-Sensitive Validation

Imagine an application where certain users can only enter values within a specified range, and different ranges apply for different user roles.

```
MODULE check_salary_based_on_role INPUT.
  IF user_role EQ 'Admin'.
    IF salary > 50000 AND salary < 200000.
      CONTINUE.
    ELSE.
      MESSAGE 'Valid salary range for Admin is 50,000-200,000' TYPE 'E'.
    ENDIF.
  ELSEIF user_role EQ 'User'.
    IF salary > 10000 AND salary < 50000.
      CONTINUE.
    ELSE.
      MESSAGE 'Valid salary range for User is 10,000-50,000' TYPE 'E'.
    ENDIF.
  ENDIF.
ENDMODULE.
```

This implementation highlights how role-based logic can ensure that users adhere to proper data constraints specific to their access level.

Handling Validation Errors and User Feedback

The manner in which validation errors are handled directly impacts user experience. Clear, informative error messages and guidance enable users to correct mistakes efficiently.

- **Consistent Error Messaging**: Messages should consistently inform users of what went wrong, where, and suggest possible corrective actions without ambiguity.

6.5. MANAGING USER INPUT AND VALIDATION

- **Error Visual Indicators**: Utilize visual cues such as highlighting erroneous fields or using pop-up messages to capture attention.

- **Detailed Descriptions**: Providing concise yet detailed descriptions of validation failures facilitates quicker resolution and enhances user engagement.

Integration with Backend Systems

Robust input management often requires integration with backend systems for validation and processing. SAP systems utilize BAPIs or RFCs to communicate between the front-end and back-end, leveraging centralized business logic for input validation.

Example of Backend Integration for Validation

In a scenario where an SAP GUI application needs to validate an input against data in the enterprise database, an RFC can be invoked.

```
CALL FUNCTION 'Z_VALIDATE_CUSTOMER'
  EXPORTING
    customer_id = input_customer_id
  IMPORTING
    is_valid = valid_flag
  EXCEPTIONS
    not_found = 1
    internal_error = 2.

IF sy-subrc = 1 OR valid_flag = 'X'.
  MESSAGE 'Invalid Customer ID' TYPE 'E'.
ENDIF.
```

By validating inputs against back-end data, SAP applications ensure the inputs maintain integrity throughout the system, leveraging existing business rules and data.

Best Practices for User Input Management and Validation

Ensuring successful user input handling necessitates adherence to several best practices.

- **Comprehensive Input Checks**: Implement multiple layers of validation covering field-level, form-level, and business rule validation.

- **User Involvement in Design**: Involve end-users in screen design to understand practical user actions, guiding efficient UI structures and validation flows.

- **Performance Considerations**: Balance validation thoroughness with system performance. Excessive validations may hinder seamless user experiences.

- **Regular Rule Reviews**: Periodically review and update validation rules to reflect changes in business logic, ensuring ongoing relevance and compliance.

Managing user input and validation is a fundamental component of SAP dialog programming, vital for maintaining data quality, security, and compliance. By employing structured techniques, SAP applications can efficiently capture, process, and validate user inputs, providing robust and interactive interfaces that facilitate business processes seamlessly. Through effective design, advanced validation techniques, and integration with backend systems, developers can build SAP GUI interfaces that are reliable, intuitive, and responsive, ultimately contributing to improved enterprise system performance and user satisfaction.

6.6 Implementing Navigation and Flow Logic

In SAP dialog programming, effective navigation and flow logic are crucial to creating user-friendly applications that guide the user smoothly from one interface to another. Proper navigation ensures coherence in user interactions and aids in structuring complex processes into manageable steps. Flow logic, on the other hand, defines the interaction sequence and response actions based on user inputs. This section delves into the principles of designing navigation paths, implementing flow logic using PBO (Process Before Output) and PAI (Process After Input) events, and best practices to ensure optimal user experience in SAP GUI applications.

Principles of SAP GUI Navigation

6.6. IMPLEMENTING NAVIGATION AND FLOW LOGIC

Navigation in SAP GUI involves designing a logical path through which users can progress during their interaction with an application. Thoughtfully designed navigation helps users accomplish tasks efficiently by minimizing confusion and reducing the potential for errors.

Key aspects of navigation include:

- **Screen Sequencing**: Determining the logical order in which screens appear as users embark on specific tasks or processes. Effective sequencing typically reflects natural workflows, ensuring users move seamlessly from one step to the next.

- **User Control**: Providing users with mechanisms to navigate forward, backward, or to jump to particular screens as needed. This control is facilitated through buttons like 'Next', 'Back', 'Exit', and potentially 'Skip'.

- **Consistency and Predictability**: Ensuring navigation follows a predictable, consistent pattern reduces the cognitive load on users. Consistency in button placement, screen layout, and navigation controls fosters efficiency and user confidence.

- **Feedback and Guidance**: Integrating navigational feedback, such as confirmations and error messages, guides users through the process, helping them understand their current position within the workflow.

Implementing Flow Logic with PBO and PAI

Flow logic is implemented in SAP GUI using the PBO and PAI events. These form the backbone of screen management, dictating execution sequences, handling events, and controlling navigation between screens.

- **PBO (Process Before Output)**: This event is triggered every time a screen is called or refreshed. PBO is used for initializing screen elements, setting default values, and managing UI elements' properties such as visibility and input readiness.

- **PAI (Process After Input)**: Executed after user input has been processed, this event captures the action taken by the user, validates input data, and determines subsequent navigation or processes to trigger.

Example: Basic Navigation using PBO and PAI

Consider an SAP application with a sequence of screens to manage order processing.

```
PROCESS BEFORE OUTPUT.
  MODULE set_order_screen_status.

PROCESS AFTER INPUT.
  MODULE user_command_handling.

*----------------------------------------------------------------*
* PBO Module for Initializing Order Screen
*----------------------------------------------------------------*
MODULE set_order_screen_status OUTPUT.
  SET TITLEBAR 'ORDERSCREEN'.
  CLEAR: order_number, order_date, customer_id.
  PERFORM setup_dropdown_lists.
ENDMODULE.

*----------------------------------------------------------------*
* PAI Module for Handling User Commands
*----------------------------------------------------------------*
MODULE user_command_handling INPUT.
  CASE ok_code.
    WHEN 'NEXT'.
      PERFORM validate_order.
      IF sy-subrc = 0.
        LEAVE TO SCREEN '0200'.
      ENDIF.
    WHEN 'BACK'.
      LEAVE TO SCREEN '0100'.
    WHEN 'EXIT'.
      LEAVE PROGRAM.
    WHEN OTHERS.
      MESSAGE 'Invalid Command' TYPE 'E'.
  ENDCASE.
ENDMODULE.
```

In this example, PBO configures the screen with relevant data and screen elements, while PAI handles user commands to navigate between screens.

Advanced Navigation Techniques

Advanced navigation techniques in SAP GUI applications ensure that users are not only guided through linear workflows but also have the flexibility to handle complex, multi-path tasks.

6.6. IMPLEMENTING NAVIGATION AND FLOW LOGIC

- **Dynamic Navigation**: Sometimes, navigation paths require conditional logic based on user input or data states. This entails programmatically controlling movement between screens dynamically.

  Example: Conditional Navigation Based on Input

  ```
  MODULE determine_next_screen INPUT.
    IF order_status EQ 'AUTHORIZED'.
      LEAVE TO SCREEN '0300'.
    ELSEIF order_status EQ 'PENDING'.
      LEAVE TO SCREEN '0400'.
    ELSE.
      MESSAGE 'Invalid Order Status' TYPE 'E'.
    ENDIF.
  ENDMODULE.
  ```

- **Navigation Stack**: Implementing a stack-like mechanism allows realistic revisiting of screens, maintaining state-information that users might want to return to during validation or review.

- **Tabstrip Control Navigation**: Integrating tabstrips creates a navigational method within a single screen but across multiple contexts or datasets. Users can switch contexts without leaving the overarching screen, enhancing the flexibility of data processes.

Best Practices in Designing Navigation and Flow Logic

Creating intuitive and efficient navigation paths and robust flow logic involves adherence to several best practices, ensuring enhanced interaction in SAP GUI applications.

- **Logical Task Segmentation**: Break down tasks into logical screens and steps that are manageable and intuitive to users. This approach not only simplifies the process but reduces the potential for confusion and error.

- **Visibility and Accessibility**: Ensure navigational elements are consistently placed and easily accessible, helping users navigate effortlessly. The placement of buttons and controls should align with user expectations and platform standards.

- **Validation and Feedback**: Integrate validation checks and provide immediate feedback to users. If navigation needs to redirect users based on input inaccuracies, do so with explanatory messages.

- **Error Handling**: Craft error messages that help users understand what went wrong, why it happened, and how they can rectify it. Error handling should be tied into navigation logic to ensure seamless recovery paths.

- **Prioritizing Efficiency within Screen Loads and Navigational Paths**: Ensure that elements essential for navigation–like menus, buttons, and links–are optimized for speed to prevent sluggish user experience, particularly where large datasets are involved in processes.

Implementing navigation and flow logic in SAP GUI applications involves careful design and logic considerations that promote intuitive, efficient, and seamless user experiences. By leveraging PBO and PAI events, developers can create robust dialog systems that accommodate complex workflows and dynamic navigation requirements. Advanced techniques such as conditional navigation and tabstrip utilization enrich the user interface, ensuring flexibility and adaptability in enterprise processes. By adhering to established best practices, SAP applications can achieve high usability and efficiency, ultimately contributing to streamlined business operations and improved user satisfaction.

6.7 Enhancing User Experience with Custom Controls

Enhancing user experience (UX) within SAP GUI applications involves the strategic integration of custom controls that extend beyond standard user interface elements. Custom controls provide additional functionality, a richer interaction environment, and improved aesthetic appeal, significantly impacting usability and satisfaction. This section explores the concept and implementation of custom controls, examining how they can augment the standard SAP GUI experience, the adjust-

6.7. ENHANCING USER EXPERIENCE WITH CUSTOM CONTROLS

ments needed for seamless integration, and the best practices to ensure their effective use in dialog applications.

Understanding Custom Controls in SAP GUI

Custom controls in SAP GUI are specialized user interface elements that offer extended capabilities beyond standard components such as basic input fields, buttons, or tables. These controls can be integrated to provide users with more interactive and dynamic experiences, facilitate complex data manipulations, or enhance visualizations.

Types of Custom Controls:

- ALV Grids/Reports: Allow for advanced data representation and are highly configurable for sorting, filtering, and data aggregation operations.

- Tree Controls: Enable hierarchical display of structured data, facilitating intuitive navigation through nested information.

- HTML Viewer: Allows integrating web-based content into SAP GUI screens, which can be used for rendering dynamic content or instructions.

- Graphical Controls: Include elements like charts or diagrams that visually represent data trends or relationships, assisting in data comprehension.

- Picture Boxes: Display images or icons, enriching the visual appeal and providing contextual cues in the user interface.

Implementing ALV Grids for Data Representation

The ALV (ABAP List Viewer) Grid is one of the most powerful custom controls in the SAP GUI, designed to enhance data presentation and functionality in applications. It allows for a wide array of interactive features like sorting, filtering, editing, and exporting, making data processing more efficient and user-friendly.

Basic Implementation Steps:

- Data Preparation: Define an internal table that serves as the data source for the ALV grid.

- Field Catalog Definition: Set up a field catalog specifying which fields of the internal table should be displayed, their labels, and display characteristics.

- ALV Function Module: Utilize an ALV function module, such as REUSE_ALV_GRID_DISPLAY, to render the data in a grid format within the SAP GUI.

Example: Integrating an ALV Grid

```
DATA: lt_data TYPE TABLE OF spfli,
    lt_fcat TYPE lvc_t_fcat,
    ls_fcat TYPE lvc_s_fcat.

* Prepare data for display
SELECT * FROM spfli INTO TABLE lt_data.

* Define field catalog
CLEAR ls_fcat.
ls_fcat-fieldname = 'CARRID'.
ls_fcat-seltext_m = 'Carrier ID'.
APPEND ls_fcat TO lt_fcat.

ls_fcat-fieldname = 'CONNID'.
ls_fcat-seltext_m = 'Connection ID'.
APPEND ls_fcat TO lt_fcat.

CALL FUNCTION 'REUSE_ALV_GRID_DISPLAY'
  EXPORTING
    it_fieldcat = lt_fcat
  TABLES
    t_outtab = lt_data.
```

This example defines an ALV grid for a flight data table (spfli) with specific fields and labels, utilizing a function module to handle display.

Utilizing Tree Controls for Hierarchical Data

Tree controls represent a sophisticated custom control used in SAP GUI to display hierarchical information. This control is beneficial for visualizing nested structures or complex data relationships, where a tree view can enhance understanding and navigation.

Implementation Overview:

- Create Tree Model: Prepare data in a suitable structure, reflecting the hierarchical nature of the content.

- Instantiate Tree Control: Use SAP GUI tree control functions to instantiate, populate, and manage the tree items.

6.7. ENHANCING USER EXPERIENCE WITH CUSTOM CONTROLS

Example: Creating a Navigation Tree

```
DATA: gt_nodes TYPE TABLE OF mynodeline,
      gs_node TYPE mynodeline.

* Prepare nodes for the tree
CLEAR gs_node.
gs_node-node_key = 'ROOT'.
gs_node-description = 'Root Node'.
APPEND gs_node TO gt_nodes.

gs_node-node_key = 'CHILD1'.
gs_node-parent_key = 'ROOT'.
gs_node-description = 'Child Node 1'.
APPEND gs_node TO gt_nodes.

CALL FUNCTION 'RS_TREE_CONSTRUCT'
  EXPORTING
    father_node = 'ROOT'
  TABLES
    nodes = gt_nodes.
```

This example illustrates constructing a simple tree, with parent-child relationships established within the node table.

Incorporating HTML Viewers for Dynamic Content

HTML viewers in SAP GUI allow the embedding of web-based content directly into the user interface, enriching the functionality and enabling the integration of dynamic elements such as interactive guides, media, or other web applications.

Steps to Implement an HTML Viewer:

- Prepare HTML Content: Create or source the desired HTML content that will be displayed within the viewer.

- Configure Viewer Object: Use HTML control methods to configure and load the web content.

Example: Creating an HTML Viewer

```
DATA: lo_html TYPE REF TO cl_gui_html_viewer,
      lo_container TYPE REF TO cl_gui_custom_container.

* Place an HTML viewer in a custom container
CREATE OBJECT lo_container
  EXPORTING container_name = 'HTML_CONTAINER'.

CREATE OBJECT lo_html
  EXPORTING container = lo_container.
```

```
lo_html->load_data( url = 'http://example.com/sap-help.html' ).
```

Here, an HTML Viewer displays web-based content from a specified URL, facilitating enriched user guidance directly within the application.

Best Practices for Using Custom Controls in SAP GUI

Ensuring a smooth and effective application design when implementing custom controls involves adherence to several best practices:

- User Needs and Context: Choose custom controls that align directly with user tasks and requirements. Overly complex controls can overwhelm users if they do not add significant value to the process.

- Performance Considerations: Evaluate the performance impact of custom controls, especially when dealing with large datasets or high-traffic applications. Adequate performance tuning and tests are crucial.

- Consistency Across Applications: Maintain consistency in the implementation of custom controls across different screens and applications to ensure a cohesive user experience.

- Integration with Standard Elements: Seamlessly integrate custom controls with standard SAP GUI components, ensuring unified look and feel and consistent interactions.

- Accessibility and Usability: Design custom control implementations to be accessible to users with different needs and levels of experience, fostering inclusivity and ease of use.

Enhancing the user experience with custom controls in SAP GUI applications offers ample opportunities to improve functionality, interactivity, and user satisfaction. By skillfully integrating elements such as ALV grids, tree controls, and HTML viewers, developers can craft rich, efficient applications tailored to enterprise requirements. Adhering to best practices ensures optimized performance and consistency, enabling SAP applications to provide continually transformative user experiences that contribute significantly to productivity and operational success.

Chapter 7

File Handling and Data Transfer

This chapter addresses the crucial aspects of file handling and data transfer within ABAP applications. It begins with the foundational operations for effectively reading and writing flat files, and expands on managing both sequential and binary files. Various data transfer methods, including techniques for file uploads and downloads, are explored to facilitate seamless interaction between SAP systems and external environments. Additionally, the chapter covers file management on the application server, focusing on access, security, and data conversion. Strategies for ensuring data consistency during transfers and guidance on integrating with legacy systems are also provided, ensuring comprehensive coverage of these essential operations.

7.1 File Handling Basics in ABAP

In ABAP (Advanced Business Application Programming), understanding file handling is crucial for developing robust and efficient applications. File handling refers to the process of storing, retrieving, and updating data stored in files, which are often used for persistent storage or data interchange. This section delves into the fundamental operations needed to read from and write to flat files using ABAP statements, presenting a necessary skill set for any ABAP developer.

File handling involves basic operations such as opening a file, reading from a file, writing to a file, and closing a file. In the context of ABAP, these operations predominantly involve datasets and employ specific ABAP commands and functions to manage file operations.

In ABAP, files are typically handled using either the Open Dataset, Read Dataset, Transfer, or Close Dataset statements. Each of these statements plays a key role in file management, enabling the seamless exchange of data between SAP systems and storage files.

Open Dataset initiates the file handling process. This command is responsible for opening a file and preparing it for reading or writing. The syntax, as detailed below, requires specifying the mode (either reading or writing) as part of its parameters.

```
OPEN DATASET <file_name> FOR OUTPUT IN <mode>.
```

Here, <file_name> represents the path of the file, and <mode> can be BINARY MODE or TEXT MODE. The FOR OUTPUT option indicates that the file is being opened with the expectation of writing data to it.

To efficiently read from a file, the statement **Read Dataset** is employed. This command extracts data from the opened file into an ABAP variable for further processing. The key is to structure the reading operation such that it captures the data correctly according to the file's contents.

```
READ DATASET <file_name> INTO <variable>.
```

Here, <variable> will store the data read from <file_name>. To ensure that the data aligns with the expected types and formats, it is often beneficial to define <variable> with the appropriate data type.

Writing data to a file in ABAP is managed via the **Transfer** statement. It directs the output of data processing operations in the program into a specified file, ensuring persistent storage.

```
TRANSFER <value> TO <file_name>.
```

7.1. FILE HANDLING BASICS IN ABAP

In this instance, <value> signifies the data to be written, which could be a variable or a hardcoded string. It is crucial to maintain data integrity by ensuring that <value> is in a compatible format for the file's expected content.

Finally, once the necessary file operations are complete, it is important to close the dataset using **Close Dataset**. This action ensures that system resources are freed and that the file is no longer open for unintended operations, preventing potential data corruption or loss.

```
CLOSE DATASET <file_name>.
```

ABAP provides a robust framework for handling files, supported by a number of parameters and options that enhance its functionality. By default, files are processed in text mode, and the system's code page is applied unless specified otherwise. However, BINARY MODE can be invoked when dealing with binary data, ensuring no conversion between character codes is performed, preserving the exact bit patterns.

Additionally, two further specifications allow for more tailored file interactions. The MESSAGE addition provides system-specific error messages on failure, which can be leveraged for debugging:

```
OPEN DATASET <file_name> FOR INPUT IN BINARY MODE MESSAGE <msg>.
```

Here, <msg> collects the system message upon error, which requires pre-definition typically as a string.

To demonstrate basic file handling, consider the following illustrative example, which reads from a file and then writes data to another file. This example assumes access permissions have been granted and explores both reading and writing data.

```
DATA: lv_file_read TYPE string,
      lv_file_write TYPE string,
      lv_file_line TYPE string.

lv_file_read = '/usr/sap/tmp/input.txt'.
lv_file_write = '/usr/sap/tmp/output.txt'.

OPEN DATASET lv_file_read FOR INPUT IN TEXT MODE ENCODING
    DEFAULT.
IF sy-subrc <> 0.
  WRITE: / 'Failed to open file for reading'.
  RETURN.
ENDIF.
```

```
OPEN DATASET lv_file_write FOR OUTPUT IN TEXT MODE ENCODING
    DEFAULT.
IF sy-subrc <> 0.
  WRITE: / 'Failed to open file for writing'.
  CLOSE DATASET lv_file_read.
  RETURN.
ENDIF.

DO.
  READ DATASET lv_file_read INTO lv_file_line.
  IF sy-subrc = 0.
    TRANSFER lv_file_line TO lv_file_write.
  ELSE.
    EXIT.
  ENDIF.
ENDDO.

CLOSE DATASET lv_file_read.
CLOSE DATASET lv_file_write.
WRITE / 'File handling operations completed successfully'.
```

In the example above, a file input.txt is read line-by-line, and its content is transferred to output.txt. Error checking is performed immediately after the OPEN DATASET command to ensure that the files are accessed correctly, and appropriate responses are programmed for potential issues.

Furthermore, logical protection against errors during file manipulation in ABAP can be reinforced using the TRY-CATCH structure, which enables exception handling.

```
TRY.
    OPEN DATASET lv_file_read FOR INPUT IN TEXT MODE ENCODING
        DEFAULT.
  CATCH cx_sy_file_open.
    WRITE: / 'File read open error'.
    EXIT.
ENDTRY.

TRY.
    OPEN DATASET lv_file_write FOR OUTPUT IN TEXT MODE ENCODING
        DEFAULT.
  CATCH cx_sy_file_open.
    WRITE: / 'File write open error'.
    CLOSE DATASET lv_file_read.
    EXIT.
ENDTRY.
```

The above illustrations showcase both technical implementation and the integration of error management within ABAP file handling operations, promoting resilience and robustness in the applications developed.

Moreover, a deeper understanding of character encoding and text formatting can further complement file handling proficiencies. When engaging with text-based data, character encoding defines how characters are stored in files. ABAP supports multiple encoding formats, including UTF-8 and the default system code page, which can be specified in the OPEN DATASET statement using the ENCODING addition:

```
OPEN DATASET lv_file_read FOR INPUT IN TEXT MODE ENCODING UTF-8.
```

This selection dictates how text is interpreted and ensures compatibility with various external systems which may use different encoding schemes.

Ultimately, mastering file handling in ABAP lays the groundwork for executing broader data transfer operations across systems, providing a strong foundation for handling diverse data processing tasks efficiently. Understanding these principles not only facilitates fundamental file manipulations but also paves the way for more complex interactions, such as file conversions and transformations addressed in subsequent sections. The methodical application of these basics assures data integrity and control within SAP-driven processes, enabling seamless and precise data exchanges.

7.2 Working with Sequential and Binary Files

As an integral component of data management within ABAP, handling different file types is essential for efficient system operations. Among them, sequential and binary files are frequently encountered, necessitating a clear understanding of their unique characteristics and handling methods. This section delves into these file types' fundamentals and procedures, emphasizing the specific approaches and statements in ABAP necessary to manage such files proficiently.

Sequential files, often referred to as text files, are composed of sequences of characters or text data organized in a particular order. These files are typically line-based, where each line represents a record.

The data in sequential files is stored as strings, making them easily readable by humans and text-processing programs alike. They are favored for their simplicity and ease of handling when dealing with line-oriented text data or logs.

Handling a sequential file in ABAP entails opening the file using the OPEN DATASET command with the TEXT MODE specification. This mode facilitates correct interpretation and transformation of character data according to the designated encoding, providing a seamless interface for both reading and writing operations.

```
DATA: lv_file TYPE string,
      lv_line TYPE string.

lv_file = '/usr/sap/tmp/sequential.txt'.

OPEN DATASET lv_file FOR INPUT IN TEXT MODE ENCODING DEFAULT.
IF sy-subrc <> 0.
  WRITE: / 'Failed to open sequential file'.
  RETURN.
ENDIF.

DO.
  READ DATASET lv_file INTO lv_line.
  IF sy-subrc <> 0.
    EXIT.
  ENDIF.
  WRITE: / lv_line.
ENDDO.

CLOSE DATASET lv_file.
```

In the example above, a file is opened for reading, and each line is read into the variable lv_line. Each record, i.e., line, displays on-screen to demonstrate the sequential retrieval of entries until the end-of-file condition disrupts the loop.

Writing to a sequential file follows similar principles but requires preparation of data to conform to line-based structures, ensuring consistent appending of textual records.

```
DATA: lv_output_line TYPE string.

lv_file = '/usr/sap/tmp/sequential_output.txt'.

OPEN DATASET lv_file FOR OUTPUT IN TEXT MODE ENCODING DEFAULT.
IF sy-subrc <> 0.
  WRITE: / 'Failed to open file for writing'.
  RETURN.
ENDIF.
```

7.2. WORKING WITH SEQUENTIAL AND BINARY FILES

```
DO 10 TIMES.
  lv_output_line = 'This is line' && sy-index.
  TRANSFER lv_output_line TO lv_file.
ENDDO.

CLOSE DATASET lv_file.
WRITE / 'Sequential write complete'.
```

This code snippet illustrates writing multiple lines, each prefixed with a text string, denoting sequential indices. The iteration over ten cycles showcases repeatability while appending formatted text data to a sequential file.

Conversely, binary files encapsulate data as serial streams of bytes, accommodating various data types beyond mere textual representation. These files are conducive to storing images, executables, or any data requiring precise bit control, untouched by encoding transformations. Managing binary files in ABAP necessitates employing the BINARY MODE within the OPEN DATASET command, appropriate when fidelity to byte patterns is paramount.

```
DATA: lv_bin_file TYPE string,
      lv_bin_data TYPE xstring.

lv_bin_file = '/usr/sap/tmp/binary_file.bin'.

OPEN DATASET lv_bin_file FOR INPUT IN BINARY MODE.
IF sy-subrc <> 0.
  WRITE: / 'Failed to open binary file'.
  RETURN.
ENDIF.

READ DATASET lv_bin_file INTO lv_bin_data MAXIMUM LENGTH 255.
IF sy-subrc = 0.
  WRITE / 'Binary data read successfully'.
ELSE.
  WRITE / 'No data or end of file reached'.
ENDIF.

CLOSE DATASET lv_bin_file.
```

The above example illustrates the reading of binary data into an xstring type variable, crucial for handling binary streams. The use of MAXIMUM LENGTH ensures the capturing of byte chunks up to a specified length, facilitating structured data processing.

Writing to binary files mirrors the reading structure, emphasizing the accurate placement of byte streams into persistent storage.

CHAPTER 7. FILE HANDLING AND DATA TRANSFER

```
DATA: lv_data_chunk TYPE xstring.

lv_data_chunk = '01020304'.

OPEN DATASET lv_bin_file FOR OUTPUT IN BINARY MODE.
IF sy-subrc <> 0.
  WRITE: / 'Failed to open file for writing'.
  RETURN.
ENDIF.

TRANSFER lv_data_chunk TO lv_bin_file.
CLOSE DATASET lv_bin_file.
WRITE / 'Binary data write complete'.
```

In this case, an explicit xstring assignment to lv_data_chunk ensures writing a representative stream of bytes to the designated binary file. This formats the data as a raw byte pattern without any character set interpretation.

It is crucial to adopt careful error handling strategies when engaging with file operations. Syndicating the use of ABAP's exception handling constructs, namely TRY-CATCH, incorporates resilience against errors during file access and manipulations, safeguarding against issues like permission denials or non-existent paths.

```
TRY.
  OPEN DATASET lv_bin_file FOR OUTPUT IN BINARY MODE.
  CATCH cx_sy_file_open INTO DATA(lx_error).
  WRITE / lx_error->get_text( ).
  RETURN.
ENDTRY.
```

This approach, utilizing the cx_sy_file_open exception class, permits a graceful exit and diagnostic feedback in case of file operation failures, thereby enforcing reliable file interactions.

Understanding file access and data validation in conjunction with sequential and binary files provides additional robustness. Implementing efficient data schema checks and integrating pre-processing steps ascertain the correctness and appropriateness of data formats, averting potential downstream errors during operations.

Moreover, awareness of system-specific limitations, like maximum file size and access permissions, enhances situational responses and aligns practices with organizational policies, thus ensuring compliance with security and operational guidelines.

In summary, working with sequential and binary files in ABAP not only requires a well-rounded knowledge of file handling syntax and commands but also demands a robust implementation of validation and exception management strategies. By pooling these aspects, developers can manage file system interactions with meticulous precision, contributing to the sustainable and secure operation of SAP-based applications. Understanding these core file types enables developers to leverage data interchange proficiently, maintaining a seamless flow of data within and across technical ecosystems.

7.3 Data Transfer Methods: Upload and Download

Data transfer is a critical operation in enterprise systems involving the movement of data between diverse platforms, thus ensuring seamless integration across various IT environments. In SAP ABAP, facilitating robust mechanisms for data uploads and downloads enables efficient data interchange between SAP systems and external entities. This section elaborates comprehensively on these methods, considering various scenarios and underlying techniques crafted within ABAP for handling such operations.

Upload refers to the process of importing data from an external source into the SAP system. This functionality is often required to initialize or update data repositories, involving complex datasets and formats received from legacy systems, data providers, or external databases. Effective upload strategies aim for minimal data loss and high integrity while accommodating diverse data formats, such as CSV, Excel, or plain text files.

```
DATA: lv_file_path TYPE string VALUE '/usr/sap/tmp/data_upload.csv',
      lt_data TYPE TABLE OF string,
      lv_line TYPE string,
      lv_delimiter TYPE c VALUE ','.

OPEN DATASET lv_file_path FOR INPUT IN TEXT MODE ENCODING
    DEFAULT.
IF sy-subrc <> 0.
  WRITE: / 'Failed to open file for upload'.
  RETURN.
ENDIF.
```

```
DO.
    READ DATASET lv_file_path INTO lv_line.
    IF sy-subrc <> 0.
        EXIT.
    ENDIF.
    SPLIT lv_line AT lv_delimiter INTO TABLE lt_data.
    " Process lt_data as per business requirements
ENDDO.

CLOSE DATASET lv_file_path.
WRITE / 'File upload completed successfully'.
```

In this simple upload case, a CSV file is parsed line-by-line, with each line split by a delimiter to form a tabular data structure. Each row mapped as a list of strings allows further manipulation based on specific business logic.

A structured approach to uploading employs the GUI_UPLOAD function, designed to harness SAP's graphical interface for user-assisted file selection and data ingestion.

```
DATA: lv_user_path TYPE string,
      lt_upload TYPE TABLE OF string,
      lw_message TYPE string.

CALL METHOD cl_gui_frontend_services=>file_open_dialog
    EXPORTING
        window_title = 'Select a File to Upload'
    CHANGING
        file_table = lt_upload
        rc = sy-subrc
        user_action = lv_user_path.

IF NOT lv_user_path IS INITIAL.
    CALL FUNCTION 'GUI_UPLOAD'
        EXPORTING
            filename = lv_user_path
            filetype = 'ASC'
        TABLES
            data_tab = lt_upload
        EXCEPTIONS
            file_open_error = 1
            file_read_error = 2
            no_batch = 3
            gui_refuse_filetransfer = 4
            OTHERS = 5.

    IF sy-subrc = 0.
        " Proceed with processing lt_upload
    ELSE.
        WRITE: / 'Upload error, please review input file'.
    ENDIF.
ENDIF.
```

7.3. DATA TRANSFER METHODS: UPLOAD AND DOWNLOAD

Here, the function GUI_UPLOAD engages a user interface to select and read files into an internal table. Automatic handling of delimiters and encoding makes this approach advantageous for varied client environments, promoting widespread usability.

Download operations in ABAP involve writing data from SAP systems to an external location, meeting needs for archival storage, report generation, or data interchange to non-SAP platforms. Ensuring data accuracy and format adherence is critical in download operations, requiring a structured approach with explicit format definitions.

```
DATA: lv_out_file TYPE string VALUE '/usr/sap/tmp/data_download.txt',
      lt_output_data TYPE TABLE OF string,
      lv_out_line TYPE string.

APPEND 'Field1,Field2,Field3' TO lt_output_data.
APPEND 'Data11,Data12,Data13' TO lt_output_data.
APPEND 'Data21,Data22,Data23' TO lt_output_data.

OPEN DATASET lv_out_file FOR OUTPUT IN TEXT MODE ENCODING
    DEFAULT.
IF sy-subrc <> 0.
  WRITE: / 'Failed to open file for download'.
  RETURN.
ENDIF.

LOOP AT lt_output_data INTO lv_out_line.
  TRANSFER lv_out_line TO lv_out_file.
ENDLOOP.

CLOSE DATASET lv_out_file.
WRITE / 'File download completed successfully'.
```

This code illustrates a practical download task whereby SAP data is formatted as CSV and written to a file. By using OPEN DATASET and TRANSFER, it ensures structured output with consistent delimiters for accurate data interpretation externally.

Download operations may also harness SAP GUI facilities to enable direct user interaction for file output, using the GUI_DOWNLOAD function module.

```
DATA: lv_client_save_path TYPE string.

CALL FUNCTION 'GUI_DOWNLOAD'
  EXPORTING
    filename = 'c:\path\to\file.csv'
    write_field_separator = 'X'
    filetype = 'ASC'
  TABLES
    data_tab = lt_output_data
```

CHAPTER 7. FILE HANDLING AND DATA TRANSFER

```
EXCEPTIONS
    file_write_error = 1
    no_batch = 2
    gui_refuse_filetransfer = 3
    invalid_filetype = 4
    no_authority = 5
    OTHERS = 6.

IF sy-subrc <> 0.
    WRITE: / 'Download error, check permissions and file path'.
ENDIF.
```

With this approach, user accessibility to specify download paths and controlled handling of specific download options like separators provides a versatile environment for exporting data. Its flexible nature caters to various modes of data consumption beyond SAP confines.

By integrating FIELD-SYMBOLS and RTTS (Runtime Type Services) in ABAP upload/download logic, system developers ensure adaptable and dynamic data frame processing, automatically tailoring field structures to different dataset formats.

```
FIELD-SYMBOLS: <lt_data> TYPE ANY TABLE,
               <ls_line> TYPE any.

ASSIGN lt_output_data TO <lt_data> CASTING.

LOOP AT <lt_data> ASSIGNING <ls_line>.
    " Processing logic utilizing <ls_line> attributes
ENDLOOP.
```

Such advanced methodologies allow generic data handling without rigid dependencies on explicit type definitions, fostering a more scalable and maintainable codebase. This approach is useful in multi-format integrations—where datasets exhibit varied structures—enabling handling flexibility.

In complex enterprise environments, ensuring secure and high-fidelity data upload/download is of paramount importance. Embracing validation measures, checksum mechanisms, or encryption, developers prevent inadvertent data corruption or unauthorized access during transitions.

Data Integrity involves ensuring completeness, accuracy, and consistency during upload and download. Techniques such as checksum comparison prior to file closing, or validating data records post-upload, secure data transactions.

```
* Calculate checksum for data validation
DATA: lv_checksum TYPE string.

CALL FUNCTION 'CALCULATE_CHECKSUM'
  EXPORTING
    file_path = lv_file_path
  IMPORTING
    checksum = lv_checksum.
```

Employing such measures corroborates transfer precision by allowing developers to verify that data remains unaltered and authentic from source to destination.

Security facets include encryption and authorization management. File transfers should integrate secure communication protocols and access restrictions to block illicit file manipulations or interceptions.

```
* Example call to encrypt data prior to download
CALL FUNCTION 'SSFC_BASE64_ENCODE'
  EXPORTING
    input = lv_out_line
  IMPORTING
    output = lv_encoded_line.
```

In this encryption example, encoding data in Base64 prior to download ensures non-readable transfer data, adherent to safety protocols, and guarding against unauthorized reads or captures.

Mastering data transfer methods within ABAP empowers developers to construct reliable, efficient interfaces for cross-platform data flow. Emphasizing not only the technicalities of upload/download routines but also integrating sound principles on data validation and security extends an organization's ability to operate securely within heterogeneous network architectures. This foundational expertise guarantees value continuity as systems evolve and extend, upholding functional harmony across sophisticated technological ecosystems.

7.4 Using Application Server for File Management

Application servers in an SAP environment serve a crucial function in file management, enabling controlled file operations in a centralized, secure manner. Leveraging application servers for file handling activities such as creation, access, and management of files fosters streamlined data processing and enhanced security through centralized access control and logging. This section delves into the concepts, methodologies, and best practices involved in using SAP application servers for file management.

At the core of server-side file management is the **Open Dataset** command, which provides structured methods for reading and writing files on the application server. Unlike GUI-based operations, application server handling allows processes to run independently of user interfaces, facilitating automated, non-interactive scripts essential for backend operations.

```
DATA: lv_server_file_path TYPE string VALUE '/usr/sap/trans/global/datafile.txt',
      lv_data_line TYPE string.

OPEN DATASET lv_server_file_path FOR OUTPUT IN TEXT MODE ENCODING
    DEFAULT.
IF sy-subrc <> 0.
  WRITE: / 'Error: Cannot open file on application server'.
  RETURN.
ENDIF.

lv_data_line = 'Server-side file management content'.
TRANSFER lv_data_line TO lv_server_file_path.

CLOSE DATASET lv_server_file_path.
```

In this example, a text file is opened on the application server for writing data derived from automated processes without user interaction, empowering seamless integration into routine system tasks like log aggregation or report generation.

Server-side file handling mainly focuses on persistent storage and secure access. As application servers often host sensitive data, access permissions are a primary concern. Addressing these through role and profile management ensures that only authorized users and programs manipulate files, adhering to organizational security protocols.

SAP employs authorization objects (for instance, S_DATASET) that enable security administrators to assign file operation privileges selectively, aligning system accessibility with job roles without compromising data safety.

```
AUTHORITY-CHECK OBJECT 'S_DATASET'
  ID 'ACTVT' FIELD '02'
```

7.4. USING APPLICATION SERVER FOR FILE MANAGEMENT

```
  ID 'FILENAME' FIELD '/usr/sap/trans/global/datafile.txt'.
IF sy-subrc <> 0.
  WRITE: / 'Unauthorized: Access to application server file denied'.
  RETURN.
ENDIF.
```

The AUTHORITY-CHECK function ensues validity of file operations, eliciting authorization failure responses versus unauthorized attempts, consequently bolstering sensitive data safeguards.

Moreover, leveraging the application server's reach, systematic file management activities broaden to embrace error handling and logging. System logs archive interaction records, helping trace operations and troubleshoot errors. Implementing robust error logging overcomes interaction ambiguities by providing explicit feedback loops.

```
OPEN DATASET lv_server_file_path FOR INPUT IN TEXT MODE ENCODING
    DEFAULT.

IF sy-subrc <> 0.
  WRITE: / 'Cannot open server file for reading, logging error'.
  CALL FUNCTION 'BAL_LOG_MSG_ADD'
    EXPORTING
      i_s_msg = 'File access denied'
      i_s_data = 'Error during file read operation'.
ENDIF.
```

The use of logging through mechanisms like the Business Application Log (BAL) ensures granulated traceability over file operations, crucial for system audits and performance analysis.

An interesting facet of application server file management is the **Batch Processing** capability it renders possible. Here, batch jobs executing non-interactive time-consuming tasks exploit file management APIs to automate large-scale data procedures, optimizing resource allocation without impacting active user sessions.

```
SUBMIT report_name
  WITH parameter EQ 'value'
  VIA JOB job_name NUMBER job_number
  AND RETURN.
```

This snippet reflects on the submission of background processes where integration with file management practices on the server allows efficient batch operations exclusive of user interface confines.

Proficiency in using application servers for file management extends to understanding the advantages of operating in diverse environments. Centralizing files on the server simplifies accessibility for distributed application instances, eliminates redundancy, and maintains improved synchronization and reporting channels across enterprise systems.

File Middleware features such as the ArchiveLink create sophisticated file management frameworks within SAP landscapes by facilitating diverse file types like PDFs, images, or EDI documents' seamless handling, abstraction, and long-term storage.

Clear guidelines on file naming conventions and path structures prevent common pitfalls in server file management, ensuring systematic file organization and retrieval. Conventional standards include maintaining file paths relative to system directories, consistent naming with timestamps or identifiers, and adherence to standard formats warranting readiness for audits or cross-references.

Finally, coupling file management with comprehensive testing protocols guarantees minimized disruption in live environments. Unit tests, integration checks, and performance metrics ensure file operation logic is robust, scalable, and aligned with policy requirements.

To summarize, managing files on the application server via ABAP involves a multifaceted approach brought together through versatile command use, security protocol adherence, automation tools, and vigilant logging/governance frameworks. As systems advance and data exchange surges, these proficiencies in server-based file management ensure that businesses maintain resilient, secure, and effective operational backbones, ultimately supporting enhanced enterprise agility and responsiveness.

7.5 Managing File Access and Security

In the intricate landscape of enterprise systems, managing file access and security is paramount to ensuring data protection, compliance with regulations, and maintaining the integrity of business operations. Within SAP environments, ABAP developers must employ a robust set of mechanisms to govern file access and apply stringent security measures. This section explores the techniques and strategies pivotal for

7.5. MANAGING FILE ACCESS AND SECURITY

controlling file access and enhancing security while implementing file operations in ABAP.

File access security in SAP encompasses several dimensions: ensuring only authorized personnel and processes can access critical data files, protecting file integrity during operations, and maintaining audit trails for monitoring and analysis. At the heart of managing file access in ABAP are **authorization checks**, specifically leveraging SAP's role-based access model which aligns with an organization's security policies to prevent unauthorized access and modifications.

Authorization management within SAP involves using AUTHORITY-CHECK statements which check permissions against predefined authorization objects. One such object is S_DATASET, which determines user permissions concerning file operations on the application server. This allows administrators to specify which users or roles have rights to create, read, delete, or change files.

```
AUTHORITY-CHECK OBJECT 'S_DATASET'
    ID 'ACTVT' FIELD '03' " Activity: read
    ID 'FILENAME' FIELD '/usr/sap/trans/global/datafile.txt'.
IF sy-subrc <> 0.
    WRITE: / 'Access Denied: You do not have permission to read this file'.
    RETURN.
ENDIF.
```

In this example, the AUTHORITY-CHECK confirms whether the user has read permissions ('03') for the specified file. This early intervention prevents unauthorized access attempts, preserving data confidentiality and integrity.

Furthermore, file path management is critical in security—avoiding hard-coded paths may limit exposure to unnecessary file access. Instead, leveraging dynamic paths and maintaining relative references ensures that unauthorized parties do not predictively access or manipulate files.

Beyond checking access, it is critical to protect files from unauthorized modifications, deletions, or corruptions. To this end, implementing checksum verifications can provide assurances of file integrity, confirming that the content remains unaltered throughout transmission or storage.

```
DATA: lv_checksum_original TYPE string,
      lv_checksum_current TYPE string.
```

```
CALL FUNCTION 'CALCULATE_CHECKSUM'
  EXPORTING
    file_path = lv_file_path
  IMPORTING
    checksum = lv_checksum_original.

" After file operations, recheck the file integrity
CALL FUNCTION 'CALCULATE_CHECKSUM'
  EXPORTING
    file_path = lv_file_path
  IMPORTING
    checksum = lv_checksum_current.

IF lv_checksum_original <> lv_checksum_current.
  WRITE: / 'Warning: File integrity compromised'.
  RETURN.
ENDIF.
```

This example demonstrates how leveraging checksum methodologies can guard against data integrity breaches by continuously verifying the consistency of file contents.

Encrypting sensitive data files before storage or transmission adds another layer of security. Encoding files using secure cryptographic functions offers protection from unauthorized access to file content, especially during file transfers over less secure channels.

```
DATA: lv_raw_data_hex TYPE xstring,
      lv_encoded_data TYPE string.

CALL FUNCTION 'SSFC_BASE64_ENCODE'
  EXPORTING
    input = lv_raw_data_hex
  IMPORTING
    output = lv_encoded_data.

" Subsequent download or write to storage
OPEN DATASET lv_file_path FOR OUTPUT IN TEXT MODE ENCODING
    DEFAULT.
IF sy-subrc = 0.
  TRANSFER lv_encoded_data TO lv_file_path.
  CLOSE DATASET lv_file_path.
ELSE.
  WRITE: / 'Error: Unable to open file for writing encrypted data'.
ENDIF.
```

In this snippet, Base64 encoding is applied to raw data, transforming it into a secure format fit for transmission or storage. Such precautions mitigate the risk of data exposure in case of unauthorized access.

Another dimension of file security involves the logical segregation of

7.5. MANAGING FILE ACCESS AND SECURITY

data. Utilizing directories with controlled access permissions and restricting file operations by directory can ensure files are compartmentalized based on their security classifications.

Administratively, SAP Basis administrators can define policies on allowable storage locations or file operations within transaction codes such as SM49 and SM69, managing permissible paths and external commands for file operations within SAP.

The **Logging and Monitoring** of file access events is indispensable not only for regulatory compliance but also for proactive threat detection. Implementing log files for file operations helps in tracing unauthorized activities and creating an alert mechanism.

```
CALL FUNCTION 'BAL_LOG_MSG_ADD'
  EXPORTING
    i_s_msg = 'File Access Event'
    i_s_data = 'User accessed restricted file'.
```

The Business Application Log (BAL) allows for capturing detailed events regarding file access, helping administrators in forensic analyses if security breaches occur. Such log entries should include user details, operation type, file path, and timestamp for clarity.

For seamless integration, consider optimizing user interfaces and processes for secure file operations by adopting secure practices from UI design through to backend implementation. Employ GUI restrictions, avoid file sharing via unsafe channels, and educate employees about security policies.

In summary, managing file access and security in ABAP involves a composed strategy of authorization management, cryptography, data integrity checks, logical segregation, and vigilant monitoring. By combining these tactics, organizations can create robust defenses against unauthorized file access and manipulation, ensuring the reliability and security of critical SAP data assets. The development of secure file access protocols fortifies the overall stability and trust in enterprise-wide SAP systems while adhering to established compliance and security standards.

7.6 Data Conversion and Formatting

Data conversion and formatting are pivotal processes in ABAP, as they ensure data consistency, integrity, and usability during its transition between systems or datasets. These operations are essential for seamless data interchange between SAP environments and other platforms, each potentially utilizing distinct data formats and conventions. This section addresses the thorough methodologies and insights encompassing data conversion and formatting within ABAP.

Data conversion is the process of changing data from one format or type into another. This could involve converting character strings to numerical values, date formats, or transforming entire datasets to align with specific schema requirements. In SAP ABAP, conversion routines are integral in guaranteeing that data adheres to predefined standards, hence maintaining precision and relevance.

Numeric and Date Conversion: ABAP offers various built-in functions that facilitate the conversion of numeric values and dates to and from strings. Formatting numeric data correctly is crucial when dealing with financial reports or statistics, where precision is non-negotiable.

```
DATA: lv_char_number TYPE char10 VALUE '123456',
      lv_num_value TYPE i.

lv_num_value = lv_char_number.
" Error handling required if type conversion fails
IF sy-subrc <> 0.
  WRITE: / 'Error: Conversion failed from char to int'.
ELSE.
  WRITE: / 'Numeric conversion successful', lv_num_value.
ENDIF.
```

This example demonstrates converting a character-type field into an integer. It is imperative to manage exceptions or errors that may arise from such operations, as invalid characters could lead to conversion failures.

Date conversion, on the other hand, involves transferring dates from one format to another, which may be required when interfacing your SAP system with external applications that utilize different date standards. One often-used function is CONVERT_DATE_FORMAT, which facilitates such transformations.

7.6. DATA CONVERSION AND FORMATTING

```abap
DATA: lv_date TYPE d,
      lv_new_date TYPE string.

lv_date = '20211213'.

CALL FUNCTION 'CONVERT_DATE_FORMAT'
  EXPORTING
    date_in = lv_date
    in_date_format = 'YYYYMMDD'
    out_date_format = 'MM/DD/YYYY'
  IMPORTING
    date_out = lv_new_date.

IF sy-subrc = 0.
  WRITE: / 'Date conversion successful: ', lv_new_date.
ELSE.
  WRITE: / 'Error: Date conversion failed'.
ENDIF.
```

Efforts to standardize date formats prevent misinterpretation of data, especially in multinational engagements where region-specific formats prevail.

String Manipulation and Formatting: Handling strings in ABAP involves various operations: trimming, padding, concatenation, and transformation, which ensure that text data is presented correctly.

```abap
DATA: lv_first_name TYPE string,
      lv_last_name TYPE string,
      lv_full_name TYPE string.

lv_first_name = 'John'.
lv_last_name = 'Doe'.

CONCATENATE lv_first_name lv_last_name INTO lv_full_name SEPARATED BY space.
WRITE: / 'Full name: ', lv_full_name.

SHIFT lv_first_name LEFT DELETING LEADING 'J'.
WRITE: / 'Shifted first name: ', lv_first_name.
```

Here we concatenate first and last names with a space separator to form a full name. By leveraging operations like CONCATENATE and SHIFT, one can manipulate string data efficiently to suit specific application needs.

ABAP also offers formatting routines for various string transformations necessary for interfacing with systems that require strict data input formats.

Handling Complex Data Structures: ABAP's ability to deal with complex data structures like internal tables or nested fields is invaluable when dealing with large datasets that must be converted or formatted to fit consensual data models.

```
TYPES: BEGIN OF ty_employee,
       emp_id TYPE i,
       name TYPE string,
       salary TYPE p DECIMALS 2,
       END OF ty_employee.

DATA: lt_employees TYPE TABLE OF ty_employee,
      ls_employee TYPE ty_employee,
      lv_xml_output TYPE string.

ls_employee-emp_id = 1001.
ls_employee-name = 'Alice Smith'.
ls_employee-salary = '50000.00'.
APPEND ls_employee TO lt_employees.

CALL TRANSFORMATION id
  SOURCE employees = lt_employees
  RESULT XML lv_xml_output.

WRITE lv_xml_output.
```

In this example, a structured transformation translates internal table data into XML format, facilitating data exchange with external systems that utilize XML schemas.

Automated and Batch Conversion: Much routine data conversion can be automated as batch operations within ABAP programs, ensuring efficiency and reducing the risk of manual errors. Batch conversion routines often iterate over datasets, applying conversion rules, and outputting converted data.

```
DATA: it_source TYPE TABLE OF string,
      it_target TYPE TABLE OF string,
      lv_line TYPE string.

APPEND '100,John,3000' TO it_source.
APPEND '101,Jane,3500' TO it_source.

LOOP AT it_source INTO lv_line.
  SPLIT lv_line AT ',' INTO TABLE it_target.
  " Process each entry for conversion
  MODIFY lt_employees INDEX sy-tabix FROM <target_struct>.
ENDLOOP.
```

After parsing each line in the source data, this batch processing style automates the reconstitution into structured datasets, ready for subsequent operations or transfers.

Data Type Casting and Precision Handling: The need for precise data type conversions is especially pressing in financial or scientific computations, where detail specificity is essential. ABAP's prowess in handling customized type casting with its inherent CASTING features and declaration of field symbols for dynamic access offers significant control over data precision and validation processes.

Such conversion and formatting approaches form the backbone of robust, synchronized interactions in diverse SAP-based operations. They elevate business IT transformation initiatives by promoting seamless data flow and reducing cycle times associated with data corrections or reconciliations necessitated by misaligned data types and formats. As businesses continue embracing complex, integrated IT landscapes, these conversion capabilities maintain their critical importance, ensuring accuracy and consistency as organizations leverage both SAP and non-SAP technologies in tandem.

7.7 Integrating with Legacy Systems

Integrating with legacy systems is an essential aspect of modern enterprise IT strategy, particularly for organizations relying on SAP solutions. Legacy systems, typically defined as outdated computing systems, applications, or technologies that continue to serve essential business functions, present unique challenges when integrating with contemporary SAP environments. Bridging this gap requires a comprehensive understanding of technologies, methodologies, and tools necessary to ensure seamless data flow and operational harmony. This section explores the strategies, technical issues, and practical implementations geared towards integrating ABAP systems with legacy infrastructures.

Legacy systems often use antiquated software and hardware, providing limited interoperability with modern systems due to differences in data formats, communication protocols, and processing capabilities. Effective integration necessitates a broad spectrum of approaches tailored to specific environmental constraints and business demands.

CHAPTER 7. FILE HANDLING AND DATA TRANSFER

- **Data Exchange and Transformation**

  A critical integration challenge is managing disparate data formats. Legacy systems may operate with exclusive encodings or proprietary data structures that differ from SAP standards. Data exchange thus requires efficient transformation strategies, involving stepwise data format modification and cleansing.

- **Using Common Data Formats**

  One approach involves employing widely-accepted data interchange formats like XML or JSON, serving as transitional mediums. SAP's ABAP language natively supports these formats via transformation tools that map data between incompatible structures.

```
DATA: lv_json_input TYPE string,
      lt_datastore TYPE TABLE OF ty_datastore,
      lv_err_msg TYPE string.

lv_json_input = '{"data":[{"id":1,"name":"Legacy Item","value":123.45}]}'.

CALL FUNCTION 'JSON_TO_DATA'
  EXPORTING
    json = lv_json_input
  IMPORTING
    data = lt_datastore
  EXCEPTIONS
    json_syntax_error = 1
    others = 2.

IF sy-subrc <> 0.
  lv_err_msg = 'Error in JSON conversion'.
ENDIF.
```

This example illustrates how JSON serves as an intermediary to handle data exchanges where legacy systems initially output data in a compatible format.

- **Custom Transformation Logic**

  For cases involving proprietary formats, custom parsing logic may be necessary. ABAP's string manipulation capabilities, including employing REGEX operations, cater to such distinct translation needs.

```
DATA: lv_input_line TYPE string,
      lt_fields TYPE TABLE OF string,
      lv_err_msg TYPE string.
```

7.7. INTEGRATING WITH LEGACY SYSTEMS

```
lv_input_line = '01|LegacyData|250.0'.

IF lv_input_line CONTAINS REGEX '^\d{2}\|[A-Za-z]+\|\d+(\.\d{1,2})?$'.
  SPLIT lv_input_line AT '|' INTO TABLE lt_fields.
  " Proceed to map lt_fields to target fields
ELSE.
  lv_err_msg = 'Error parsing legacy format'.
ENDIF.
```

The above code fragments leverage regular expressions and string splitting to parse data, transforming it from legacy formats into structured SAP-compliant datasets.

- **Communication Protocols and Middleware**

  Choosing appropriate communication protocols is crucial when integrating SAP with legacy systems. Middleware solutions—such as SAP PI/PO, MuleSoft, or IBM MQ—act as mediators that facilitate robust communication between disparately configured environments.

- **Using Remote Function Calls (RFC)**

  SAP's Remote Function Call (RFC) mechanism provides synchronous and asynchronous communication between SAP and non-SAP systems. With fluent integration capabilities and built-in conversion options, RFCs are an attractive choice for linking legacy systems to SAP.

```
CALL FUNCTION 'RFC_REMOTE_FUNCTION'
  DESTINATION 'LEGACY_SYSTEM'
  EXPORTING
    input_value = 'SomeValue'
  IMPORTING
    output_value = lv_received_data
  EXCEPTIONS
    communication_failure = 1
    system_failure = 2
    others = 3.

IF sy-subrc <> 0.
  WRITE: / 'Communication with legacy system failed'.
ENDIF.
```

This example executes an RFC to communicate with a legacy system, passing input data and receiving results back to ABAP.

- **Implementing Middleware Solutions**

CHAPTER 7. FILE HANDLING AND DATA TRANSFER

Middleware platforms simplify complex integrations by insulating system-specific protocol dependencies. These platforms enable message routing, queuing, transformation, and service orchestration, effectively bridging SAP to legacy systems across heterogeneous networks.

- **Transaction Monitoring and Data Validation**

  Ensuring successful data integration requires rigorous transaction monitoring and validation mechanisms to preserve data integrity across both systems.

- **Implementing Logging and Exception Handling**

  Design strategies integrating robust error logging and exception handling pinpoint potential disruptions at all transaction stages, enhancing system reliability.

  ```
  TRY.
      CALL FUNCTION 'PERFORM_DATA_EXCHANGE'
        EXPORTING
          legacy_input = lv_input_data
        IMPORTING
          sap_output = lt_processed_data.
      CATCH cx_standard_error INTO DATA(lx_error).
      WRITE: / 'Processing Error: ', lx_error->get_text( ).
      " Log error details for audit
  ENDTRY.
  ```

  This sample code demonstrates encapsulating the function call within a TRY-CATCH block, ensuring systematic error handling while recording exceptions for future diagnosis.

- **Security Considerations**

  As legacy systems may lack modern security features, integrating them with current SAP solutions introduces specific security risks. Implementing data encryption, user authentication, access control, and monitoring are necessary to mitigate security threats.

  ```
  DATA: lv_encrypted_data TYPE string.

  CALL FUNCTION 'SSFC_BASE64_DECODE'
    EXPORTING
      input = lv_encrypted_legacy_data
    IMPORTING
      output = lv_decrypted_data
    EXCEPTIONS
  ```

7.7. INTEGRATING WITH LEGACY SYSTEMS

```
    others = 1.
IF sy-subrc <> 0.
  WRITE: / 'Decryption failed, unauthorized data'.
ENDIF.
```

By decrypting data received from legacy systems, risks of data exposure are minimized, contributing to successfully integrated secure SAP landscapes.

- **Sustainable Integration Architecture**

  Ultimately, maintaining a sustainable integration architecture necessitates comprehensive documentation, such as defining integration patterns, data mappings, communication endpoints, security standards, audit logs, and periodic reviews to address technical debts accruing from persistent legacy system dependence.

Integrating SAP ABAP systems with legacy infrastructures is a multifaceted yet essential endeavor underscored by attention to data and communication nuances between contrasting environments. Combining technical solutions like data transformation, protocol compatibility, middleware, security, and error management collectively enables seamless interactions, ensuring data coherency and system harmony. These practices significantly enhance the robustness and adaptability of enterprise-wide IT systems operating amidst the dynamic evolution of technological standards.

Chapter 8

Object-Oriented Programming in ABAP

This chapter delves into Object-Oriented Programming (OOP) in ABAP, presenting a modern approach to enhancing code modularity and reusability. It outlines the core principles of OOP, including class and object definitions, inheritance, and polymorphism, tailored specifically for the ABAP environment. The chapter guides readers through the creation and management of classes, focusing on encapsulation and data hiding to protect data integrity. It explores dynamic method calls to achieve polymorphism, along with techniques for effective instance management. Additionally, the chapter addresses exception handling within an OOP context, promoting robust and maintainable ABAP programming practices.

8.1 Fundamentals of Object-Oriented Concepts

The concept of Object-Oriented Programming (OOP) serves as a foundation for modern software development, including ABAP (Advanced Business Application Programming). OOP is oriented around building software as a collection of discrete objects that combine data and functionality. This paradigm brings a robust structure to programming by allowing developers to conceptualize designs in terms of real-world entities. Key principles of OOP include classes, objects, inheritance, and polymorphism. Each of these concepts contributes distinctly to the versatility and efficiency of the code created within an object-oriented framework like ABAP.

Classes are the blueprint from which objects are created. In ABAP, a class is defined by encapsulating data, through variables or properties known as attributes, and behavior, through functions or methods. The definition of a class specifies what data an object will contain, and how that data can be operated upon. Understanding how classes work paves the way for object creation, a pivotal aspect of OOP, as objects are instances of classes. They represent specific realizations of the class blueprint, possessing concrete attribute values and accessible operations provided by class methods.

```
CLASS car DEFINITION.
  PUBLIC SECTION.
    DATA: model TYPE string,
          speed TYPE i.
    METHODS: start,
             stop.
ENDCLASS.
CLASS car IMPLEMENTATION.
  METHOD start.
    WRITE: / 'Car started'.
  ENDMETHOD.
  METHOD stop.
    WRITE: / 'Car stopped'.
  ENDMETHOD.
ENDCLASS.
```

In the above example, the 'car' class defines two public attributes, 'model' and 'speed', reflecting characteristics that a car object might have. Two methods, 'start' and 'stop', provide the behaviors directly associated with a car.

8.1. FUNDAMENTALS OF OBJECT-ORIENTED CONCEPTS

Objects, as instances of classes, embody the properties and functionalities defined within their respective blueprints. When an object is created, or instantiated, it inherits the structure of its class, meaning it possesses all defined methods and attributes. Instantiation is a crucial concept, transforming a class definition from an abstract specification into a usable component in the program.

```
DATA: my_car TYPE REF TO car.
CREATE OBJECT my_car.
my_car->model = 'Sedan'.
my_car->speed = 0.
my_car->start().
```

In this instantiation example, an object 'my_car' is created from the class 'car'. The 'model' and 'speed' attributes of 'my_car' are assigned values, and its 'start' method is invoked, effectively simulating a functional car instance.

The principle of inheritance allows a new class to inherit characteristics from an existing class, known as the parent or superclass. This process not only promotes code reusability by eliminating redundancy but also provides a mechanism to introduce specific enhancements or alterations in derived classes. A subclass can extend the features of its parent class while maintaining the option to override methods, tailoring the inherited behavior as required.

```
CLASS sports_car DEFINITION INHERITING FROM car.
  PUBLIC SECTION.
    METHODS: turbo_boost.
ENDCLASS.
CLASS sports_car IMPLEMENTATION.
  METHOD turbo_boost.
    speed = speed + 50.
    WRITE: / 'Turbo boost activated, speed:', speed.
  ENDMETHOD.
ENDCLASS.
```

In the above code, 'sports_car' is a subclass inheriting from the 'car' class. It inherits all properties and methods of 'car', and additionally, it includes a new method 'turbo_boost', enhancing the behavior of 'sports_car' objects by extending the base functionality.

Polymorphism is a defining aspect of OOP, characterized by the ability of different objects to respond, individualized, to the same operation or method call. This is often implemented through method overriding, where a subclass provides its specific implementation of a method already defined in a superclass. Polymorphism bolsters flexibility, enabling the same operation to behave differently on various classes derived from a common superclass.

```
METHOD sports_car->start REDEFINITION.
  WRITE: / 'Sports car started with extra power'.
ENDMETHOD.
```

The 'start' method in 'sports_car' overrides the inherited 'start' method from 'car', illustrating polymorphism at work. When 'start' is called on a 'sports_car' object, the overridden version is executed, showcasing a dynamic method dispatch as unique to the object's class type.

An analysis of these fundamental OOP concepts reveals their significance in augmenting software design and functionality. Classes serve as structural blueprints, shaping the contours within which objects operate. Through inheritance, classes allow for the expansion and refinement of existing code, fostering a layered, modular design. Polymorphism further refines this model, instilling versatility within method interactions, thus making the design intuitive and adaptable.

In ABAP, understanding and leveraging these principles leads to enhanced code that is not only robust and scalable but also maintainable. This paradigmatic approach ensures code redundancy is minimized and that clearly defined class hierarchies emerge. These hierarchies promote ease of understanding and navigation, proving advantageous in both individual and collaborative programming contexts.

In summary, the comprehensive detailing of OOP core tenets – classes, objects, inheritance, and polymorphism – within ABAP underscores the transformative power of this paradigm. Proper utilization of these elements equips developers with the tools needed to construct programs that are both efficient and adaptable, equipped to meet diverse application requirements. This object-oriented approach inherently increases the modularity of systems, ensuring that ABAP solutions remain versatile, scalable, and aligned with modern development practices.

8.2 Defining and Implementing Classes

Creating classes and implementing them in ABAP (Advanced Business Application Programming) is a fundamental skill in developing object-oriented applications. Classes define the template for objects, encapsulating data in the form of attributes and functionality in the form of methods. By defining and implementing classes thoughtfully, programmers can build reusable and maintainable software components. This section delves deeply into the intricacies of class definition, attribute specification, method implementation, and the role of interfaces in ABAP.

In ABAP, a class is defined using the CLASS keyword followed by class components such as sections, attributes, and methods. A typical ABAP class is divided into interface and implementation sections, primarily the PUBLIC, PROTECTED, and PRIVATE sections. Each section dictates the level of access provided to the class attributes and methods. Proper demarcation of these sections ensures encapsulation, a cornerstone principle of OOP.

```
CLASS vehicle DEFINITION.
  PUBLIC SECTION.
    DATA: vehicle_type TYPE string READ-ONLY,
          number_of_wheels TYPE i.
    METHODS: display_info IMPORTING color TYPE string.
  PROTECTED SECTION.
    METHODS: calculate_range RETURNING VALUE(distance) TYPE i.
  PRIVATE SECTION.
    DATA: fuel_capacity TYPE i.
    METHODS: adjust_fuel_capacity IMPORTING new_capacity TYPE i.
ENDCLASS.
```

In this vehicle class definition, different sections reveal varying degrees of accessibility and data encapsulation:

- **Public Section**: Contains vehicle_type and number_of_wheels, which are accessible to any client program. The display_info method can be invoked directly from outside the class to display the vehicle's color.

- **Protected Section**: The calculate_range method can be accessed by subclasses of vehicle, allowing them to utilize and potentially refine the basic functionality.

- **Private Section**: The fuel_capacity attribute and the adjust_-fuel_capacity method are strictly accessible within the vehicle class, ensuring that fuel management is tightly controlled internally.

Implementing the class involves writing method definitions that specify executable operations for class instances. Methods can manipulate class attributes and facilitate interactions both within the class and with external entities. Method implementation backs the promises made by method declarations in the interface section.

```
CLASS vehicle IMPLEMENTATION.
  METHOD display_info.
    WRITE: / 'Vehicle Type:', vehicle_type,
           / 'Number of Wheels:', number_of_wheels,
           / 'Color:', color.
  ENDMETHOD.

  METHOD calculate_range.
    distance = fuel_capacity * 15. "Assuming a fuel efficiency"
  ENDMETHOD.

  METHOD adjust_fuel_capacity.
    fuel_capacity = new_capacity.
  ENDMETHOD.
ENDCLASS.
```

The vehicle class implementation details how data and functionality are combined:

- display_info **Method**: Provides a description of the vehicle, outputting attributes and method-imported values.

- calculate_range **Method**: Utilizes the private fuel_capacity to return an estimated range, demonstrating the protected logic that can be shared with subclasses.

- adjust_fuel_capacity **Method**: Offers a controlled way to modify the fuel_capacity, ensuring proper encapsulation by restricting direct access to the attribute.

Attributes in ABAP classes hold data pertinent to the class function. They can be static (shared across all instances) or instance-specific. Instance attributes reflect the class blueprint, unique to each object, while static attributes retain consistent values across class instances.

8.2. DEFINING AND IMPLEMENTING CLASSES

Proper use of attributes enhances the class's ability to maintain state and store necessary information.

```
CLASS navigation_system DEFINITION.
  PUBLIC SECTION.
    CLASS-DATA default_language TYPE string VALUE 'English'.
    DATA: current_location TYPE string,
          destination TYPE string.
    METHODS: set_destination,
             show_navigation IMPORTING language TYPE string DEFAULT
                             default_language.
ENDCLASS.
```

In navigation_system, default_language is a class attribute, consistent across all system instances, whereas current_location and destination vary per instance. Managing these attributes well ensures that class instances maintain appropriate, context-sensitive information.

Method implementation is core to a class's behavior in an object-oriented program. Proper method design in ABAP involves:

- Defining explicit inputs and outputs (e.g., IMPORTING, EXPORTING, CHANGING, and RETURNING specifications).

- Ensuring methods perform singular, clear tasks to maintain clarity and minimize side effects.

- Engaging class attributes thoughtfully, modifying states when necessary while preserving significant context.

```
CLASS navigation_system IMPLEMENTATION.
  METHOD set_destination.
    destination = 'Office'.
  ENDMETHOD.

  METHOD show_navigation.
    WRITE: / 'Navigation from', current_location, 'to', destination,
           / 'Language:', language.
  ENDMETHOD.
ENDCLASS.
```

Here, set_destination assigns a target, while show_navigation conveys directional guidance in the specified language. Precision in these method implementations targets coherent, step-wise execution paramount to clear program flow.

Interfaces in ABAP enable the separation of the definition from implementation, fostering modularity and contract-based development.

Through interfaces, a class commits to implementing specified methods without dictating their execution strategy, enhancing flexibility and future scalability.

```
INTERFACE i_vehicle_operations.
  METHODS: start_engine,
           stop_engine.
ENDINTERFACE.

CLASS motorbike DEFINITION.
  PUBLIC SECTION.
    INTERFACES: i_vehicle_operations.
    DATA: is_running TYPE abap_bool.
ENDCLASS.

CLASS motorbike IMPLEMENTATION.
  METHOD i_vehicle_operations~start_engine.
    is_running = abap_true.
    WRITE: / 'Motorbike engine started.'.
  ENDMETHOD.

  METHOD i_vehicle_operations~stop_engine.
    is_running = abap_false.
    WRITE: / 'Motorbike engine stopped.'.
  ENDMETHOD.
ENDCLASS.
```

The motorbike class uses i_vehicle_operations interface, guaranteeing method provision for start_engine and stop_engine. This interface ensures consistency in how engine operations are defined, allowing for diverse class implementations without sacrificing standardization.

The structuring of classes within ABAP significantly contributes to a program's clarity, robustness, and adaptability by drawing upon carefully defined attributes, methods, and interfaces. This structure aligns with OOP principles by facilitating encapsulation, modularization, and reuse. Methodical class definitions and implementations, as seen here, equip developers with powerful tools for crafting sophisticated, maintainable programs that adhere to modern development standards.

8.3 Inheritance and Interfaces

Inheritance and interfaces form integral aspects of Object-Oriented Programming (OOP) and are essential in ABAP (Advanced Business Application Programming) for crafting complex, modular applications. These paradigms facilitate the reuse of existing software components,

8.3. INHERITANCE AND INTERFACES

enhance extensibility, and promote uniformity through well-defined contracts. Applying these principles effectively requires a solid understanding of their mechanics and a strategic approach to leveraging their benefits.

Inheritance allows a class, known as the child or subclass, to acquire attributes and methods from another class, referred to as the parent or superclass. This mechanism eliminates redundancy, as common functionality need not be redefined in every new class but can instead be inherited from a parent class. In ABAP, inheritance is implemented using the INHERITING FROM clause in the child class definition, indicating the parent class from which the subclass derives.

```
CLASS vehicle DEFINITION.
  PUBLIC SECTION.
    DATA: speed TYPE i,
          fuel_level TYPE i.
    METHODS: start,
             stop,
             refuel IMPORTING amount TYPE i.
ENDCLASS.

CLASS vehicle IMPLEMENTATION.
  METHOD start.
    WRITE: / 'Vehicle started with speed:', speed.
  ENDMETHOD.

  METHOD stop.
    WRITE: / 'Vehicle stopped.'.
  ENDMETHOD.

  METHOD refuel.
    fuel_level = fuel_level + amount.
    WRITE: / 'Refueled:', amount, 'units. Current fuel level:', fuel_level.
  ENDMETHOD.
ENDCLASS.
```

In the vehicle class, core functionalities for starting, stopping, and refueling are encapsulated. The class also maintains speed and fuel level attributes, allowing subclasses to inherit this shared behavior and state.

```
CLASS car DEFINITION INHERITING FROM vehicle.
  PUBLIC SECTION.
    METHODS: open_trunk,
             honk.
ENDCLASS.

CLASS car IMPLEMENTATION.
  METHOD open_trunk.
    WRITE: / 'The car trunk is opened.'.
  ENDMETHOD.
```

```
METHOD honk.
  WRITE: / 'Honking the car horn.'.
ENDMETHOD.
ENDCLASS.
```

In car, a subclass of vehicle, the inherent vehicle methods and attributes are accessible without redefinition. Additional methods open_trunk and honk further refine the subclass to embody characteristics specific to cars.

Inheritance grants subclasses the flexibility to override or extend parent class functionalities. Method overriding happens when a subclass provides its implementation of a method defined in the superclass, enabling polymorphic behavior.

```
CLASS sports_car DEFINITION INHERITING FROM car.
  PUBLIC SECTION.
    METHODS: start REDEFINITION,
             activate_turbo.
ENDCLASS.

CLASS sports_car IMPLEMENTATION.
  METHOD start.
    speed = 200.
    WRITE: / 'Sports car starts with a boost. Speed:', speed.
  ENDMETHOD.

  METHOD activate_turbo.
    speed = speed + 50.
    WRITE: / 'Turbo activated! Current speed:', speed.
  ENDMETHOD.
ENDCLASS.
```

Sports_car extends car, overriding the start method to accelerate with increased speed, exemplifying polymorphism. It also introduces activate_turbo, demonstrating method addition specific to the subclass. By employing inheritance, subclasses adapt inherited attributes and methods effectively, whether by enhancing existing functionalities or by integrating new ones.

Interfaces offer a different means of establishing a contract in ABAP by abstractly defining method blueprints without prescribing their implementations. An interface dictates a set of methods a class must implement, ensuring consistent application behavior when multiple classes share an interface. This approach facilitates standardized communication across disparate classes, promoting cohesion and reducing dependencies.

8.3. INHERITANCE AND INTERFACES

```
INTERFACE i_drivable.
  METHODS: accelerate,
           brake.
ENDINTERFACE.

CLASS bicycle DEFINITION.
  PUBLIC SECTION.
    INTERFACES: i_drivable.
    DATA: current_speed TYPE i.
ENDCLASS.

CLASS bicycle IMPLEMENTATION.
  METHOD i_drivable~accelerate.
    current_speed = current_speed + 5.
    WRITE: / 'Bicycle accelerates. Current speed:', current_speed.
  ENDMETHOD.

  METHOD i_drivable~brake.
    current_speed = 0.
    WRITE: / 'Bicycle stopped. Speed:', current_speed.
  ENDMETHOD.
ENDCLASS.
```

The bicycle class, implementing the i_drivable interface, adheres to its contract by providing concrete implementations for accelerate and brake. This illustrates that despite varying class contexts, consistent method names and expected outcomes are maintained.

```
CLASS motorbike DEFINITION.
  PUBLIC SECTION.
    INTERFACES: i_drivable.
    DATA: current_speed TYPE i.
ENDCLASS.

CLASS motorbike IMPLEMENTATION.
  METHOD i_drivable~accelerate.
    current_speed = current_speed + 20.
    WRITE: / 'Motorbike accelerates rapidly. Current speed:', current_speed.
  ENDMETHOD.

  METHOD i_drivable~brake.
    current_speed = 0.
    WRITE: / 'Motorbike stopped aggressively. Speed:', current_speed.
  ENDMETHOD.
ENDCLASS.
```

The motorbike class, also implementing i_drivable, showcases varied method implementations under a unified interface, highlighting the adaptability and specificity enabled by this approach.

The combination of inheritance and interfaces allows for sophisticated OOP designs where inheritance supports hierarchical organization and shared behavior enhancement, while interfaces facilitate cross-cutting concerns and design by contract. Both paradigms, when prudently applied, foster a systematic and logical structure in ABAP applications, emphasizing maintainability and reducing complexity.

Through inheritance, code is composed in hierarchy levels, ensuring that shared attributes and methods are centralized within superclasses, thereby eliminating duplication and enhancing code sustainability. Meanwhile, interfaces guide the integration of shared method signatures, incorporating flexibility into the system's architecture. This dual-pronged approach, balancing the robustness of inheritance with the agility of interfaces, stands as a testament to the power of OOP in developing sophisticated software solutions in ABAP.

By drawing on both inheritance and interfaces, ABAP developers can design adaptable, scalable applications, leveraging the strengths of each concept to craft efficient, purpose-driven software. Such programs are not only reflective of sound coding practices but also exhibit clarity and precision, embodying the fundamental principles of object orientation within the ABAP landscape.

8.4 Working with Objects and Instances

In Object-Oriented Programming (OOP) within ABAP (Advanced Business Application Programming), objects and instances are the fundamental units of data interaction and manipulation. Understanding how to work proficiently with these units is crucial for developing effective, maintainable applications. This section delves into the creation and management of objects, the nuances of instantiation, object lifecycle, and the dynamics of object interactions in ABAP.

An object is essentially an instance of a class, embodying the blueprint defined within the class. Objects encapsulate data and provide functionalities as defined by their class attributes and methods. The instantiation of a class results in the creation of an object, marking the transition from a mere class definition to a functional program component.

In ABAP, object creation is realized through the 'CREATE OBJECT' statement which initializes a class instance. This process involves allocating memory for the object and optionally initializing it with specified

8.4. WORKING WITH OBJECTS AND INSTANCES

parameters. The life of an object begins with its creation and continues until it is no longer reachable, allowing for garbage collection.

```
CLASS air_conditioner DEFINITION.
  PUBLIC SECTION.
    DATA: temperature TYPE i,
          power_state TYPE abap_bool.
    METHODS: switch_on,
             switch_off,
             set_temperature IMPORTING new_temperature TYPE i.
ENDCLASS.

CLASS air_conditioner IMPLEMENTATION.
  METHOD switch_on.
    power_state = abap_true.
    WRITE: / 'Air conditioner is now ON'.
  ENDMETHOD.

  METHOD switch_off.
    power_state = abap_false.
    WRITE: / 'Air conditioner is now OFF'.
  ENDMETHOD.

  METHOD set_temperature.
    temperature = new_temperature.
    WRITE: / 'Temperature set to:', temperature.
  ENDMETHOD.
ENDCLASS.
```

In the air_conditioner class defined above, its instantiation and subsequent interaction are demonstrated below:

```
DATA: my_ac TYPE REF TO air_conditioner.
CREATE OBJECT my_ac.
my_ac->switch_on( ).
my_ac->set_temperature(18).
```

Here, 'CREATE OBJECT' generates an instance of air_conditioner stored in my_ac. Through this object reference, the air conditioner's state and attributes are manipulated by invoking methods like switch_on and set_temperature.

One of the advantages of OOP is the ability to manage complex interactions and states through objects. By creating multiple instances of a class, each with its distinct set of attributes and methods, an application in ABAP can handle numerous entities dynamically and independently.

Instances in ABAP are crucial for maintaining object states. Each instance has its attribute set, allowing each object to operate independently. This characteristic of OOP simplifies the modeling of complex systems where individual component behavior must be tracked distinctly.

```
DATA: ac_family_room TYPE REF TO air_conditioner,
      ac_living_room TYPE REF TO air_conditioner.

CREATE OBJECT ac_family_room.
ac_family_room->set_temperature(22).
ac_family_room->switch_on( ).

CREATE OBJECT ac_living_room.
ac_living_room->set_temperature(20).
ac_living_room->switch_on( ).
```

In this illustration, two independent instances of air_conditioner, one for a family room and another for a living room, are individually created and manipulated. By maintaining separate object references, each air conditioner operates according to its specified attributes and methods.

Object lifecycle management is a crucial consideration in ABAP programming. Managing resource allocation and cleanup efficiently ensures the robust performance of applications. ABAP's memory management is primarily automatic, with the garbage collector handling unused objects. Nevertheless, explicit object dereferencing using 'FREE' can be employed to release resources when an object's continuity is assuredly unnecessary.

```
FREE ac_living_room.
```

Call to 'FREE' in this example makes the object ac_living_room eligible for resource cleanup, stimulating efficient memory management in the application.

Object interaction, another central OOP element, facilitates complex communications and data exchanges between objects while respecting encapsulation. In ABAP, method invocations govern such interactions, enabling an object to exploit functionalities of another, thus coordinating cohesive application processes.

```
CLASS thermostat DEFINITION.
  PUBLIC SECTION.
    METHODS: regulate_temperature
      IMPORTING ac_device TYPE REF TO air_conditioner
        SETTING desired_temp TYPE i.
ENDCLASS.
```

8.4. WORKING WITH OBJECTS AND INSTANCES

```abap
CLASS thermostat IMPLEMENTATION.
  METHOD regulate_temperature.
    IF ac_device->temperature <> desired_temp.
      ac_device->set_temperature( desired_temp ).
    ENDIF.
  ENDMETHOD.
ENDCLASS.
```

In this example, the thermostat class interacts with an air_conditioner object to regulate its temperature. The regulate_temperature method shows how objects exchange data and influence each other's state.

Moreover, constructors in ABAP enhance object initialization, providing defined states and ensuring consistency upon object creation. Constructors, signified by the 'CONSTRUCTOR' keyword, run automatically whenever an object of the class is instantiated.

```abap
CLASS television DEFINITION.
  PUBLIC SECTION.
    DATA: current_channel TYPE i,
          volume_level TYPE i.
    METHODS: turn_on,
             constructor IMPORTING start_channel TYPE i DEFAULT 1.
ENDCLASS.

CLASS television IMPLEMENTATION.
  METHOD constructor.
    current_channel = start_channel.
    volume_level = 10.
  ENDMETHOD.

  METHOD turn_on.
    WRITE: / 'Television ON at channel:', current_channel,
           / 'with volume level:', volume_level.
  ENDMETHOD.
ENDCLASS.
```

In the television class, the constructor method sets the initial channel and volume levels, streamlining object creation settings to default values unless specified otherwise.

```abap
DATA: my_tv TYPE REF TO television.
CREATE OBJECT my_tv EXPORTING start_channel = 5.
my_tv->turn_on( ).
```

The above ABAP snippet depicts object initialization with a specified starting channel, showcasing constructor utility in providing default configurations.

Understanding the distinction between class (static) and instance (dynamic) data is critical to effective object-oriented design. Static attributes are shared across all instances, whereas each instance maintains its copy of non-static attributes. This distinction is fundamental in designing how objects will store and handle data.

The utilization of object-oriented design in ABAP, focusing on objects and instances, bestows significant benefits: isolation of concerns, enhanced modularity, easier troubleshooting, and code that mirrors real-world systems behavior more closely. As ABAP evolves, incorporating such paradigms equips developers with capabilities to address complexities of modern applications efficiently.

Given this overview, working with objects and instances in ABAP is not merely a matter of syntax but involves employing strategies that maximally exploit OOP's potential. Methodical design, appropriate object referencing, lifecycle management, and interface utilization all contribute to coherent ABAP applications poised for diverse, sophisticated requirements. By mastering these elements, developers can harness the full power of ABAP, facilitating effective software solutions consistent with object-oriented principles.

8.5 Encapsulation and Data Hiding

Encapsulation and data hiding are foundational principles of Object-Oriented Programming (OOP) and are pivotal in ABAP (Advanced Business Application Programming) for managing complexity while promoting robustness and security within applications. By encapsulating data and controlling access, developers shield the internal state of objects, thereby enforcing boundaries and minimizing unintended interference. This section provides an in-depth exploration of encapsulation techniques and the implementation of data hiding within the ABAP context, highlighting its benefits and offering illustrative examples to emphasize its importance in developing maintainable software systems.

Encapsulation refers to the practice of bundling data (attributes) and methods (functions or procedures) that operate on the data into a single cohesive unit, or class. By encapsulating these elements, a class

8.5. ENCAPSULATION AND DATA HIDING

maintains control over its own data while exposing a well-defined interface for outside interaction. This controlled exposure ensures that the internal state is modified only through specific methods designed for interaction, preventing unauthorized or erroneous alterations.

In ABAP, encapsulation is achieved through the strategic use of access specifiers: PUBLIC, PROTECTED, and PRIVATE. These access specifiers delineate the visibility and accessibility of class members, crucially determining which parts of a class can be used externally and which remain internal.

```
CLASS bank_account DEFINITION.
  PRIVATE SECTION.
    DATA: account_balance TYPE p LENGTH 8 DECIMALS 2,
          account_number TYPE string.
    METHODS: update_balance,
             calculate_interest.
  PUBLIC SECTION.
    METHODS: deposit IMPORTING amount TYPE p LENGTH 8 DECIMALS 2,
             withdraw IMPORTING amount TYPE p LENGTH 8 DECIMALS 2
                      RETURNING VALUE(success) TYPE abap_bool,
             get_balance RETURNING VALUE(balance) TYPE p LENGTH 8
                         DECIMALS 2.
ENDCLASS.

CLASS bank_account IMPLEMENTATION.
  METHOD deposit.
    account_balance = account_balance + amount.
  ENDMETHOD.

  METHOD withdraw.
    IF account_balance >= amount.
      account_balance = account_balance - amount.
      success = abap_true.
    ELSE.
      success = abap_false.
    ENDIF.
  ENDMETHOD.

  METHOD get_balance.
    balance = account_balance.
  ENDMETHOD.

  METHOD update_balance.
    "Private method logic for updating account balance"
  ENDMETHOD.

  METHOD calculate_interest.
    "Private method logic to compute interest"
  ENDMETHOD.
ENDCLASS.
```

In the bank_account class, encapsulation ensures data integrity and security:

- **Private Section**: Critical data such as account_balance and account_number, along with internal methods like update_balance and calculate_interest, are made private, safeguarding them from unauthorized access.

- **Public Section**: Methods such as deposit, withdraw, and get_balance are exposed to provide controlled operations on the account, maintaining a strict interface through which the account state can be changed.

Data hiding assists in concealing the internal representation of an object from the outside, minimizing interdependencies and allowing for changes within a class without affecting external systems. This not only reinforces data security but also promotes flexibility since the internal workings can be modified without altering the external contract.

In practice, aligning encapsulation and data hiding ensures that while necessary functionalities are accessible, the precise details of how they are accomplished remain hidden. Data hiding, a byproduct of encapsulation, allows developers to alter a class's internal implementation safely, provided the external interface remains consistent.

Consider the extension of the bank_account to incorporate account types with interest rates, wherein data hiding and encapsulation become pivotal in managing complexity without external disruption.

```
CLASS savings_account DEFINITION INHERITING FROM bank_account.
  PRIVATE SECTION.
    DATA: interest_rate TYPE f.
  PUBLIC SECTION.
    METHODS: set_interest_rate IMPORTING rate TYPE f,
             apply_interest.
ENDCLASS.

CLASS savings_account IMPLEMENTATION.
  METHOD set_interest_rate.
    interest_rate = rate.
  ENDMETHOD.

  METHOD apply_interest.
    calculate_interest( ).
    account_balance = account_balance + account_balance * interest_rate / 100.
  ENDMETHOD.

  METHOD calculate_interest.
    "Overridden method for interest calculation specific to savings accounts"
```

8.5. ENCAPSULATION AND DATA HIDING

```
ENDMETHOD.
ENDCLASS.
```

In savings_account, a subclass of bank_account, private member interest_rate exemplifies data hiding, allowing internal use for interest calculations without exposing it within the class interface. Encapsulation governs the addition method logically and securely, letting clients modify interest rates and apply interest without exposing the calculation logic.

Key advantages of encapsulation and data hiding in ABAP are evident through the tractability and modularity they introduce. A well-encapsulated class contains all necessary information to perform its duties, insulated from interference unless explicitly permitted. This established boundary simplifies the complexity of larger systems by isolating functionality and promoting a clear architecture. Moreover, implementing encapsulation protects data integrity by ensuring that interactions strictly adhere to defined protocols.

This encapsulation paradigm extends naturally to mutable states, sensitive to inappropriate manipulations. ABAP facilitates encapsulation by encouraging thoughtful attribute exposure and strictly controlling access via methods. Such structures evoke high cohesion in class design, as closely related functionalities cluster within, and low coupling, since classes interact only through controlled interfaces.

By applying these principles, ABAP applications benefit from improved scalability—the interface consistency remains intact as internal details evolve—and reduction in maintenance overheads—future changes predominantly confine to internal implementations.

Ultimately, encapsulation and data hiding are more than tactical choices in ABAP. They represent a commitment to producing sustainable, graceful code adaptable to inevitable requirements shifts and enhancement opportunities. Correct implementation of these principles yields a foundationally strong software design, ready to support evolving business dynamics while fostering a secure, maintainable ecosystem.

Throughout ABAP application development, harnessing encapsulation with data hiding efficiently balances performance and protection, ensuring developers craft robust programs that cogently organize functionality behind secure façades. The principles explored herein are steadfast allies for creating manageability, adaptability, and elegance in ABAP's OOP environment, serving both as a methodology guide and as a milestone against which developers can measure their architectural strategies.

8.6 Polymorphism and Dynamic Method Calls

Polymorphism and dynamic method calls are significant pillars of Object-Oriented Programming (OOP) and play influential roles in developing sophisticated ABAP (Advanced Business Application Programming) applications. These concepts introduce flexibility and scalability in software design, enabling objects to be processed more generically and methods to be invoked dynamically based on runtime information. Understanding these facets of OOP deepens a developer's ability to craft applications that are both reusable and extensible.

Polymorphism in OOP allows objects to be treated as instances of their parent class rather than their actual class. This ability is crucial in creating flexible and interoperable systems, wherein a single interface can accept various types of objects. ABAP supports polymorphism through interfaces and class inheritance, enabling programmers to define method operations common to a set of classes without knowing exact object types at compile time.

Polymorphism relies heavily on the concept of method overriding, where a subclass implements a method with the same signature as a method in its superclass. This feature allows derived classes to offer specific implementations while maintaining a consistent interface, ensuring that subclasses remain interchangeable.

```
CLASS vehicle DEFINITION.
  PUBLIC SECTION.
    METHODS: move.
ENDCLASS.

CLASS vehicle IMPLEMENTATION.
  METHOD move.
    WRITE: / 'Generic vehicle moves.'.
  ENDMETHOD.
ENDCLASS.
```

8.6. POLYMORPHISM AND DYNAMIC METHOD CALLS

```
CLASS car DEFINITION INHERITING FROM vehicle.
  PUBLIC SECTION.
    METHODS: move REDEFINITION.
ENDCLASS.

CLASS car IMPLEMENTATION.
  METHOD move.
    WRITE: / 'Car drives on the road.'.
  ENDMETHOD.
ENDCLASS.

CLASS airplane DEFINITION INHERITING FROM vehicle.
  PUBLIC SECTION.
    METHODS: move REDEFINITION.
ENDCLASS.

CLASS airplane IMPLEMENTATION.
  METHOD move.
    WRITE: / 'Airplane flies in the sky.'.
  ENDMETHOD.
ENDCLASS.
```

In this example, 'vehicle' defines a generic 'move' method. Subclasses 'car' and 'airplane' redefine this method to offer specific behavior. Through polymorphism, both 'car' and 'airplane' can be treated as 'vehicle' instances, allowing their unique 'move' implementations to be invoked dynamically.

```
DATA: my_vehicle TYPE REF TO vehicle,
      my_car TYPE REF TO car,
      my_airplane TYPE REF TO airplane.

CREATE OBJECT my_car.
CREATE OBJECT my_airplane.

my_vehicle = my_car.
my_vehicle->move( ). "Output: Car drives on the road."

my_vehicle = my_airplane.
my_vehicle->move( ). "Output: Airplane flies in the sky."
```

The above ABAP code snippet exemplifies polymorphism by assigning 'my_car' and 'my_airplane' to 'my_vehicle'. The 'move' method invoked reflects the specific subclass's behavior, demonstrating polymorphic competency in handling diverse object types uniformly.

Dynamic method calls represent another tenet of OOP in ABAP, facilitating method invocation determined at runtime rather than compile time. This flexibility endows applications with the capability to respond to varying conditions and data structures within their operational context, promoting versatility and responsiveness.

In ABAP, dynamic calls are made using the 'CALL METHOD' statement, in which method names can be replaced by values computed at runtime. Such calls empower developers to build applications accommodating a wide array of operational scenarios without hardcoding method names.

```
CLASS temperature_controller DEFINITION.
  PUBLIC SECTION.
    METHODS: set_cooling,
             set_heating.
ENDCLASS.

CLASS temperature_controller IMPLEMENTATION.
  METHOD set_cooling.
    WRITE: / 'Cooling system activated.'.
  ENDMETHOD.

  METHOD set_heating.
    WRITE: / 'Heating system activated.'.
  ENDMETHOD.
ENDCLASS.

DATA: command TYPE string,
      controller TYPE REF TO temperature_controller.

CREATE OBJECT controller.

command = 'set_cooling'.

CALL METHOD controller->(command). "Output: Cooling system activated."

command = 'set_heating'.

CALL METHOD controller->(command). "Output: Heating system activated."
```

In this demonstration, 'temperature_controller' dynamically executes 'set_cooling' and 'set_heating' based on the 'command' variable, showcasing dynamic method invocation's adaptability in varying operation contexts.

Achieving Polymorphic Behavior Through Interfaces

In addition to inheritance, interfaces also enable polymorphic behavior by allowing different classes to implement the same interface in diverse ways. This approach decouples class hierarchies and offers flexibility beyond traditional inheritance polymorphism.

```
INTERFACE i_payment_processor.
  METHODS: process_payment.
ENDINTERFACE.
```

8.6. POLYMORPHISM AND DYNAMIC METHOD CALLS

```
CLASS credit_card_processor DEFINITION.
  PUBLIC SECTION.
    INTERFACES: i_payment_processor.
ENDCLASS.

CLASS credit_card_processor IMPLEMENTATION.
  METHOD i_payment_processor~process_payment.
    WRITE: / 'Processing credit card payment.'.
  ENDMETHOD.
ENDCLASS.

CLASS paypal_processor DEFINITION.
  PUBLIC SECTION.
    INTERFACES: i_payment_processor.
ENDCLASS.

CLASS paypal_processor IMPLEMENTATION.
  METHOD i_payment_processor~process_payment.
    WRITE: / 'Processing PayPal payment.'.
  ENDMETHOD.
ENDCLASS.

DATA: payment_processor TYPE REF TO i_payment_processor,
      cc_processor TYPE REF TO credit_card_processor,
      pp_processor TYPE REF TO paypal_processor.

CREATE OBJECT cc_processor.
CREATE OBJECT pp_processor.

payment_processor = cc_processor.
payment_processor->process_payment( ). "Output: Processing credit card payment."

payment_processor = pp_processor.
payment_processor->process_payment( ). "Output: Processing PayPal payment."
```

The above example demonstrates polymorphic behavior achieved through an interface 'i_payment_processor'. Both 'credit_card_processor' and 'paypal_processor' implement the interface, allowing interchangeable usage while providing distinct processing logic.

Analysis and Benefits

The benefits of polymorphism and dynamic method calls in ABAP extend to enhancing code manageability, reducing duplication, and supporting the Open/Closed principle from SOLID design: software entities should be open for extension but closed for modification.

- Code Flexibility: By allowing objects to adhere to multiple behaviors, polymorphism facilitates the creation of more adaptable systems.

- Reduced Coupling: Systems utilizing polymorphism boast reduced dependencies, resulting in components that can evolve autonomously.

- Maintainability: Changes in polymorphic methods typically require modification within those methods only, minimizing cascading effects across the system.

- Dynamic Behavior: Dynamic method calls enhance systems' adaptability, executing varied operations based on runtime conditions and priorities.

- Extensibility: As new types or functionalities emerge, a polymorphic architecture allows easy integration without widespread alterations, adhering to robust software design principles.

The integration of polymorphism and dynamic method calls within ABAP enhances application adaptability, maintainability, and scope for growth. They represent strategic functionalities enabling programmers to navigate complex design challenges with ease, reinforcing applications' resilience and responsiveness to the dynamic business environment. Employing these principles ensures optimal use of object-oriented power, reinforcing the production of flexible, efficient, and future-proof ABAP software systems.

8.7 Exception Handling in Object-Oriented Approach

Exception handling is a critical aspect of robust application development, and within the object-oriented paradigm of ABAP (Advanced Business Application Programming), it takes on strategic importance. The ability to manage unexpected conditions gracefully and to maintain application stability is paramount for ensuring software reliability and resilience. In this section, we delve into the intricacies of exception handling using an object-oriented approach, examining its principles, applications, and benefits within ABAP.

In object-oriented programming, exceptions are anomalous conditions or errors that occur during the execution of a program. They disrupt

8.7. EXCEPTION HANDLING IN OBJECT-ORIENTED APPROACH

the normal flow, requiring special processing. Exception handling provides a structured method of catching these errors and taking appropriate corrective actions, thus preventing system crashes or unpredictable behavior. In ABAP, exceptions are integral to maintaining program control flow, allowing developers to implement error-catching mechanisms that align closely with object-oriented principles.

ABAP's exception handling primarily utilizes the class-based approach, allowing exceptions to be defined and managed as classes. This object-oriented technique enhances modularity and reusability by treating exceptions as objects that can be instantiated and manipulated like any other class instances.

Defining Exception Classes

Creating custom exception classes provides a tailored mechanism for handling specific error situations that cannot be effectively managed using standard exceptions. Exception classes in ABAP inherit from predefined exception superclasses such as CX_NO_CHECK, CX_STATIC_CHECK, or CX_DYNAMIC_CHECK, each designating different checking levels and scenarios where the exceptions are utilized.

```
CLASS cx_insufficient_funds DEFINITION INHERITING FROM cx_static_check.
  PUBLIC SECTION.
    DATA: requested_amount TYPE p LENGTH 8 DECIMALS 2,
          available_balance TYPE p LENGTH 8 DECIMALS 2.
    METHODS: constructor IMPORTING request TYPE p LENGTH 8 DECIMALS 2
                                   balance TYPE p LENGTH 8 DECIMALS 2.
ENDCLASS.

CLASS cx_insufficient_funds IMPLEMENTATION.
  METHOD constructor.
    super->constructor( ).
    requested_amount = request.
    available_balance = balance.
  ENDMETHOD.
ENDCLASS.
```

In the cx_insufficient_funds exception class, financial constraints are encapsulated, capturing both the requested amount and the available balance in the event of insufficient funds. The constructor method initializes these attributes, providing contextually relevant details for troubleshooting.

Raising Exceptions

Raising exceptions is an intentional act by which control is transferred to an exception-handling block. This is typically done when invalid conditions are detected that preclude successful method completion. In ABAP, exceptions are raised using the RAISE EXCEPTION statement, which specifies an instance of the exception class to be activated.

```
CLASS bank_account DEFINITION.
  PUBLIC SECTION.
    DATA: balance TYPE p LENGTH 8 DECIMALS 2.
    METHODS: withdraw IMPORTING amount TYPE p LENGTH 8 DECIMALS 2
             RAISING cx_insufficient_funds.
ENDCLASS.

CLASS bank_account IMPLEMENTATION.
  METHOD withdraw.
    IF amount > balance.
      RAISE EXCEPTION TYPE cx_insufficient_funds
        EXPORTING request = amount
                  balance = balance.
    ELSE.
      balance = balance - amount.
    ENDIF.
  ENDMETHOD.
ENDCLASS.
```

The withdraw method in bank_account demonstrates how the cx_insufficient_funds exception is raised when a withdrawal amount exceeds the balance, offering a structured means to handle this unexpected scenario.

Catching Exceptions

Catching exceptions involves intercepting a raised exception and executing a specialized block of code to address the error. This is typically done using the TRY...ENDTRY construct, with specific clauses such as CATCH to define actions for different exceptions.

```
DATA: my_account TYPE REF TO bank_account.

CREATE OBJECT my_account.
my_account->balance = 500.00.

TRY.
    my_account->withdraw( 600.00 ).
  CATCH cx_insufficient_funds INTO DATA(insufficient_funds).
    WRITE: / 'Withdrawal failed. Requested:',
             insufficient_funds->requested_amount,
             ' | Available:',
             insufficient_funds->available_balance.
ENDTRY.
```

This example illustrates a TRY block where an attempted withdrawal

8.7. EXCEPTION HANDLING IN OBJECT-ORIENTED APPROACH

leads to catching the cx_insufficient_funds exception. The accompanying CATCH block outputs informative messages, ensuring users are aware of the specific error conditions.

Reusability and Customization

An object-oriented approach to exception handling promotes code reusability, allowing developers to craft exception classes that encapsulate detailed error information. These classes can be reused across applications, ensuring consistent handling of similar error conditions. Custom exception classes also provide a straightforward way to integrate business logic with error management, delivering context-specific resolutions to error situations that standard exceptions may not address.

Hierarchical Exception Handling

Exception handling is inherently hierarchical, with exception classes forming part of an inheritance hierarchy. This hierarchy helps to organize exceptions in a logical manner and allows broader exception classes to catch multiple related error types unless specifically overridden by more specialized exceptions.

```
CLASS cx_transaction_error DEFINITION INHERITING FROM cx_static_check.
ENDCLASS.

CLASS cx_network_error DEFINITION INHERITING FROM cx_transaction_error.
ENDCLASS.

CLASS cx_timeout_error DEFINITION INHERITING FROM cx_network_error.
ENDCLASS.
```

In this hierarchical structure, cx_timeout_error inherits from cx_network_error, which in turn inherits from cx_transaction_error. This setup allows handling broad categories of exceptions or more specific ones, depending on the granularity required in error resolution.

```
TRY.
    "Some transactional operations"
  CATCH cx_timeout_error INTO DATA(timeout).
    WRITE: / 'Operation timed out. Please try again.'.
  CATCH cx_network_error.
    WRITE: / 'Network related error occurred.'.
  CATCH cx_transaction_error.
    WRITE: / 'A general transaction error was encountered.'.
ENDTRY.
```

This TRY block demonstrates prioritization in handling specific errors (cx_timeout_error) over more general categories (cx_network_error and cx_transaction_error), ensuring detailed and situation-appropriate responses.

Analyzing the Benefits

Effective exception handling in an object-oriented manner confers multiple benefits:

- **Error Localization**: By handling exceptions locally, objects can ensure that only relevant code blocks react to specific error conditions, resulting in more accurate and reliable error management.

- **Improved Readability**: Structuring exceptions as part of the class hierarchy and using semantic method names upgrades code readability and maintainability.

- **Controlled Fault Recovery**: Exception handling allows programs to recover gracefully from faults, offering opportunities for retry logic, fallback operations, or user notifications, thereby enhancing overall application resilience.

- **Simplified Debugging**: Detailed and contextual exception information facilitates quicker and more effective debugging, allowing developers to trace and address root causes with greater precision.

- **Flexible Error Handling Strategies**: Object-oriented exception handling supports diverse strategies tailored to different scenarios, ranging from log-based tracking to real-time corrective measures, underpinning robust and context-aware programming paradigms.

Exception handling through an object-oriented lens in ABAP reinforces the paradigm's strengths—modularity, extensibility, and encapsulation—while addressing the critical need for solid error management. It empowers developers to craft applications capable of anticipating, identifying, and resolving error conditions effectively, ensuring stability and reliability in complex, dynamic environments. Through thoughtful design and systematic application of these principles, ABAP developers can sustain the robustness and adaptability of their software solutions, even amidst the uncertainty of runtime anomalies.

Chapter 9

SAP Enhancement Options and User Exits

This chapter examines the mechanisms available for customizing SAP systems through enhancements and user exits, facilitating tailored solutions without altering core functionalities. It details the SAP Enhancement Framework, highlighting the use of user exits, customer exits, and Business Add-Ins (BADIs) to extend system capabilities. Techniques for implementing enhancement points and sections are discussed, alongside the distinctions between implicit and explicit enhancements. The Switch Framework is introduced to manage enhancements efficiently. By adhering to best practices, developers can ensure that modifications are sustainable and compatible with future SAP updates, promoting flexible and adaptable system customization.

9.1 Overview of Enhancement Framework

The SAP Enhancement Framework is a critical component of SAP systems, serving as a robust mechanism for customizing standard applications without modifying the core code. This framework provides a structured and systematic approach to extend the functionality of SAP applications, thereby ensuring their adaptability to meet specific business requirements. Understanding the nuances of this framework is essential for developers who aim to maximize the capabilities of their SAP environments while maintaining the integrity and upgradeability of the base system.

Within the SAP system, enhancements are designed to introduce new features or modify existing functionalities. The core principle of the Enhancement Framework is to allow these modifications in a non-intrusive manner. This ensures that any customizations or enhancements made are preservable, even during system upgrades or patches. Consequently, businesses can benefit from personalized SAP solutions while minimizing the risks associated with direct modifications to the SAP standard code.

At its core, the SAP Enhancement Framework consists of several key components: enhancement points, enhancement sections, and Business Add-Ins (BADIs). Each of these components offers distinct mechanisms for extending SAP applications, and understanding their interrelationship is crucial for effective application enhancement.

Enhancement points and sections allow for static and predefined positions within the SAP code where custom logic can be introduced. These can either be explicit, predefined by SAP, or implicit, which are system-generated at specific locations within the code. The explicit enhancement points are strategically placed by SAP to accommodate anticipated extension scenarios, thus offering a predictable and reliable way to insert custom functionalities.

For instance, consider that a business requirement emerges where the company needs to add a custom validation check in a standard SAP transaction. In such a scenario, a thorough examination of the relevant standard programs would reveal explicit enhancement points where

9.1. OVERVIEW OF ENHANCEMENT FRAMEWORK

the custom validation logic can be inserted. Utilizing these enhancement points enables the custom functionality to be isolated from the main codebase, ensuring that future upgrades or patches do not overwrite the enhancements.

The implicit enhancement options, on the other hand, are more pervasive throughout the SAP code and allow developers to insert custom code at predetermined locations, such as at the end of a code block, at the beginning, or just before a subroutine call. One of the primary advantages of implicit enhancements is their ubiquity, providing extensive possibilities for customization even in parts of the SAP code where explicit enhancement options might not be available. This flexibility is instrumental in fulfilling unique business requirements that were not originally anticipated during SAP development.

Moreover, the framework includes comprehensive tools for managing these enhancements. These tools facilitate the creation, modification, activation, and deactivation of enhancements, thereby enabling developers to experiment with various configurations without compromising the stability of the production system.

The Enhancement Framework is complemented by the concept of Business Add-Ins (BADIs). BADIs are object-oriented enhancements that leverage the polymorphism and encapsulation benefits of object-oriented programming, providing a powerful and flexible mechanism for extending SAP functionality. BADIs offer an interface-based approach to enhancements, allowing for multiple implementations and promoting a more modular architecture.

For instance, a BADI might be provided by SAP for enhancing the behavior of a standard report. Developers can create multiple implementations for this BADI to cater to different scenarios or user requirements. The BADI framework manages these implementations and determines which one to execute based on selection criteria specified by the developer. This approach contrasts with the single-option nature of user exits, providing a more flexible enhancement strategy.

Understanding how to implement and manage both enhancement points and BADIs is vital for creating stable and maintainable custom solutions. Consider the following example of defining a simple BADI in ABAP for enhancing a standard SAP transaction:

CHAPTER 9. SAP ENHANCEMENT OPTIONS AND USER EXITS

```
INTERFACE if_my_enhancement_badi PUBLIC.
  METHODS:
    my_custom_method
      IMPORTING iv_parameter TYPE string
      RETURNING VALUE(rv_result) TYPE string.
ENDINTERFACE.

CLASS my_enhancement_badi DEFINITION.
  PUBLIC SECTION.
    INTERFACES: if_my_enhancement_badi.
  PROTECTED SECTION.
  PRIVATE SECTION.
ENDCLASS.

CLASS my_enhancement_badi IMPLEMENTATION.
  METHOD if_my_enhancement_badi~my_custom_method.
    rv_result = iv_parameter && ' enhanced'.
  ENDMETHOD.
ENDCLASS.

DATA: instance TYPE REF TO if_my_enhancement_badi.

CREATE OBJECT instance TYPE my_enhancement_badi.
DATA(lv_result) = instance->my_custom_method( 'SAP' ).
WRITE: / lv_result.
```

In this example, a simple interface 'if_my_enhancement_badi' is defined, introducing a method 'my_custom_method' for processing enhancement logic. A class 'my_enhancement_badi' implements this interface, defining the logic for appending the word 'enhanced' to the input string. Consequently, when the BADI is instantiated and executed, it modifies the typical transaction flow as defined by the BADI implementation.

The core benefit of using the Enhancement Framework is its capability to integrate seamlessly into the SAP development lifecycle. It allows for enhancements to be developed in a transportable manner, thus promoting a clean separation between custom logic and standard SAP code. This modularity is crucial for sustaining enhancements across system upgrades, patches, and customization projects.

Moreover, the use of the Enhancement Framework mitigates the "modification hell" frequently encountered when directly altering standard SAP code. When employing the framework, customizations are encapsulated in enhancements that SAP recognizes and preserves across system evolutions, markedly reducing the effort and risk involved in maintaining such systems.

A critical consideration for SAP developers when leveraging the Enhancement Framework is to align the design of enhancements with architectural principles that favor maintainability and scalability. In practice, this means designing enhancements in a way that minimizes dependencies on specific version features, adhering instead to broader API contracts or enhancement interfaces provided by SAP.

Furthermore, the careful selection of enhancement points, especially in complex systems, requires a sound understanding of the standard SAP application to prevent unintended side-effects. Testing becomes paramount, as custom logic introduced through enhancement points might interact in unforeseen ways with standard processes or other enhancements. Consequently, a robust testing strategy that includes both unit and integration testing is indispensable.

The SAP Enhancement Framework remains a cornerstone of modern SAP customization strategies. Its principles of modularity, separation, and preservation align with best practices in software engineering, offering a versatile and targeted approach for extending SAP solutions. By expertly leveraging enhancement points, sections, and BADIs, developers can build adaptable, scalable, and maintainable SAP environments that align with the dynamic needs of their business operations without compromising the stability and upgradeability of the SAP system itself. The framework's structured approach ensures that enhancements are both effective in addressing unique business requirements and sustainable in the long-term evolution of the enterprise IT landscape.

9.2 User Exits and Customer Exits

User exits and customer exits are essential mechanisms within the SAP ecosystem that provide predefined hooks, allowing developers to enhance and extend standard functionalities of SAP applications. These exits enable the insertion of custom code into standard SAP programs, ensuring that specific business processes are adequately supported without necessitating direct modifications to the core codebase. This section delves into the intricacies of both user exits and customer exits, examining their differences, use cases, and implementation details.

At their core, user exits and customer exits are part of the broader

SAP enhancement concept designed to facilitate customized business solutions. Businesses often need to adapt standard SAP applications to fit unique organizational processes, legal requirements, or regional mandates. By utilizing these exits, organizations can introduce custom logic that interacts with SAP's standard offerings, thus tailoring the system to better meet specific needs.

User Exits:

User exits typically relate to enhancements within the SAP SD (Sales and Distribution) module. These enhancements usually involve subroutines in standard SAP programs where custom code can be implemented. User exits are procedural in nature, as they were initially introduced in earlier iterations of SAP before object-oriented programming became the standard.

A typical scenario for user exits might involve altering the sales order creation process. For example, if a business needs to include custom validation rules during order entry, a user exit can be employed to inject validation logic that checks additional conditions before finalizing the order.

To find and implement a user exit, SAP developers often follow a structured approach:

- **Identifying Relevant User Exits:** Developers can use transaction SMOD to list available user exits and their associated enhancements. Searching based on transaction codes or relevant keywords can help identify potential exits pertinent to specific processes.

- **Creating a Project:** Once appropriate user exits are identified, the developer creates a project in transaction CMOD. This project serves as a container for enhancements and is crucial for structuring and organizing customizations.

- **Implementing the Custom Logic:** The developer writes the custom logic within the subroutine function modules specified by the user exits. Below is an example of a basic user exit implementation in SAP:

```
FUNCTION userexit_save_document_prepare.
" Custom code to check custom conditions before saving a sales document
```

9.2. USER EXITS AND CUSTOMER EXITS

```
    IF sales_document_type = 'ZSALE' AND NOT check_custom_condition
        (sales_document).
        MESSAGE e001(zsales) WITH 'Custom validation failed'.
    ENDIF.
ENDFUNCTION.
```

In this code snippet, the function userexit_save_document_prepare intercepts the save operation for a sales document. It evaluates whether custom conditions are met and raises an error if validation fails. This rudimentary example highlights how user exits can inject custom business logic seamlessly.

- **Testing:** After implementation, rigorous testing is carried out to ensure the custom logic integrates well with the standard SAP operations and does not introduce unintended side effects.

Customer Exits:

Customer exits, introduced with SAP R/3, represent a more advanced and structured enhancement method compared to user exits. These exits are designed with integration points within SAP applications through function module exits, screen exits, and menu exits.

The primary distinction of customer exits lies in their adaptability via SAP's modular architecture. Customer exits are object-oriented and enable enhancements within a wider context beyond the Sales and Distribution module, making them applicable across different SAP components.

- **Function Module Exits:** These exits are associated with specific business processes and are defined in SAP via function modules. The implementation typically involves creating an additional include program where developers write custom code to modify or enhance the functionality of the standard function module.

- **Screen Exits:** Screen exits allow for the modification of SAP standard screens via the inclusion of new subscreens. This capability is particularly useful for adding custom fields or interface elements that capture additional data pertinent to business processes.

- **Menu Exits:** Menu exits facilitate the insertion of new menu items within the SAP GUI, allowing for the extension of navigational paths to integrate custom business functions or reports.

The implementation of a customer exit involves multiple steps:

- **Identification:** Similar to user exits, customer exits can be identified using transaction SMOD, where developers search for enhancements pertinent to the desired customization.

- **Project Initialization:** Developers create or modify an existing project in CMOD, linking the required enhancements to the project.

- **Implementation of Code:** Depending on the type of exit, developers will implement the necessary logic, whether it be via additional screens, menu items, or function module code changes. Consider the following implementation example for a customer exit using a function module:

```
ENHANCEMENT-SECTION z_my_custom_exit SPOTS es_sap_name
    STATIC.
" Implement custom business logic here
IF sy-tcode = 'VA01' AND check_custom_business_rule(sales_order).
    " Modify sales order structure based on custom rules
    sales_order-items[] = modify_order_logic( sales_order-items[] ).
ENDIF.
END-ENHANCEMENT-SECTION.
```

In this example, the developer utilizes an enhancement section to introduce custom logic within a SAP transaction. Using the enhancement framework, the code handles specific business rules that influence the processing of a sales order.

- **Verification:** Comprehensive testing is conducted to validate that the new functionality works harmoniously with existing SAP features, ensuring that custom enhancements fulfill business objectives without causing regressions.

User exits and customer exits prove indispensable for businesses leveraging SAP, providing the flexibility required to meet evolving business needs. Despite their power, developers must exercise caution, implementing exits in a manner that balances customization with the need for maintainability and future system updates.

Both user exits and customer exits reflect parallel philosophies to customization:

- **User Exits:** Provide straightforward hooks primarily for legacy applications, favoring procedural coding practices.

- **Customer Exits:** Offer a modular, object-oriented approach, affording greater integration across SAP's expansive module ecosystem.

Furthermore, in a landscape where new enhancement techniques such as BADIs and the Enhancement Framework are prevalent, user exits and customer exits continue to hold relevance, particularly in scenarios where legacy systems or precise SAP module compatibility is of concern.

A critical consideration when implementing these exits is adherence to SAP's enhancement best practices. Developers need to ensure encapsulation of custom logic through modular design patterns, thus allowing for coherent updates, maintenance, and debugging. This requirement underscores the importance of documentation, version control, and collaborative development practices, which are integral to successful long-term SAP enhancement strategies. By maintaining a disciplined approach, SAP development teams can create robust and flexible applications that adapt to the inevitable changes in business processes and technological evolution.

9.3 BADIs (Business Add-Ins)

Business Add-Ins (BADIs) represent a sophisticated SAP enhancement technique, offering unparalleled flexibility and robustness compared to traditional methods like user exits and customer exits. BADIs empower developers to implement custom logic in an object-oriented paradigm, fully aligned with contemporary software design principles. This section elucidates the fundamentals of BADIs, their implementation mechanisms, and detailed examples illustrating their versatile capabilities in SAP environments.

CHAPTER 9. SAP ENHANCEMENT OPTIONS AND USER EXITS

SAP introduced BADIs to address the growing complexity and demanding requirements of enterprise applications. They enable enhancements that are both modular and encapsulated, complying with object-oriented programming (OOP) principles. BADIs significantly extend the adaptability of standard SAP applications by allowing multiple simultaneous enhancements without compromising system integrity. This design inherently supports reusability and scalability, as well as a clear separation of standard and custom code.

At the heart of BADI implementation is the Interface Programming paradigm, where business-specific enhancements are achieved via well-structured interfaces. Here, BADIs play a pivotal role in extending and customizing SAP applications in a manner that remains decoupled from the core SAP codebase. This decoupling is essential for maintaining system integrity during upgrades and patches.

BADI Architecture:

- **Definition and Interface:** BADIs begin with the definition of an enhancement spot and its corresponding interface. SAP packages standard functionality within these enhancement spots, allowing clients to implement solutions through interfaces rather than altering base code directly.

- **Implementations:** Developers can create their implementations of these interfaces, providing the flexibility to adapt SAP processes precisely to business requirements. These implementations can coexist, allowing multiple customized behaviors for different scenarios or datasets.

- **Filter Criteria:** One of the most robust features of BADIs is the ability to execute different implementations based on filter conditions. This capability allows developers to dynamically select which BADI implementation to invoke at runtime, based on context such as organizational data or transaction type.

Creating and Implementing a BADI:

Developing a BADI in SAP involves several steps, from defining the BADI itself to implementing and testing it. This process emphasizes the importance of proper design and understanding of the business processes involved.

9.3. BADIS (BUSINESS ADD-INS)

- **BADI Definition:** Using the Enhancement Builder tool (Transaction SE18), a developer defines a BADI. They define filter-dependent or filter-independent BADIs. The interface specifies method signatures that encapsulate the enhancement logic.

```
INTERFACE if_ex_my_custom_badi.
  METHODS:
    custom_method
      IMPORTING
        iv_parameter TYPE string
      EXPORTING
        ev_result TYPE string.
ENDINTERFACE.
```

In this example, the interface if_ex_my_custom_badi outlines a method custom_method, essential for implementing the desired enhancement logic. The method accepts and returns string parameters, providing the foundation for custom business logic.

- **BADI Implementation:** Developers create implementations via Transaction SE19. They instantiate the interface in a concrete class, encapsulating the logic for process customization.

```
CLASS lcl_my_custom_badi DEFINITION
  INHERITING FROM cl_badi_base
  FINAL
  CREATE PUBLIC.
  PUBLIC SECTION.
    INTERFACES if_ev_my_custom_badi.
  PROTECTED SECTION.
  PRIVATE SECTION.
ENDCLASS.

CLASS lcl_my_custom_badi IMPLEMENTATION.
  METHOD if_ex_my_custom_badi~custom_method.
    ev_result = iv_parameter && ' processed'.
  ENDMETHOD.
ENDCLASS.
```

The class lcl_my_custom_badi implements if_ex_my_custom_badi, defining the custom logic for the method custom_method. Here, the code appends the word "processed" to the input parameter, demonstrating a basic string manipulation as part of the enhancement logic.

- **Activation and Testing:** Once implemented, the BADI must be activated, ensuring its availability in the context of the SAP environment. Rigorous testing in both development and quality testing systems is vital for validating that the BADI fulfills business expectations without disrupting standard operations.

Use Cases for BADIs:

BADIs serve a multitude of use cases, from enhancing data processing logic to customizing user interactions. Common scenarios include:

- **Business Validation:** Implement additional validation checks within transactional processes to enforce company-specific business rules. By leveraging BADIs, SAP solutions can dynamically adapt validation logic based on complex, rule-driven conditions.

- **Data Integration:** Use BADIs for seamless integration of SAP systems with external applications, ensuring that data processes are harmonized and continuous.

- **User Interface Enhancements:** BADIs can also extend the user interface, providing business-critical data views or additional decision-making tools. This capability is crucial for enterprises looking to enrich the user experience without overwhelming the core system with custom coding.

Advantages of BADIs:

BADIs offer significant advantages over their predecessors:

- **Object-Oriented Design:** The encapsulation and inheritance principles facilitate cleaner, maintainable, and scalable code structures.

- **Multiple Implementations:** The ability to create numerous implementations for a single BADI allows unparalleled flexibility, supporting diverse business processes under varying conditions without interference.

- **Upgrade-Proof:** BADIs maintain system compatibility with SAP updates, as enhancements are implemented separately from standard SAP code.

- **Dynamic Selection:** Filter criteria permit dynamic selection of BADI implementations, providing precise control over which functionality to apply under specific conditions.

Implications and Considerations:

Harnessing the power of BADIs requires an astute understanding of SAP architecture and business processes. Thoughtful implementation involves aligning BADI logic closely with business objectives while considering future scalability and maintenance:

- **Performance Concerns:** Ensure that BADI implementations are optimized to prevent performance impacts, particularly in high-transaction-volume scenarios.

- **Governance and Documentation:** Maintain clear documentation of BADI implementations to facilitate developer handoffs and future enhancement initiatives. This documentation is vital for supporting transparent governance processes in IT environments, outlining the rationale, functionality, and dependencies of each BADI.

- **Strategic Alignment:** Align BADI deployments with broader IT and business strategies. Understand the implications of enhancements on both existing and planned system landscapes to prevent architectural incongruence.

Business Add-Ins encapsulate the infinite potential for SAP customizations, enabling enterprises to remain agile and responsive in ever-changing business environments. Harnessing BADIs effectively necessitates an integrated approach combining technical expertise, business acumen, and strategic foresight. By embedding this flexible enhancement technique within the SAP framework, developers can craft solutions that not only fulfill immediate needs but advocate for sustained competitive advantage through continuous innovation and efficiency. As businesses continue to demand more from their ERP systems, BADIs stand poised as a cornerstone of adaptive, custom-fit SAP landscapes.

9.4 Enhancement Points and Sections

Enhancement points and enhancement sections are integral elements of the SAP Enhancement Framework, serving as pivotal constructs for extending the standard SAP system logic without altering the original code base. These mechanisms empower developers to insert custom code at predefined locations in SAP programs, enabling tailored system behavior that aligns with unique business requirements. This section delves deeply into the workings of enhancement points and sections, provides practical coding examples, and discusses best practices for their effective utilization.

Understanding Enhancement Points and Sections:

Enhancement points and sections provide strategic locations within SAP programs where developers can introduce custom modifications. These customization techniques are preferred in scenarios where businesses require specific adaptations of standard processes — such as integrating company-specific validations, augmenting processing logic, or customizing output formats — while maintaining the integrity and upgradeability of the SAP environment.

- **Enhancement Points:** These are designated spots within the source code where additional logic can be injected. Unlike other forms of modification, enhancement points allow for the inclusion of additional processing logic without requiring modifications to the original code. Enhancement points can be implemented in two ways: explicit or implicit.

Explicit Enhancement Points: Specifically defined in SAP by the standard developers, these points anticipate where custom logic might reasonably be inserted. Developers typically access them using pre-designated enhancement spots already embedded in the SAP system.

Implicit Enhancement Points: Generated automatically by the SAP kernel, these are available at established locations within the program (such as the start or end of a method, or before a return statement). The advantage of implicit enhancement points lies in their ubiquity, which grants developers increased flexibility in customizing standard programs.

- **Enhancement Sections:** These are similar to enhancement points but offer greater flexibility by replacing entire blocks of standard code rather than inserting additional processing logic before or after an existing sequence.

9.4. ENHANCEMENT POINTS AND SECTIONS

Case Study for Enhanced Understanding:

Consider a scenario where a company has a custom pricing calculation that must run in addition to standard SAP pricing logic. An explicit enhancement point could be used to integrate this requirement seamlessly. The business users specified this customization should occur after the standard price determination but before the final pricing is presented to the user.

Implementing an Enhancement with Enhancement Points:

The implementation of an enhancement using enhancement points involves several key steps, involving both system exploration and code integration:

- **Identifying Enhancement Points:** Navigate within the software repository to identify enhancement points that support desired modifications. The program explorer or code inspector tools are instrumental in surfacing explicit enhancements embedded by SAP. Developers will be able to search for enhancement points within the code base by using the transaction SE80 or SE24.

- **Creating Enhancement Implementation:** Leverage the Enhancement Builder (transaction SE20) to create a custom implementation of the enhancement point.

    Define an enhancement implementation within the context of an enhancement spot, as shown in the example:

```
ENHANCEMENT-POINT price_determination_spot SPOTS es_price_logic.
ENHANCEMENT-SECTION custom_price_logic_spot SPOTS es_price_logic
    STATIC.
  " Custom pricing calculations
  IF rd_price IS INITIAL.
    rd_price = custom_calculation_logic( rv_material, rv_quantity ).
  ENDIF.
END-ENHANCEMENT-SECTION.
```

In this example, 'price_determination_spot' is the enhancement point where custom logic is injected. Through the corresponding 'custom_price_logic_spot' section, the customized pricing logic integrates seamlessly with existing operations.

- **Testing and Validation:** As with any SAP customization, rigorous testing in both controlled and live environments is a critical step in validating enhancements. It is essential to ensure the modified logic behaves as expected and adheres to prescribed business rules without inadvertently affecting related processes or transactions.

Advantages of Using Enhancement Points and Sections:

The primary advantages include:

- **Non-Intrusive Customizations:** Enhancement points and sections offer a safe harbor for extending program logic by leaving the original code untouched, thereby promoting maintainable and upgrade-compatible enhancements.

- **Flexibility and Scalability:** These constructs enhance system adaptability by aligning process customizations with evolving business needs. Their dynamic nature facilitates the ready adaptation of new development requirements as business demands change.

- **Robustness and Reliability:** Unlike temporary workarounds or direct code modifications, enhancements made at designated points are durable. This durability ensures long-term compatibility with system updates and SAP patches, reducing maintenance overhead.

Best Practices:

Leveraging enhancement points and sections requires thoughtful consideration, particularly about system architecture, development requirements, and compliance with SAP and organizational standards:

- **Maintain Comprehensive Documentation:** Accurately document where enhancement points and sections occur, detailing the business logic, reason for the enhancement, and all connecting business process dependencies. This practice helps future development and supports organizational transparency.

- **Align with SAP Standards:** While crafting enhancement implementations, developers must adhere to SAP software engineering best practices, ensuring consistent naming conventions, clear code comments, and active version management strategies.

- **Ensure Intuitive Design:** Distinct enhancements should be self-contained and seamlessly integrated, balancing the need for custom functionality against the architectural integrity of the existing system.

- **Implement Robust Testing Strategies:** Rigorous testing encompassing unit testing, integration tests, and user acceptance tests are vital to confirm the alignment of the enhancement with business rules and processes.

Enhancements offered by enhancement points and sections remain in high demand within the SAP ecosystem, particularly as enterprises continue to evolve digitally amid constant market and industry changes. The enhancement framework maintains both systematorial and business logic integrity, enabling seamless integration across disparate operations. By effectively utilizing these SAP enhancement techniques, organizations gain substantial competitive advantages, reducing time-to-market for customized solutions, maintaining robust operational support, and overall improving responsiveness to customer and market needs. The strategic application of enhancement points and sections—whether to solve business-critical demand for information, processes, or system interoperability—forms a cornerstone of efficient and effective SAP architecture management today and into the future.

9.5 Implicit and Explicit Enhancements

Implicit and explicit enhancements are fundamental concepts within the SAP Enhancement Framework that provide predefined extension points in SAP programs. These enhancements enable developers to embed custom logic directly into SAP's standard processes, facilitating the seamless integration of company-specific functionalities. This section explores the detailed mechanics of implicit and explicit enhancements, distinguishing their operational principles, use cases, and implementation strategies.

Understanding the SAP Enhancement Framework:

The SAP Enhancement Framework was developed as part of SAP's shift towards more open and extensible software systems, allowing for efficient adaptations without modifying the core codebase. By design, this framework provides hooks—implicit and explicit enhancements—that serve as touchpoints for integrating custom extensions into SAP applications.

- **Implicit Enhancements:** Implicit enhancements are automatically provided by SAP at strategic locations within the code. These points offer the opportunity to introduce custom logic without predefined opportunities explicitly detailed by SAP developers. They arise at the beginning or end of methods, forms, and function modules, as well as at other strategic transitions, like right before or after SELECT queries. Implicit enhancements are not visible in the source code editor unless specifically enabled, offering flexible customization options at nearly every logical block of code.

- **Explicit Enhancements:** Contrasting with implicit enhancements, explicit enhancements are predefined by SAP, where specific enhancement points and enhancement sections are embedded in the code. These points are strategically chosen by SAP, based on widespread customer scenarios and anticipated business extensions. Unlike their implicit counterparts, explicit enhancements can be a planned part of the development, clearly marked in the code as enhancement spots where extensions can be purposefully integrated.

Separating the Subtleties of Implicit and Explicit Enhancements:

While both implicit and explicit enhancements serve the broader goal of system extensibility, they cater to different customization strategies due to their nature and placement within the system.

- **Locational Flexibility:**

9.5. IMPLICIT AND EXPLICIT ENHANCEMENTS

- Implicit enhancements offer ubiquity, appearing at standard logical division points within the code, ensuring that developers can access typical transaction segments globally, rendering the system highly adaptable to almost any specialized requirement.

- Explicit enhancements are precise, appearing only where explicitly determined by SAP developers, thereby making them optimal for planned adaptations aligned with well-understood business processes.

- **Implementation Strategy:**

- Implicit enhancements require developers to identify potential enhancement points within the broader program architecture, leveraging specific transaction keys (e.g., SE24, SE80) and enhancement settings to access and modify code.

- Explicit enhancements, on the other hand, mandate no additional identification effort since such points are visible and ready for configuration by default.

Example Implementation: Implicit Enhancements:

Consider a scenario where a company requires additional logging information every time a financial transaction entry is saved. The implicit enhancement could be added at the end of the transaction saving method to automatically insert the desired logging logic.

```
ENHANCEMENT 1 ZFIN_TRX_SAVE
  SPOTS es_implicit_saves.
  DATA log_info TYPE string.
  log_info = 'Transaction Saved: ' && sy-datum.
  CALL FUNCTION 'WRITE_LOG_ENTRY'
    EXPORTING
      message = log_info.
ENDENHANCEMENT.
```

This snippet demonstrates using an implicit enhancement point at the transaction save block, dynamically inserting a log entry each time a transaction is saved. By leveraging the automatic presence of implicit enhancements, this customization is introduced with minimal disruption to program flow.

Example Implementation: Explicit Enhancements:

Consider an example where specific validations need to be implemented during the order processing sequence after form input is finalized. An explicit enhancement point explicitly can manage this need.

```
ENHANCEMENT-POINT order_validation_check SPOTS es_order_mgmt.
" Perform custom validation logic for order
IF NOT validate_order_data( order ).
   MESSAGE e001 WITH 'Order validation failed'.
   EXIT.
ENDIF.
END-ENHANCEMENT-POINT.
```

Here, the enhancement point order_validation_check is already embedded at a logical control point anticipated by SAP. By implementing validation logic here, developers ensure that order data meets organizational requirements every time the transaction progresses through this phase.

Advantages and Challenges:

- **Advantages:**

    - **Separation of Concerns:** Enhancements promote clear separation between standard application logic and custom logic, fostering maintenance, scalability, and system consistency.

    - **Upgrade Stability:** By maintaining core program codebase integrity, enhancements remain stable across upgrades, reducing potential rework during software updates.

    - **Comprehensive Integration:** Implicit and explicit enhancements together offer developers flexibility, ensuring that no matter the need, logical access points are available for customization.

- **Challenges:**

    - **Complexity and Management Overhead:** With power comes complexity—managing multiple enhancements across vast applications necessitates proper version management and documentation to prevent internal conflicts.

9.5. IMPLICIT AND EXPLICIT ENHANCEMENTS

- **Risk of Misuse:** Misapplication or overuse of enhancement points can lead to performance issues, added complexity, and hard-to-maintain code if systemic integration principles are ignored.

Best Practices for Enhancement Implementation:

- **Start with a Detailed Analysis:** Understand the core operation flow first and identify where customization points must logically integrate into the system.

- **Utilize Robust Design Constructs:** Define enhancements that are modular and encapsulated, ensuring they align with architectural best practices and support future scaling efforts.

- **Limitative, Not Exceeding:** Focus on ensuring enhancement logic executes responsibly—enhancements should not attempt to overstep SAP core functions, which could otherwise maintain data integrity and application consistency.

- **Coordinate Thorough Testing:** Comprehensive testing pathways should validate enhancements. Regression tests must be unsparingly applied to ensure business processes remain undistorted.

- **Documentation and Code Clarity:** Maintain accurate documentation of all enhancements and their impact to avoid hidden technical debt or reliance on individual developer knowledge over time.

Implicit and explicit enhancements stand as pillars of adaptability within the SAP programming environment. Their design ensures enterprises can infuse individualized business logic without compromising SAP standards or upgrade pathways. These enhancements grant systems resilience and flexibility, ensuring a robust response to evolving business demands over time. Therefore, by methodically applying these enhancements, organizations can achieve superior alignment, drawing potent value from their SAP investment and sustaining competitive advantage in the dynamic enterprise application landscape.

9.6 Switch Framework and Enhancement Implementation

The Switch Framework within the SAP system comprises a crucial infrastructure component that provides structured control over custom enhancements, allowing for their systematic activation or deactivation based on business requirements. This feature is instrumental in managing complexity, as it enables enterprises to adapt SAP landscapes efficiently while maintaining high levels of flexibility for business innovations. Leveraging the Switch Framework for enhancement implementation ensures adaptability in evolving business landscapes with minimal disruption to core operations.

Understanding the Switch Framework:

The Switch Framework is designed to offer selective control over the capabilities and features in the SAP environment. It achieves this by allowing developers to turn certain enhancements or modules on or off using switch objects—a fundamental aspect of SAP NetWeaver.

- **Switch Objects:** These are the main building blocks of the Switch Framework, forming logical constructs that define what functionality can be managed. A switch object controls the behavior of specific software layers or components, making adjustments to system capabilities as easy as flipping a switch based on configuration settings.

- **Business Functions:** Business functions refer to bundles of functionality that can be toggled as a unit through the Switch Framework. By grouping related enhancements or capabilities, business functions allow system administrators to adaptively cater to evolving business processes or phases of deployment.

- **Switchable Components:** Anything within the SAP ecosystem that supports a switch object can be enabled or disabled through the framework, including function groups, classes, methods, and individual code blocks.

Implementing Enhancements with the Switch Framework:

9.6. SWITCH FRAMEWORK AND ENHANCEMENT IMPLEMENTATION

Implementing enhancements using the Switch Framework involves a strategic approach, addressing not only the technical requirements but also aligning system changes with broader organizational goals. This implementation encompasses the development and management of switch objects and how they get associated with specific enhancements.

1. **Creation of Switch Objects:** The first step in managing enhancements with the Switch Framework is creating switch objects. Use the transaction SFW1 to define new switch objects, specifying the components, capabilities, and preliminary configurations needed to manage new or existing functionalities.

2. **Association with Business Functions:** After creating the switch objects, these are associated with business functions using transaction SFW2. Business functions group related functional advancements or enhancements under a single umbrella, providing structure for activation.

```
REPORT zswitch_example.

" Define a switch object for enhancements
DATA: lv_switched(1) TYPE c VALUE ' '.

IF swc_switch_active( 'YOUR_SWITCH_OBJECT' ) EQ abap_true.
  lv_switched = 'X'.
ENDIF.

IF lv_switched = 'X'.
  " Enhancement logic when switch is active
  PERFORM enhanced_processing.
ELSE.
  " Standard processing when switch is inactive
  PERFORM standard_processing.
ENDIF.

FORM enhanced_processing.
  WRITE: / 'Enhanced functionality active'.
ENDFORM.

FORM standard_processing.
  WRITE: / 'Standard functionality active'.
ENDFORM.
```

In this example, swc_switch_active checks if a specific switch object—'YOUR_SWITCH_OBJECT'—is active, thus altering the executed process path accordingly. This flexibility underscores the framework's ability to adapt system behavior based on preset configurations without needing significant changes in the code structure.

3. **Activation and Testing:** System administrators utilize transaction SFW5 to activate business functions—making enhancements available in production systems where necessary. Proper planning ensures synchronization between code deployment and functional activation, guarding against inconsistencies.

4. **Maintenance and Management:** Given that business needs evolve, managing active enhancements in live systems requires diligent maintenance. The Switch Framework aids in decisions about when to deprecate or shelve certain functionalities, supporting strategic alignment with long-term business objectives.

Benefits of Using the Switch Framework:

The Switch Framework proffers multifaceted benefits that extend beyond simplistic functional control, enhancing both technical and business operations.

- **Structured Adaptability:** By controlling the activation and deactivation of system features, this framework provides measured adaptability, allowing businesses to transition through periodic changes or new strategic directions efficiently.

- **System Integrity:** By toggling functionalities based on business requirements, the Switch Framework ensures system stability, allaying risks associated with over-modification and potential feature-breaking changes.

- **Deployment Flexibility:** Supporting phased deployments, the framework accommodates multi-stage rollouts by enabling iterative activation of new features or enhancements, matching project timelines or phased business integrations.

Best Practices for Enhancement Implementation Using the Switch Framework:

9.6. SWITCH FRAMEWORK AND ENHANCEMENT IMPLEMENTATION

1. **Align with Business Strategy:** Ensure that the controlling structures within the Switch Framework align seamlessly with organizational and IT strategies, supporting proactive capabilities management instead of reactive decision-making.

2. **Plan for Lifecycle Management:** Define clear lifecycle states for switch objects and business functions, planning for iterative improvements, phased shutdowns, or necessary deprecations within strategic planning.

3. **Document Key Structures:** Maintain comprehensive documentation regarding each switch object's definition, intent, and business function associations. This ensures transparent governance processes and effective communication within the IT landscape.

4. **Incorporate Robust Testing Framework:** Systematically test all function switch toggles, including their cross-functional impacts and integration points. Ensure regular validation in both simulation and live scenarios to minimize the risk of unintended consequences.

5. **Facilitate Cross-Organizational Collaboration:** Coordinate enhancements implementation across various stakeholders within the organization, from product teams to business users, promoting shared understanding and coherent decision-making.

Strategic Implications and Considerations:

The Switch Framework for enhancement implementation embodies SAP's vision of adaptive ERP systems, providing a holistic means for managing business process innovations with precision. The framework ensures that enhancements are not merely patches or alterations but are integral adaptations of business logic, systematically applied—mirroring both technical and business complexity with accuracy.

For organizations, employing the framework allows IT and business leaders strategic latitude, offering timely avenues for responding to competitive pressures, emerging opportunities, and regulatory shifts. Empowered by this structured facilitation of change management, enterprises can position their SAP systems as formidable enablers of innovation, seamlessly integrating new functionalities under structured governance models that support sustained growth and market advantage.

Harnessing the Switch Framework within the SAP environment represents an evolution in managing ERP complexities—shaping strategic pathways that align technology with business needs even amid heightened operational demands. By effectively integrating the framework mastery into daily practices, enterprises secure an agile enterprise resource planning system capable of steering and supporting decisive digital improvements both present and future.

9.7 Best Practices for Implementing Enhancements

Implementing enhancements within SAP systems necessitates a strategic approach that harmonizes technical proficiency with organizational objectives. The vast capabilities offered by the SAP Enhancement Framework, including techniques like user exits, customer exits, BADIs, and enhancement spots, provide developers with potent tools for tailoring SAP environments. However, careful execution, alignment with business needs, and adherence to best practices are crucial to ensure enhancements maintain system stability and scalability. In this section, we detail the best practices for implementing SAP enhancements effectively, focusing on methodology, strategic foresight, and comprehensive execution.

- **Align Enhancements with Business Objectives:**

  Aligning enhancements with clearly defined business objectives forms the backbone of any successful SAP implementation strategy. Developers must engage with business stakeholders to comprehensively understand process requirements and core objectives behind the desired enhancements.

  - **Requirements Gathering:** Perform thorough requirements-gathering sessions involving key stakeholders to detail explicit business needs, ensuring enhancements address specific operational gaps or opportunities for improvement.

9.7. BEST PRACTICES FOR IMPLEMENTING ENHANCEMENTS

- **Business Process Analysis:** Use process mapping techniques to uncover precise enhancement points within workflows. Mapping tools help visualize current processes and inform where enhancements can provide maximum value or efficiency gains.
- **Strategic Fit:** Evaluate proposed enhancements against strategic company objectives, ensuring alignment with long-term organizational vision, compliance standards, and market positioning.

- **Emphasize Modularity and Reusability:**

  Encapsulating enhancement logic into modular, reusable components ensures that solutions are flexible, maintainable, and adaptable to future changes. Adhering to modular design patterns enhances code quality and facilitates iterative improvements.

  - **Encapsulated Logic:** Implement encapsulated methods or classes containing all enhancement logic, minimizing dependencies on core units and promoting reusability across different modules or processes.
  - **Interface Implementation:** Leverage interfaces within BADIs or enhancement spots to promote consistent coding practices and facilitate easier integration with other system parts. By providing adaptable entry points, interfaces standardize how custom logic interacts with standard processes.
  - **Reusable Components:** Design enhancements using reusable components, allowing for adaptation to new projects or requirements without substantial redevelopment. Avoid hardcoding values or logic specific to single scenarios to foster component flexibility.

- **Maintain System Consistency and Stability:**

  System stability is paramount when implementing enhancements. Careful consideration must be given to how custom logic interacts with existing processes, ensuring enhancements integrate seamlessly without causing disruptions.

- **Pre-Enhancement Impact Assessment:** Conduct impact assessments before implementing enhancements to ascertain potential effects on related processes or data integrity. Identify areas where enhancements may influence existing operations, resources, or transactions.

- **Adherence to Standards:** Follow SAP and organizational coding standards to enforce uniformity across all enhancement implementations, supporting consistent readability, understanding, and maintainability.

- **Regular Reviews and Audits:** Establish regular reviews and audits of enhancement logic and processes to identify opportunities for optimization and to ensure alignment with updated standards and best practices.

- **Comprehensive Testing and Validation:**

  Thorough testing and validation processes are indispensable for verifying that enhancements function as intended across varying scenarios and environments. A robust testing strategy safeguards against unexpected system behavior or performance degradation.

  - **Unit Testing:** Develop detailed unit tests for each enhancement component, validating individual functionality under edge conditions and typical use cases to prevent integration-level failures.

  - **Integration Testing:** Implement integration tests to verify the seamless operation of enhancements within larger processes. Test interactions between enhancements and existing SAP modules to confirm connectivity and operational logic.

  - **User Acceptance Testing (UAT):** Conduct user acceptance testing to validate that enhancements meet business user expectations and integrate effectively into daily operations. Collect feedback from end-users to refine functionality and user experience.

  - **Performance Testing:** Assess the performance of enhancements within typical workload contexts, ensuring they do not introduce processing slowdowns or resource bottlenecks.

- **Governance and Documentation:**

  Comprehensive documentation and governance structures underpin sustainable enhancement practices, providing transparency and informed decision-making capabilities.

  - **Formal Documentation:** Document all aspects of enhancement projects, including business requirements, technical specifications, impact analyses, testing procedures, and deployment strategies. Thorough documentation supports future development and facilitates informed enhancement evolution.

  - **Version Control:** Utilize version control systems to manage code changes, enhancements, and configurations systematically. Effective version management supports traceability, rollback capabilities, and collaborative development efforts.

  - **Enhancement Registers:** Maintain detailed enhancement registers within the organization to track implemented enhancements, their purposes, associations, and dependencies. Registers shall act as central repositories of enhancement knowledge, supporting continuity across projects and personnel changes.

  - **Governance Frameworks:** Establish governance frameworks to oversee enhancement implementation, ensuring compliance with organizational standards, resource allocation efficiency, and alignment with business objectives.

- **Facilitate Cross-functional Collaboration:**

  Successful enhancement implementation involves extensive collaboration across multiple departments and functions. Engaging key stakeholders ensures enhancements complement broader strategic initiatives and deliver maximum value.

  - **Cross-Functional Teams:** Assemble cross-functional teams involving technical experts, business analysts, project managers, and end-users to engage in requirement gathering, solution design, and validation as a cohesive unit.

– **Regular Communications:** Conduct frequent communication sessions with stakeholders to update progress, surface challenges, and align deliverables with evolving requirements or changes in business strategy.

– **Feedback Loops:** Create feedback loops during testing phases to incorporate suggestions from business users or other development teams, ensuring that the end solution holistically fulfills user needs and expectations.

- **Plan for Future Updates and Scalability:**

Building enhancements with scalability and future rewritability in mind ensures they remain adaptable to evolving requirements and technology landscapes.

– **Scalability Factors:** Design enhancements considering potential future scaling needs. Architects should account for anticipated increases in transaction volumes, new data sources, and integration with potential systems or platforms.

– **Refactoring Pathways:** Allow for the potential refactoring of enhancement logic as business priorities or technology evolve. Clear coding and documentation facilitate smooth refactoring processes that align enhancements with new technological directions.

– **Continuous Improvement:** Commit to continuous improvement initiatives, regularly evaluating enhancements for opportunities to optimize, refactor, or expand their functionality according to emerging best practices or user feedback.

Conclusion:

Enacting SAP enhancements with best practices ensures systems remain stable, flexible, and scalable, fulfilling business needs while supporting ongoing innovation. By following these structured guidelines,

9.7. BEST PRACTICES FOR IMPLEMENTING ENHANCEMENTS

developers manage enhancements efficiently, respecting both technical constraints and business imperatives. Through meticulous alignment with organizational strategy, adherence to robust coding practices, diligent testing methodologies, active documentation, and collaborative engagement, effective enhancement practices future-proof SAP systems, aiding in long-term enterprise success. With the ability to rapidly deploy new features, address emergent business opportunities, and pivot quickly in response to change, organizations secure transformative capabilities and market leadership using adaptable and well-implemented SAP enhancements.

Chapter 10

Best Practices and Performance Optimization

This chapter focuses on strategies for enhancing the quality and efficiency of ABAP programming through best practices and performance optimization. It covers adherence to coding standards and the importance of consistent naming conventions to improve code clarity and maintainability. Techniques for optimizing database access and memory management are discussed to ensure resource-efficient applications. The chapter also introduces tools for performance analysis, guiding developers in identifying and mitigating bottlenecks. By exploring program flow optimizations and parallel processing techniques, developers can achieve significant performance gains. Emphasis is placed on rigorous code reviews and quality assurance to uphold high standards in ABAP development.

10.1 Coding Standards and Naming Conventions

Adhering to coding standards and using consistent naming conventions is critical in software development, including ABAP (Advanced Business Application Programming), the programming language used in SAP systems. These practices significantly enhance code readability, maintainability, and collaboration among development teams. This section delves into various coding standards and naming conventions that should be followed in ABAP programming and explains their importance in generating reliable, understandable, and scalable code.

Coding standards are a set of guidelines or rules that determine programming style, practices, and methods for a particular programming language. In ABAP, coding standards ensure uniformity and consistency in code which is crucial for seamless project management, especially in environments with multiple contributors. An ABAP coding standard often encompasses various aspects such as indentation, comment styles, program naming, and error handling.

First, indentation is vital in making code more readable. Each block of code should be indented uniformly to reflect its logical hierarchy. For instance, inside conditionals and loops, the statements should be indented uniformly to show their membership to that particular block. Appropriate use of indentation provides a visual cue to programmers as they navigate through the program.

Comments are another vital component of coding standards. Properly used comments can significantly enhance the understandability of code by providing explanations for complex logic, rationale for decisions, or the purpose of particular code blocks. In ABAP, comments can be added using an asterisk (*) at the beginning of the line or by using double quotes (") following a piece of code on the same line. It is important to avoid excessive commenting which can clutter the code. Comments should only be used to provide necessary insight that cannot be gleaned merely from reading the code itself.

Another significant aspect of ABAP coding standards is the use of language constructs that promote clarity and efficiency. For instance, expressions like IF ...ELSEIF ...ENDIF should be used instead of complex

10.1. CODING STANDARDS AND NAMING CONVENTIONS

nested IF statements which can make the code hard to follow. Similarly, using loops like DO or WHILE should be preferred over using PERFORM statements whenever possible to maintain structured programming practices.

Error handling is another cornerstone of robust coding standards. ABAP provides several mechanisms to handle exceptions and errors efficiently. Using standardized error texts, capturing exceptions with CATCH or TRY statements, and logging error contexts where applicable, are widely recommended practices. Proper error handling not only prevents potential run-time issues but also contributes towards making code more robust and user-friendly.

Naming conventions constitute another significant component of programming best practices in ABAP. Proper naming styles enhance code readability and comprehension, particularly when developers who are unfamiliar with the codebase must understand and modify existing code. Names should be descriptive, concise, and consistent across the application.

With the naming of variables, constants, methods, and classes, specific rules should be adhered to. For instance, variables should typically begin with a lower-case letter and use camelCase, while constants should be all caps with underscores separating words. For example:

```
DATA: lv_employeeName TYPE string,
      lv_employeeID TYPE i.
CONSTANTS: c_maxEmployees TYPE i VALUE 100.
```

Here, lv_employeeName and lv_employeeID follow the lower camelCase pattern for variable names, providing an immediate understanding that these variables are local. On the other hand, c_maxEmployees appears in uppercase, denoting it as a constant which inherently suggests immutability.

When it comes to classes and methods, Pascal Case is often recommended. Class names should start with an upper-case letter, while methods typically follow the camelCase style. For example:

```
CLASS LCL_Employee DEFINITION.
  PUBLIC SECTION.
    METHODS: retrieveEmployeeData,
             updateEmploymentStatus.
ENDCLASS.
```

The above convention establishes a clear distinction between classes and methods, aiding in the identification of different code elements swiftly.

In domain-specific contexts within ABAP, such as BAPI (Business Application Programming Interface), realizing consistent nomenclature across APIs is imperative. Uniform naming conventions enable developers to form a clear association between a given BAPI and its corresponding functionality, diminishing confusion and reducing errors.

In addition to the base guidelines regarding naming conventions, ABAP's language scope also extends to encouraging the use of prefixes or suffixes that denote the purpose, type, or nature of elements. For instance, prefixes like gt_, lt_, iv_, ev_, and lv_ are employed to indicate tables, work areas, import parameters, export parameters, and local variables, respectively. Here are examples showcasing this approach:

```
TABLES: gt_employeeTable.
DATA: lt_selectedEmployees TYPE TABLE OF EMPLOYEE,
    lv_salaryIncrement TYPE p LENGTH 8 DECIMALS 2,
    iv_departmentCode TYPE char4.
```

This structured naming facilitates quick comprehension concerning the role of each variable or parameter within a given program.

By instituting uniformly enforced coding standards and naming conventions, organizations can significantly improve the lifecycle management of ABAP applications. However, the correct application of these standards and conventions requires continuous practice and peer reviews. Code reviews serve not only as a measure to ensure adherence to these standards but also as a platform for sharing best practices and learning across the development team. Through rigorous code review processes, developers can identify discrepancies, optimize logic, simplify complex constructs, and enhance code performance.

Moreover, software development environments can further reinforce these practices via automated tools that check for coding guideline violations. Such tools can integrate seamlessly into the development lifecycle, allowing developers to receive immediate feedback on code compliance issues before they merge code into the broader codebase.

The symbiosis of effective coding standards and naming conventions lays the foundation for high-quality, maintainable, and scalable ABAP software. As organizations strive for innovative solutions to meet business demands, these practices serve an integral role in fostering efficient, collaborative, and adaptable development processes. Adhering to these principles not only ensures immediate gains in code quality but also sets the stage for long-term success by cultivating a culture of precision, clarity, and excellence in ABAP programming.

10.2 Efficient Database Access Techniques

Efficient database access techniques are critical in ensuring optimal performance and responsiveness of ABAP applications. As applications often rely on data retrieval and storage operations, poorly optimized database interactions can become a major bottleneck affecting overall system efficiency. This section explores key principles and techniques for optimizing database access in ABAP, focusing on SELECT statements, indexing, and buffering strategies that enhance performance while ensuring data integrity and consistency.

The SELECT statement is one of the fundamental operations for interacting with databases in ABAP. To maximize efficiency, it is crucial to retrieve only the necessary data. This involves selecting specific fields rather than all fields of a table, and filtering records using WHERE clauses to limit the result set. For instance, consider a scenario where only employee names and IDs are needed from the employee database:

```
SELECT employee_id name
  FROM employee_table
  INTO TABLE @DATA(employee_list)
  WHERE department = 'HR'.
```

In this example, by specifying only the required fields in the SELECT clause and filtering using the WHERE clause, the application efficiently retrieves the necessary data without processing excess information.

Indexing is another powerful technique that significantly improves database access times. An index creates a sorted data structure which enhances the speed of data retrieval operations. In ABAP, creating indexes on commonly queried fields, particularly those involved in WHERE clauses, can expedite data lookups. However, it's vital to strike a balance as excessive indexing may have adverse effects, such as increased storage and maintenance overhead and potential degradation of write performance. Therefore, careful analysis and profiling should be conducted before implementing indexes.

For example, if frequent queries are performed based on the employee department, indexing the 'department' field in the employee_table can drastically reduce access times.

Understanding and leveraging database buffering can also lead to substantial performance improvements, especially in scenarios involving repetitive access to static or infrequently updated data. Buffering techniques maintain copies of table data in the application server memory, reducing repeated database calls. ABAP supports various types of buffering: single-record, generic, and fully buffered. The decision to buffer a table should be based on an evaluation of its update frequency, size, and the nature of queries.

Consider using fully buffered tables when the data is read-only and rarely updated across application context. However, caution must be advised as fully buffered tables can lead to inconsistencies if concurrent updates occur.

It is also important to utilize the appropriate type of JOIN operation for multi-table queries. ABAP offers different JOIN types such as INNER JOIN, LEFT OUTER JOIN, and RIGHT OUTER JOIN, each serving a distinct purpose. Refer to the following example where INNER JOIN is appropriately used to connect employee and department tables:

```
SELECT e~employee_id e~name d~department_name
  FROM employee_table as e
  INNER JOIN department_table as d
  ON e~department_id = d~department_id
  INTO TABLE @DATA(employee_details).
```

In scenarios demanding data summarization, the GROUP BY clause is essential. However, using it indiscriminately can escalate processing time. When combined with appropriate filtering and indexing strategies, GROUP BY operations can be optimized, significantly reducing the processing load on the database server.

Advanced techniques, like using Native SQL or AMDP (ABAP Man-

10.2. EFFICIENT DATABASE ACCESS TECHNIQUES

aged Database Procedures), can also be harnessed to further optimize performance. While Open SQL in ABAP is database-independent, utilizing Native SQL can leverage specific database capabilities and optimizations that Open SQL might not provide. Similarly, AMDPs allow executing SQL Script or Native SQL directly on databases like SAP HANA, utilizing in-database optimizations and returning results efficiently.

In some use cases involving complex calculations or transformations on a vast amount of data, moving logic to the database through stored procedures could yield performance benefits by reducing data transferred between the application server and database. This strategy, however, demands a careful evaluation to prevent increased coupling between database-specific logic and the application layer.

Batch processing of database operations is also a vital strategy, especially for mass data manipulation. Transactions like UPDATE, INSERT, and DELETE should be batched whenever possible. This minimizes the number of times the database is hit, resulting in reduced latency and improved throughput.

Consider the case where adjustments to employee salaries need to be executed for an entire department:

```
MODIFY employee_table FROM TABLE lt_salary_adjustments.
```

Here, a bulk modification approach minimizes resource consumption compared to individual update statements.

Concurrency control is pivotal in ensuring data integrity when multiple operations require access to the same data sets. ABAP offers locking mechanisms like ENQUEUE and DEQUEUE to manage concurrent database access. These locks ensure that data is not compromised by conflicting operations, yet must be used judiciously to prevent bottlenecks and deadlocks.

Finally, the use of performance analysis tools in identifying bottlenecks and optimizing database access cannot be overstated. SAP provides tools such as SQL Trace (transaction ST05) that track and analyze database access patterns, pinpointing inefficient queries, or highlighting missing indexes. By leveraging these insights, developers can iteratively refine their database access strategies.

Adopting efficient database access techniques in ABAP programming is instrumental in driving application performance. Through the diligent use of optimized SELECT statements, strategic indexing, prudent buffering, appropriate JOIN operations, batching, and leveraging of performance analysis tools, developers can substantially reduce database access time and ensure responsive, robust ABAP applications. By embedding these best practices within the development lifecycle, organizations can achieve enhanced execution efficiency, fulfilling business requirements with precision and reliability.

10.3 Memory Management and Internal Table Handling

Effective memory management and internal table handling in ABAP are paramount to the performance and scalability of SAP applications. Efficient use of memory resources ensures applications run smoothly, meeting performance benchmarks and minimizing resource constraints. This section explores the principles of memory management in ABAP, delving into strategies for optimizing internal table management, minimizing memory consumption, and adopting best practices that cater to efficient data processing.

In ABAP programming, internal tables serve as dynamic arrays used to store and manipulate data in the application server's memory. They are indispensable for temporary data storage during program execution. However, without mindful handling, internal tables can consume significant memory resources, especially when dealing with large datasets, leading to potential performance degradation.

To efficiently manage memory in ABAP, developers should start by choosing appropriate data types for internal table fields to optimize memory usage. ABAP offers fixed-length and variable-length data types, each with specific memory allocation characteristics. For example, use numeric types (such as INT4 or DEC) and packed numbers PACKED for calculations and avoid using overly large types unless necessary.

Consider the following example, which demonstrates the importance of selecting an appropriate data type:

10.3. MEMORY MANAGEMENT AND INTERNAL TABLE HANDLING

```
DATA: lt_employee_data TYPE TABLE OF employee,
      lw_employee_data TYPE employee,
      l_salary TYPE p LENGTH 8 DECIMALS 2.
```

Here, l_salary is defined with the packed number type, economizing memory space compared to using a less efficient type such as FLOAT.

Defining internal tables with specific keys is another practice that affects memory and processing performance. Keys determine the uniqueness of rows, aiding in operations like searching, sorting, and deleting duplicates. While the NON-UNIQUE KEY is commonly used for flexibility, specifying UNIQUE KEYS can save memory by preventing duplicate entries and improving data integrity.

When dealing with internal tables, a pivotal aspect of memory efficiency is using appropriate table types: STANDARD, HASHED, and SORTED tables. Each type is optimized for specific operations:

- STANDARD TABLES allow generic use, supporting simple linear searches. They should be used when insertion order matters, while searches and deletions do not demand high efficiency.

- HASHED TABLES are optimized for key-based access, providing constant-time complexity for lookups, making them ideal when frequent searches are required, but elements cannot be sorted or indexed using non-unique keys.

- SORTED TABLES maintain elements in a sorted order, enabling binary searches, which are faster than linear searches. Use sorted tables when data order is important, with unique or non-unique keys facilitating access speed.

Consider the following example, illustrating different table types:

```
TYPES:
  BEGIN OF employee,
    employee_id TYPE int4,
    name TYPE string,
    salary TYPE p LENGTH 8 DECIMALS 2,
  END OF employee.

DATA: lt_std_table TYPE STANDARD TABLE OF employee WITH NON-UNIQUE
        KEY employee_id,
      lt_hashed_table TYPE HASHED TABLE OF employee WITH UNIQUE KEY
        employee_id,
```

```
lt_sorted_table TYPE SORTED TABLE OF employee WITH UNIQUE KEY
    employee_id.
```

Optimizing operations like reading, inserting, or deleting entries necessitates understanding these table differences and selecting the type that best meets the use case requirements.

Another construct that aids memory efficiency is the utilization of field symbols and data references as they provide more direct data manipulation. Field symbols function like pointers, allowing developers to perform operations without duplicating data, thereby conserving memory.

For example, instead of copying table entries to a work area before processing, field symbols can be employed as follows:

```
FIELD-SYMBOLS: <fs_employee> TYPE employee.

LOOP AT lt_employee_data ASSIGNING <fs_employee>.
    <fs_employee>-salary = <fs_employee>-salary * 1.05.
ENDLOOP.
```

Here, <fs_employee> acts as a reference to each row, enabling in-place modifications that are more memory efficient.

Data references, on the other hand, are used to dynamically allocate and manage memory. They provide a similar utility to field symbols but offer additional control through explicit dereferencing. Data references are particularly useful when dealing with complex data structures requiring dynamic memory allocation.

In addition to structural efficiencies, emptying and releasing unused resources is crucial. The FREE statement can be employed to explicitly release memory allocated to internal tables when further use is not anticipated:

```
FREE lt_employee_data.
```

Internally, this operation reclaims memory from the table but retains its description, allowing it to be reallocated efficiently if required subsequently.

Furthermore, managing the lifecycle of internal tables requires an understanding of their scope. Defining tables within localized contexts or subroutines (e.g., within FORM or FUNCTION MODULE) allows for automatic garbage collection, promoting memory conservation upon exit of these routines.

Transaction-intensive applications benefit from additional measures employing SAP's memory monitoring tools such as ST02 (Buffer Monitor) and ST06 (Operating System Monitor) to observe the usage patterns, identifying any misguided memory allocation that could be optimized.

To summarize, memory management and internal table handling in ABAP programming heavily influence the performance and scalability of applications. By adhering to best practices like selecting suitable data types, applying the correct table types, using keys wisely, and leveraging field symbols and data references, developers can significantly reduce memory usage and enhance performance. These tactics, combined with proactive memory monitoring and management, facilitate efficient data processing and resource conservation, creating resilient SAP solutions capable of handling complex business demands with ease.

10.4 Using Performance Analysis Tools

The quality and efficiency of ABAP programs can be significantly enhanced by employing performance analysis tools. These tools play a vital role in identifying performance bottlenecks, pinpointing inefficient code paths, and providing insights into system utilization, thus enabling developers to optimize their applications effectively. This section provides an overview of essential performance analysis tools available in SAP, elaborating on their functionalities and practical applications.

One of the cornerstone tools for performance analysis in ABAP is the Runtime Analysis transaction (SE30). The Runtime Analysis tool is designed to monitor ABAP programs and measure various execution metrics, such as processing time, database call frequency, and memory consumption. This tool enables developers to investigate specific sections of code and analyze their performance footprint.

To utilize Runtime Analysis effectively, developers need to enable the tool either by executing it directly from the SE30 transaction or integrating it within an ABAP program via the BREAK-POINT and BREAK statements. The tool supports detailed investigation by breaking down execution times across different components, such as the database, internal tables, or specific function modules.

Consider an example where a comprehensive Runtime Analysis is executed to profile an ABAP report.

```
REPORT z_performance_test.

* Sample code for demonstration
DATA: lt_output TYPE TABLE OF string.
FIELD-SYMBOLS: <fs_output> TYPE string.

START-OF-SELECTION.
  PERFORM load_data.

FORM load_data.
  LOOP AT lt_output ASSIGNING <fs_output>.
    * Simulate data processing
    <fs_output> = <fs_output> && ' processed'.
  ENDLOOP.
ENDFORM.
```

After executing this program, developers can go to SE30, specify the transaction or report name, and start capturing performance data. Upon completion, detailed statistics are available for examination, revealing which operations consume the most resources.

Another invaluable tool is the SQL Trace (Transaction ST05). SQL Trace offers deep insights into SQL statements executed against the database. By tracing these statements, developers can identify expensive queries, analyze their execution plans, and evaluate the actual runtime performance.

Consider a situation where a particular SELECT query in an ABAP program performs poorly:

```
SELECT * FROM employee_table
  INTO TABLE lt_employees
  WHERE department = 'IT'.
```

By activating SQL Trace just before executing this query and reviewing the trace afterwards, developers gain visibility into the exact SQL operation executed, including metadata such as execution time and index usage. Analyzing this information allows developers to refine the query, e.g., adding appropriate indexes or revising table structures to

10.4. USING PERFORMANCE ANALYSIS TOOLS

enhance access times.

SQL Trace also enables developers to deduce whether ABAP Open SQL generated effective SQL statements or if there are discrepancies between the logical database views and physical database implementations.

Moreover, the Performance Trace (Transaction ST12) consolidates both runtime and SQL traces, providing a unified environment for evaluating ABAP and database execution simultaneously. The ST12 tool is especially powerful when diagnosing issues that span multiple operational layers, offering a comprehensive view of execution dynamics.

By conducting consolidated traces, developers can correlate ABAP logic with corresponding SQL statements, uncovering opportunities for enhanced efficiency through adjustments in both ABAP code and database interactions.

To employ Performance Trace, developers activate a trace for specific users or work processes and then proceed with executing the problematic transaction or report. Upon termination of the trace, extensive analysis options enable developers to drill down into specific time-consuming operations or inefficient loops.

In large-scale environments, SAP provides additional features such as the ABAP Debugger's New Tool, making it easy to analyze memory use, statement execution frequency, and more during debugging sessions. The ABAP Debugger is equipped with functionalities to set breakpoints, evaluate expressions, and watch variable states in real-time. By capitalizing on the debugger's capabilities, developers can iteratively diagnose and rectify performance issues without disrupting the application's continuity.

System-wide performance can also be examined using the Workload Analysis transaction (ST03N), which aggregates system activity over time, offering insight into processes that contribute critical loads. This macro-level perspective focuses on transaction response times, CPU usage, database request time, and network durations.

For a more granular point of view on data transfers between databases and applications, the DBACOCKPIT tool is indispensable. It presents detailed statistics on database performance, offering an extensive suite of monitoring features that cover areas such as IO access, locks, buffer states, and SQL caches. It provides alerts and history tracking to anticipate and prevent resource shortages or contention scenarios proactively.

To enrich performance analysis and maximize its applicability, SAP provides automated checks with tools such as the Code Inspector (SCI) and the ABAP Test Cockpit (ATC). These tools automatically inspect ABAP code for potential performance issues or adherence to best practices, recommending peer-reviewed optimizations based on the latest SAP standards. These tools offer batch mode evaluations, and their integration with continuous integration pipelines assures ongoing code quality improvements.

Here's a simplified execution of a SCI check band:

```
* Initiate a code analysis session
DATA: l_sci_handle TYPE REF TO cl_sci_session.
l_sci_handle = cl_sci_session=>begin_session(
  iv_user = sy-uname
  iv_description = 'Performance Check'
  iv_ins_pack = 'PERFORMANCE'
).
* Execute the inspection
l_sci_handle->run( ).
```

In closing, mastering the use of performance analysis tools in ABAP is a cornerstone for optimizing program execution and resource management. These tools furnish a multitude of insights across different scopes, ranging from individual code elements to system-wide statistics. Through strategic application of Runtime Analysis, SQL Trace, Performance Trace, and other supplementary analysis environments, developers can unveil optimization avenues and align application performance with both technical and business objectives. By integrating performance analysis seamlessly into development practices, organizations can foster a culture of continuous enhancement and operational excellence.

10.5 Optimizing Program Flow and Logic

Optimizing program flow and logic is crucial to developing efficient, scalable, and high-performing ABAP applications. Optimization ensures that applications maintain responsiveness and consume resources judiciously while addressing complex business processes. This section delves into effective strategies and practices that focus on enhancing the flow and logic of ABAP programs, including loop optimization, minimizing computational overheads, appropriate use of constructs, and leveraging SAP-specific enhancements.

The cornerstone of optimizing program flow is the careful handling of loops and iterative processes, as they often constitute the bulk of execution time in data processing applications. A primary optimization strategy is to eliminate unnecessary iterations, which can be achieved by refining loop conditions and using loop-invariant optimizations.

Consider the classical use case of processing an internal table using a LOOP statement:

```
LOOP AT lt_orders INTO DATA(order).
  IF order-delivered = abap_true.
    " Process the delivered order
  ENDIF.
ENDLOOP.
```

In this scenario, if only delivered orders need processing, leveraging the WHERE clause can lead to a more efficient loop:

```
LOOP AT lt_orders INTO DATA(order) WHERE delivered = abap_true.
  " Process the delivered order directly
ENDLOOP.
```

Here, employing the WHERE clause restricts iterations to only those entries meeting the specific condition, reducing computational overhead.

Nested loops can pose a serious performance concern due to their multiplicative complexity. Whenever possible, simplify the logic to utilize single-level loops, or employ parallel processing structures if loops are independent, to expedite execution.

Another effective practice is to consolidate logical checks and eliminate redundant computations. For instance, logic that repeatedly evaluates the same condition or computes identical values within a loop should be hoisted outside to save processing time:

```
DATA(lv_threshold) = calculate_threshold(imeasure).
LOOP AT lt_data INTO DATA(line).
  IF line-value > lv_threshold.
    " Perform computation once rather than inside loop
  ENDIF.
ENDLOOP.
```

By calculating lv_threshold outside the loop, redundant computations for each iteration are minimized.

Additionally, leveraging ABAP SELECT loops is more efficient than transferring data to another internal table for looping. When iterating over database results, consider using SELECT ...ENDSELECT directly for immediate row processing, avoiding unnecessary data copying and memory usage:

```
SELECT * FROM employee_table INTO TABLE lt_employees.
LOOP AT lt_employees INTO DATA(employee).
...
ENDLOOP.
```

can be optimized to:

```
SELECT * FROM employee_table INTO DATA(employee).
...
ENDSELECT.
```

In cases of sorting and filtering, prefer operations directly on internal tables without creating intermediate copies unless operationally required. Using SORT and DELETE ADJACENT DUPLICATES directly on tables reduces both code complexity and execution overhead.

Conditional logic plays a critical role in program flow optimization. Employ consistent logic and choose constructs like CASE statements over intricate nested IF constructs to enhance readability and enable the underlying interpreter to optimize execution paths:

```
CASE employee-category.
  WHEN 'A'.
    ...
  WHEN 'B'.
    ...
  WHEN OTHERS.
```

10.5. OPTIMIZING PROGRAM FLOW AND LOGIC

```
...
ENDCASE.
```

CASE statements also afford superior handling of scenarios with multiple potential outcomes by facilitating clear and maintainable code paths, employing efficient branch predictions.

The use of built-in functions and operations available in the ABAP environment can significantly reduce the overhead of manually implemented computations. SAP provides a myriad of built-in functionalities for string manipulation, mathematical computations, and more. Instead of looping and processing data manually, harness these facilities:

```
DATA(string_length) = strlen(some_string).
```

This strlen function eliminates the need for manually iterating over each character to calculate string length, boasting both succinctness and performance optimization.

For complex business logic encapsulation, modularization through function modules, or methods plays an important role. While facilitating code reuse, streamlined modules reduce the bulk of conditional computations being repeated, paving the path for standardized logic management across programs or modules.

Efficient data handling and manipulation form the backbone of optimized program flow, and practices like efficient memory utilization further facilitate logical flow improvements. Ensuring that internal tables, data structures, and memory allocations are right-sized corresponding to actual usage bolsters both logic flow and execution speed.

SAP ABAP also extends advanced constructs and features, including the introduction of ABAP Managed Database Procedures (AMDP) for seamlessly executing complex database operations and logic. Utilizing such capabilities allows offloading intensive data computations to the database layer, improving data retrieval times and resource utilization.

Beyond immediate ABAP enhancements, developers should be vigilant in their use of SELECT queries, ensuring that indexed fields are prevalent in SELECT conditions. This promotes efficient lookups and minimizes program wait times associated with unoptimized data retrieval.

To sum up, optimizing program flow and logic presents broad benefits that extend to performance improvements and code maintainability. By focusing on eliminating unnecessary operations, leveraging proper language constructs, and utilizing built-in functionalities, ABAP code becomes both efficient and scalable. Integrating these techniques into development practices enables developers to achieve a symbiotic relationship between line logic and system architecture, ultimately leading to robust SAP applications that adeptly cater to diverse business requirements.

10.6 Implementing Parallel Processing

Implementing parallel processing in ABAP is a powerful approach to improving the performance of data-intensive applications. By distributing workloads across multiple processors or execution units, developers can maximize resource utilization and significantly reduce processing times. This section explores the concepts, techniques, and best practices for implementing parallel processing in ABAP, focusing on background processing, asynchronous tasks, and the use of Parallel Cursor and Parallel Processing Frameworks.

Parallel processing is particularly beneficial in scenarios where large volumes of data require manipulation, aggregation, or transformation within tight execution windows. The fundamental principle is to divide the computational workloads into smaller, independent tasks that can be executed concurrently. This approach not only accelerates program execution but also enhances application scalability, enabling systems to handle increasing data loads efficiently.

In SAP environments, parallel processing traditionally leverages the concept of background jobs—scheduled or triggered tasks that run without direct user interaction. Background jobs can be distributed across available application servers, enabling simultaneous execution threads. However, parallel processing in ABAP extends beyond simple background jobs to more sophisticated techniques like asynchronous parallel processing and parallel cursor strategies.

To implement parallel processing, a common practice involves breaking down a large dataset into smaller subsets, processing each inde-

10.6. IMPLEMENTING PARALLEL PROCESSING

pendently. The SELECT statement below illustrates such a breakdown where data is segmented by distinct criteria (e.g., divided by range of unique identifiers):

```
SELECT * FROM huge_table
  INTO TABLE lt_subset
  WHERE id BETWEEN lower_range AND upper_range.
```

Upon segmentation, each subset can be assigned a separate execution thread or process. For asynchronous parallel processing, the use of Remote Function Calls (RFC) is prevalent. Asynchronous RFCs (aRFC) enable calling function modules asynchronously, processing them in parallel without halting the main program flow.

The following is an example of an aRFC implementation in ABAP:

```
CALL FUNCTION 'Z_PROCESS_DATA'
  STARTING NEW TASK 'TASK1'
  DESTINATION IN GROUP 'PARALLEL_GROUP'
  EXPORTING
    lower_bound = lv_lower
    upper_bound = lv_upper
  EXCEPTIONS
    OTHERS = 1.
```

In this example, the function module Z_PROCESS_DATA processes a data slice defined by lower_bound and upper_bound. The STARTING NEW TASK directive initiates this operation as a separate task, executing parallelly in a preconfigured server group, 'PARALLEL_GROUP'.

SAP also supports parallel processing using Parallel Processing Frameworks like Parallel Cursor, which effectively minimizes cursor overheads by aligning data retrieval and processing. Parallel Cursor is commonly applied in SELECT-LOOP operations where internal tables are accessed sequentially:

```
LOOP AT lt_header ASSIGNING <fs_header>.
  READ TABLE lt_items WITH KEY header_id = <fs_header>-id ASSIGNING <
    fs_item>.
  IF sy-subrc = 0.
    " Process items linked to header
  ENDIF.
ENDLOOP.
```

Using a Parallel Cursor structure, the above operation can be optimized as follows:

```
DATA(index) = 1.
```

```
LOOP AT lt_header ASSIGNING <fs_header>.
  LOOP AT lt_items ASSIGNING <fs_item> FROM index.
    IF <fs_item>-header_id = <fs_header>-id.
    " Process items
    ELSEIF <fs_item>-header_id > <fs_header>-id.
      EXIT.
    ENDIF.
  ENDLOOP.
ENDLOOP.
```

This technique of maintaining a fixed cursor position minimizes unnecessary table reading and navigation, particularly useful in cases of large dataset sizes.

For more advanced implementations, leveraging SAP's Background Processing System is highly recommended, specifically for large batch-processing tasks. With the transaction SM36, developers can create and schedule background jobs efficiently, while monitoring their execution via SM37. This asynchronous job scheduling model ensures efficient load distribution across available server resources.

Additionally, the Application Link Enabling (ALE) technology allows distributing processes across different SAP systems or clients. ALE supports asynchronous transactional processing, ensuring data consistency even when systems are distributed geographically.

An exciting development in SAP technology is the use of Cloud Platform Workflow Management for enhancing parallel processing capability. SAP Cloud Platform supports microservices architecture, enabling distributed computing models. Utilizing such a platform opens avenues for incorporating concepts like event-driven architectures into ABAP stack workflows.

Furthermore, understanding and controlling locking mechanisms within parallel processes is crucial. As multiple tasks access the same data, ensuring data consistency through efficient locking (ENQUEUE and DEQUEUE) is vital to prevent race conditions and data anomalies. However, excessive or improper use of locks can lead to bottlenecks, so employ locks judiciously alongside thorough data dependency analysis.

In practice, thoroughly analyzing transaction sequences and data dependencies is fundamental when orchestrating parallel processes. While achieving parallelism offers substantial performance gains, careful task decomposition, synchronization, and integration are essential to avoid potential conflicts and inefficiencies.

Lastly, testing and fine-tuning parallel processes is an iterative activity. Developers should leverage SAP performance monitoring tools like ST07 (Application Performance Monitor) and ST03N (Workload Analysis) to measure system load distributions and identify optimization opportunities. A balance between CPU and I/O operations, alongside effective error handling, must always be maintained to capitalize on parallel processing advantages.

In summary, implementing parallel processing in ABAP transforms applications' ability to handle vast, complex datasets within constrained timeframes, aligning closely with modern business demands for agility and speed. By embracing suitable parallel processing patterns, harnessing SAP technologies, and ensuring efficient resource management, developers can markedly elevate both system performance and end-user experiences.

10.7 Code Review and Quality Assurance Procedures

Code review and quality assurance (QA) procedures are essential practices in software development, aimed at ensuring code quality, reducing defects, and maintaining high standards in program craftsmanship. In ABAP development, these practices are integral to delivering robust and optimized solutions that align with SAP's stringent requirements and best practices. This section offers a comprehensive exploration of code review processes and QA methodologies, elucidating their importance, execution strategies, and best practices, along with relevant examples that cater to ABAP.

The objective of code reviews is multifold: ensuring code correctness, adherence to coding standards, fostering knowledge transfer, and providing opportunities for mentorship among team members. In ABAP, where codebases can become complex due to intricate business logic and system integrations, reviews act as critical checkpoints to preserve code integrity and maintainability.

One effective approach to conducting code reviews is through a formalized peer review process, where team members systematically examine code contributions before they are integrated into the main codebase. The focus of these reviews should encompass the following aspects:

- **Correctness and Functionality:** Reviewers should ensure that the code behaves as expected under all specified conditions, adequately implementing the functionality outlined in the requirements.

- **Readability and Maintainability:** Code should be readable, with well-defined logic and descriptive naming conventions, adhering to the project-wide style guide. Clarity in code facilitates long-term maintainability, benefiting future enhancements or bug fixes.

- **Performance Efficiency:** Identify potential performance bottlenecks and inefficient logic that could be optimized, considering memory utilization, execution speed, and database access patterns, which are vital in ABAP environments.

- **Security and Compliance:** Code should comply with security best practices, avoiding vulnerabilities such as SQL injections or authorization bypasses, and adhere to industry standards and legal compliance as required.

- **Test Coverage and Reliability:** Ensure code is accompanied by appropriate unit tests and that testing coverage is comprehensive, simulating both typical usage scenarios and edge cases.

An effective way to conduct reviews is through modern code review tools, which can be integrated within version control systems. These tools support collaborative review processes, providing inline commenting, version tracking, and automation features such as linting checks for early detection of coding standard violations.

Within the context of ABAP, the SAP Code Inspector (SCI) and the ABAP Test Cockpit (ATC) are indispensable tools for automating portions of the review process. These tools execute static code analysis, identifying potential issues across a vast array of categories, from performance to security. They also ensure adherence to SAP naming conventions and coding guidelines.

10.7. CODE REVIEW AND QUALITY ASSURANCE PROCEDURES

A sample execution of Code Inspector might look like this:

```
* Initiate a code inspection session
DATA: l_sci_handle TYPE REF TO cl_sci_session.
l_sci_handle = cl_sci_session=>begin_session(
  iv_user = sy-uname
  iv_description = 'Code Quality Check'
  iv_ins_pack = 'QUALITY'
).
* Run the inspection process
l_sci_handle->run( ).
```

SCI and ATC integrate seamlessly with SAP's transport management systems, offering batch inspection processes that flag issues before transport to production environments.

Quality assurance, on the other hand, extends beyond code syntax and structure, encompassing the entire lifecycle of software development. It ensures the application meets the desired quality attributes by embedding testing, validation, and verification methods through strategically planned QA processes.

An effective QA strategy includes the following elements:

- **Unit Testing:** This forms the baseline of all testing efforts, where individual components are validated for correct functionality. ABAP Unit or similar frameworks can be utilized to automate test execution, ensuring code correctness at the granular level.

```
CLASS ltcl_my_test DEFINITION FINAL FOR TESTING DURATION
    SHORT RISK LEVEL HARMLESS.
  PRIVATE SECTION.
    METHODS my_test FOR TESTING.
ENDCLASS.

CLASS ltcl_my_test IMPLEMENTATION.
  METHOD my_test.
    " Implement test logic
    cl_abap_unit_assert=>assert_equals( act = act_value exp =
        exp_value ).
  ENDMETHOD.
ENDCLASS.
```

- **Integration Testing:** Integration tests validate interfaces and interactions between different application components or systems, such as remote function calls in ABAP, ensuring data flows seamlessly and accurately.

- **Regression Testing:** Automatic regression tests ensure new changes do not negatively affect existing functionalities. Utilizing ATC, regression scenarios can be defined and executed regularly, catching unforeseen impacts early on.

- **User Acceptance Testing (UAT):** UAT involves end-user participation to verify that the solution meets business requirements and user expectations. This phase typically involves executing predefined business scenarios within a test or sandbox environment.

- **Performance Testing:** Performance testing assesses the application's operational capacity under various conditions. This includes benchmarking response times, throughput, and scalability. Analyzing SAP system traces and workload metrics (ST05, ST03N) provides insights necessary to fine-tune performance attributes.

To integrate these QA practices efficiently, Continuous Integration (CI) and Continuous Deployment (CD) pipelines can be employed. SAP's integration with platforms like Jenkins or GitLab allows automated builds, testing, and deployments, enhancing QA efficiency while minimizing human intervention.

Implementation of CI/CD within ABAP environments often involves setting up automated triggers for code inspections, unit tests, and deployment checks, aligning development activities with quality goals precisely:

```
" Example Jenkins pipeline script for ABAP tests
pipeline {
    agent any
    stages {
        stage('Checkout') {
            steps {
                git 'https://github.com/yourrepo/yourabapproject.git'
            }
        }
        stage('Code Inspection') {
            steps {
                sh 'abap_sci_inspection_tool --project yourabapproject'
            }
        }
        stage('Unit Testing') {
            steps {
                sh 'abap_unit_test_runner --project yourabapproject'
            }
        }
```

10.7. CODE REVIEW AND QUALITY ASSURANCE PROCEDURES

```
        stage('Deploy') {
            steps {
                sh 'abap_deploy_tool --project yourabapproject'
            }
        }
    }
}
```

Code review and quality assurance procedures are integral components in achieving excellence in ABAP development. By fostering disciplined code reviews and embedding comprehensive QA strategies within software development cycles, organizations can deliver high-quality, reliable SAP solutions. As these practices mature, collaboration, communication, and continuous improvement become entrenched within development cultures, ensuring that desired outcomes are not only met but consistently exceeded.

www.ingramcontent.com/pod-product-compliance
Lightning Source LLC
Chambersburg PA
CBHW052142220526
45471CB00004B/1484